Position and Responsibility

Princeton Theological Monograph Series

K. C. Hanson, Charles M. Collier, and D. Christopher Spinks,
Series Editors

Recent volumes in the series:

Byron C. Bangert
Consenting to God and Nature

Michael G. Cartwright
Practices, Politics, and Performance

Poul F. Guttesen
Leaning into the Future

Gabriel Andrew Msoka
*Basic Human Rights and the Humanitarian Crisis
in Sub-Saharan Africa*

Charles Bellinger
The Trinitarian Self

Abraham Kunnuthara
*Schleiermacher on Christian Consciousness
of God's Work in History*

Paul S. Chung
Martin Luther and Buddhism

Ryan A. Neal
Theology as Hope

Philip Ruge-Jones
Cross in Tensions

David C. Mahan
An Unexpected Light

Position and Responsibility

*Jürgen Habermas, Reinhold Niebuhr,
and the Co-Reconstruction of the Positional Imperative*

Ilsup Ahn

PICKWICK *Publications* · Eugene, Oregon

POSITION AND RESPONSIBILITY
Jürgen Habermas, Reinhold Niebuhr, and the Co-Reconstruction
of the Positional Imperative

Princeton Theological Monograph Series 118

Copyright © 2009 Ilsup Ahn. All rights reserved. Except for brief quotations in critical publications or reviews, no part of this book may be reproduced in any manner without prior written permission from the publisher. Write: Permissions, Wipf and Stock Publishers, 199 W. 8th Ave., Suite 3, Eugene, OR 97401.

Pickwick Publications
A Division of Wipf and Stock Publishers
199 W. 8th Ave., Suite 3
Eugene, OR 97401

ISBN 13: 978-1-55635-634-6

Cataloging-in-Publication data:

Ahn, Ilsup.

> Position and responsibility : Jürgen Habermas, Reinhold Niebuhr, and the co-reconstruction of the positional imperative / Ilsup Ahn.
>
> x + 248 p.; 23 cm. —Includes bibliographical references and index.
>
> Princeton Theological Monograph Series 118
>
> ISBN 13: 978-1-55635-634-6
>
> 1. Habermas, Jürgen. 2. Niebuhr, Reinhold, 1892–1971. 3. Ethics. 4. Christian ethics. I. Title. II. Series.

BX4827 N5 A39 2009

Manufactured in the U.S.A.

To my parents,
Byung-Won Ahn and Nang-Geun Suh

Contents

Acknowledgments / ix

Introduction / 1

1. Delineation of the Positional Self / 13
2. The Moral Predicament of the Positional Self: Habermasian Analysis / 48
3. Habermas's Philosophical Reconstruction and the Positional Self / 87
4. The Moral Predicament of the Positional Self: Niebuhrian Analysis / 121
5. Niebuhr's Theological Reconstruction and the Positional Self / 160
6. The Co-Reconstruction of the Positional Imperative / 200

Bibliography / 235

Index / 245

Acknowledgments

THIS BOOK IS AN INTERDISCIPLINARY STUDY OF THE MORAL RESPONSIbility for today's organizational men and women who hold managerial and executive positions in political and economic organizations such as governments and corporations. This book is therefore for various position holders including policymakers, business owners, CEOs, directors, and presidents whose roles and responsibilities are significantly linked to many people's lives.

In writing this project, I am indebted to many individuals who personally as well as professionally assisted and supported its publication. In particular, I express my gratitude to Professors William Schweiker, Franklin I. Gamwell, and Don S. Browning of the University of Chicago. They read my earlier version of this book, and provided critical feedback that greatly helped in laying out the foundation of this project. I am also thankful to Professors Theodore R. Weber and Jon P. Gunnemann, who first introduced me to the theological and philosophical worlds of Reinhold Niebuhr and Jürgen Habermas during my studies at Emory University in the mid-1990s. My sincere gratitude is offered also to the humanities faculty members at North Park University, with whom I have enjoyed a collegial relationship for the past five years. I remain indebted to them for their encouragement of and accompaniment in my teaching and research at North Park. I also offer my deepest gratitude to the Wabash Center for Teaching and Learning in Theology and Religion based in Crawfordsville, Indiana. Thanks to its generous Summer Fellowship Program in 2007, I finished this project. I also would like to thank Wipf and Stock Publishers and its editorial staff for their support and assistance in publishing this book.

With deep gratitude I acknowledge that this work is the outcome of much support and encouragement from my family members. I could never fully express my deepest thanks and joy to my parents, Byungwon Ahn and Nanggeun Suh, for their unceasing love, support, and encouragement. They have always been the source of my spiritual strength and inspiration. I also offer my sincere appreciation to my sister, Heajin Ahn, for her unsparing support and assistance, which was indispensable in successfully finishing this project. Last, I want to give my deepest thanks to my wife, Jaeyeon Chung, and to my sons, Daniel and Joshua. Jaeyeon has been the closest friend of mine as well as my life companion. From its beginning stage, many ideas and insights of this book were generated and developed through many discussions she and I had together. Her heartfelt support and endurance are embedded in each page of this book. I also would like to share my joy and delight with my sons. Indeed, they have been forgiving to me throughout the whole process during which they often had to put up with my research and writing. I am truly indebted to them.

Ilsup Ahn
Glenview, Illinois
Easter 2009

Introduction

THIS BOOK IS AN INTERDISCIPLINARY STUDY OF THE MORAL MEANING of "holding positions" in political and economic organizations such as governments, corporations, and institutions. The moral responsibility of position holders, thus, becomes the subject matter of this book. Since this book purports to help position holders become moral agents in various organizational and corporate contexts, the main question for this work is, how can we help position holders become moral selves in the systemic world of organizations, corporations, and institutions? In searching for an answer to this question, I introduce a novel concept, the "positional self," which represents as a moral subject those who hold positions in political organizations and business corporations. I also develop a new methodology, the method of "co-reconstruction," in order to formulate the moral norm for the positional self. Before discussing the concepts of the positional self and the co-reconstruction, let me describe first why we should care about the moral meaning of holding positions.

In the ethical tradition of the West, the idea of the moral self has been almost exclusively construed on the conceptual paradigm of individuality. Since the dawn of Western civilization, the notion of individuality has been deeply interconnected with the political ideal of democracy. It is not too much to say that Western democracy has been grounded in the concept of individuality. The moral paradigm of individuality was even more strengthened by the emergence and the subsequent dominance of Christianity in the West. The soteriological concern for each individual soul rendered individuality a fundamental reality. It was not until the twentieth century that the West has finally developed a new paradigm in characterizing the moral self in the name of "intersubjectivity." Based on this new paradigm of intersubjectivity, a philosopher such as Jürgen Habermas has developed a new political model for Western democracy, which he calls "deliberative democracy";

he has also devised a new ethical method in light of the intersubjectivity, which he terms "discourse ethics."

It is true that with the introduction of a new conceptual paradigm, the horizon of our moral perspective has been greatly enhanced. Despite all this development, however, we still do not have effective conceptual tools to deal with the moral issues that the position holder has to face in organizational or corporate settings. Without doubt, the moral responsibilities of position holders are not confined to their individual spheres or intersubjective social realms. Due to the lack of alternative conceptual paradigms, we cannot but conceptualize position holders either in light of the paradigm of individuality or intersubjectivity. The position holder is then reduced to the kind of an individual self or to an intersubjective self. What is more, the moral norm for the conduct of position holders is reduced to a norm for the individual self or to a norm for the intersubjective self. As a result, the moral reductionism (love your neighbor) or the legal reductionism (keep the law) becomes inevitable in providing the moral guidance to position holders. These guidelines, however, beg the questions for position holders: Who is my neighbor? And, is the law good enough?

The concept of the positional self and the method of co-reconstruction are developed out of the context to overcome these conceptual and methodological shortcomings. Position holders thus come to be considered as the positional self, and their selfhood is conceived with regard to the paradigm of positionality rather than to individuality or intersubjectivity. Through this co-reconstructive study on the moral meaning of holding positions and positionality, we have a better understanding of the moral aspect of position holders: their moral predicament and moral prospect. We also have a new methodological perspective in the area of social ethics. This book particularly contributes to the professional ethics in that it attempts to lay the groundwork of all professional ethics with the concepts of the positional self and the positional imperative. It is my wish that this book will help the position holders of our society have a better understanding of who they are, what their moral norms could be, and what it means to be a positional self in today's political, economic, and legal systems. Let me now describe the concept of the positional self and the method of co-reconstruction.

What is the positional self? How should we define it? Although we deal with the concept of the positional self extensively in the following chapters, I will briefly explain the concept as a preliminary step toward its full disclosure. In a nutshell, the positional self is an organizational self whose actions are not only oriented to the good defined by the organization but also regulated by the positional imperative. Is, then, the positional self simply an alternative name or a synonym for position holders? Why do we need the words the "positional self" to indicate the position holders? It is true that the positional self points to position holders, and yet, as the purposive-normative self in position, the "positional self" refers not merely to position holders in a sense of job holders or professionals. While the term "position holders" indicates only a formal and external meaning, the "positional self" denotes an integral concept. Unlike the generic idea of position holders, the moral concept of the positional self signifies the selfhood of position holders, and it has both internal and external aspects. The internal means the freedom of position holders, while the external connotes the corporeality of the position. The positional self, thus, has both purposive and normative aspects, and its purposive-normative spheres are intrinsically interconnected with the external corporeality of position.

The positional self may be an individual self, but it is not merely an individual as a self-confined subjectivity. The positional self is more than a self-confined subjectivity because the subjectivity of the positional self is essentially combined with the nature of the position distinguishing itself from the mere individual subjectivity. The nature of the position enables the establishment of the positional self to condition its responsibility as the positional type. Differing from the mere individual self whose responsibility is confined to its subjective domain, the responsibility of the positional self transcends the horizon of the individual subjectivity. The actions of the positional self cannot be contained within the boundary of individuality. We may call the subjectivity of the positional self as the positional subjectivity here. While the subjectivity of the individual self is grounded in the individuality, the subjectivity of the positional self is based on its positionality. As we will discuss in the later chapters, the positional subjectivity is conceived as a distinguished category that is contrasted to the individual and the intersubjective type.

What makes the positional self distinct is the positional responsibility as well as the positional role. The "positional responsibility" means the distinctive responsibility for which the positional self is held as a manager or an executive of organizations and corporations. Since the concept of the positional responsibility originates in the combined nature of the external corporeality of position and the freedom of the positional self, the positional self must be distinguished from the generic concept of an individual self. This means that the positional self needs to be understood as a distinct moral self because at the core of its identity lies such moral concepts as freedom and responsibility along with its positionality. Indeed, the purposive-normative self in position is best delineated as a positional moral self. The moral characteristic of the positional self, however, is not taken for granted, because it is something to be fulfilled and established rather than to be inherently given to the position as such. In other words, the positional self is established as a positional moral self only through the realization of its moral dimension.

The moral dimension of the positional self becomes more explicit when we focus on its mediatory nature. The positional self is basically a mediated self. What does it then mediate? How is it mediated? First of all, the positional self mediates the organization where it is posited and the people who are affected by its positional actions. For example, the manager of the company mediates the diverse interests of his or her stakeholders, such as suppliers, employees, stockholders, and consumers, and the interests of his or her own company. The positional self mediates various stakes of different parties whose interests are involved with regard to the management of the organizations and corporations. If we identify the company and corporation as "group" and various stakeholders as "individuals," then the positional self can be conceived as a mediated self between the group and the individuals. Since various stakeholders can organize themselves as a group or as groups, however, the positional self does not necessarily mediate between the group and the individuals.

The positional self mediates not only the organization and its stakeholders but also the realm of tradition and culture and the world of money and power that sustains the material structure of the society. In a Habermasian way, the positional self mediates the "lifeworld" and the "system." On the one hand, as an individual person who belongs to the world of tradition and culture, the positional self is a member of the lifeworld; on the other hand, as an organizational person who belongs to the world of money and power, the positional self is a member of the system. In this regard, the positional self has a dual membership mediating two worlds. We will see more extensively in the following chapters how this element of mediation affects the moral formation of the positional self. In order to do so, I draw on an in-depth analysis of Jürgen Habermas's critical theory and Reinhold Niebuhr's early Christian realism along with the comparison of two.

There are two reasons why we need Habermas and Niebuhr in searching for a moral-ethical criterion for the conduct of the positional self. First, we discover the most critical and realistic moral accounts of "money" and "power" in the works of Habermas and Niebuhr, which may well characterize the moral predicament of the positional self. From their own methodological perspectives, Habermas and Niebuhr regard money and power as an important moral subject. For example, for Habermas, money and power are the "steering media" of the system, while language is the media of the lifeworld. Money and power, however, are not mere media, because they may be easily degenerated into the "delinguistified" media that can colonize the lifeworld for the sake of the system and its strategic purposes. If Habermas is right, then the great temptation for the positional self is to serve the system by playing the role of a "colonizer" against the lifeworld.

In contrast, for Niebuhr, money and power are somewhat differently understood as a politico-economic entity that has its own inherent tendency to concentrate itself. Money and power are more than media. They are inherently oriented toward their own concentration, which is likely to convert them into demonic sources. The great temptation for the positional self is to blindly serve money and power by rendering itself as "slave" for their concentration. In my view, Habermas and Niebuhr are indispensable in characterizing the moral condition for the positional self because managers and administrators control money and power in the systemic world. As Habermas and Niebuhr perceive, money and power are critical since they engender the various moral dilemmas and issues for the positional self. In this respect, it is important to analyze the moral nature of money and power through their critical and realistic accounts.

Second, both Habermas and Niebuhr offer valuable insights in the search for a moral-ethical criterion for the positional self. They both regard the law and its constraint and enforcement as the most important and effective measures to regulate the society, including organizations and corporations. Of course, there are others who share the same view with Habermas and Niebuhr, and they are the legal positivists. Their understanding of law is distinguished, however, in that both Habermas and Niebuhr appropriate the law from the moral perspectives of discourse ethics and Christian realism, respectively. Habermas's discourse ethics enables us to see how the positional self as a moral self can conduct itself abiding by the morally appropriated law. By developing the concept of the law not as a positivistic enactment of law but as a discursive agreement of those who are affected by its establishment, Habermas demonstrates how law can be morally appropriated. In other words, Habermas provides us with a view on how "keep the law" can thus become an important moral norm for the positional self.

Differing from Habermas, Niebuhr in his theological and psychological analysis of human nature, particularly original sin and original righteousness (*justitia originalis*), contends that there is a higher law that both completes and contradicts the law of society. Defining the higher law as "agape," which is the requirement of freedom, Niebuhr further claims that self-sacrificial, universal love lies in a dialectical relation with any standard of law. In other words, what is required for the moral conduct of the positional self is a continuous approximation toward the universal law of love beyond the mere adherence to the law of society. Niebuhr's substantive concept of law, thus, differs from Habermas's discursively conceived formal law, but both are indispensable in establishing a moral norm for the conduct of the positional self because the positional self can only constitute itself as a moral self against the backdrop of the moral and ethical appropriation of law. We should not overlook that the positional self is an organizational self posited in the system steered by money and power.

Now that I have reviewed why we need Habermas and Niebuhr in portraying the moral prospect as well as the moral predicament for the positional self, I turn to a discussion of the method of co-reconstruction. What is the co-reconstruction? How is it possible? Why is the method co-reconstructive?

This book attempts to integrate the dual moral aspects of the positional self through a co-reconstructive method. The co-reconstructionism specifically indicates a methodological endeavor to integrate two types of the reconstructionism: the philosophical reconstructionism of Habermas's discourse ethics and the theological reconstructionism of Niebuhr's Christian realism. While the former represents the formal moral aspect of the positional self, the latter embodies the substantive moral aspect of the positional self. It is my basic argument that both Habermas and Niebuhr are reconstructionists. About the difference of their reconstructionism, suffice it to say here that the key element of their reconstructionism is specified by the universal norms they have reconstructed: Habermas's universalizability principle and Niebuhr's *justitia originalis*. At the bottom of the co-reconstructionism lies a fundamental idea that the procedurally reconstructed moral vision of justice anticipates the realization of the substantive ethical norm defined as agape, whereas the theological analysis of the human nature necessitates the procedurally reconstructed moral vision of justice as a requirement for the realization of the moral ideal. In the following chapters where I discuss Habermas's discourse ethics and Niebuhr's Christian realism, the nature and scope of these two types of the reconstructionism are fully described.

How, then, is the co-reconstructionism possible as a meaningful method? In order to answer this, we need to talk about the concept of the "moral faculty" because the co-reconstructionism is deeply interrelated with the integration of the two moral faculties (communicative reason and freedom) in the positional self. The moral faculty is the moral agency that the moral self employs to fulfill its moral spheres. The moral faculty can be exemplified by such internal capacities as practical reason, free will, conscience, sentiment, purposive reason, and communicative reason. The moral faculty is crucial in reconstructing the moral identity of the positional self because the positional self becomes a moral self by adhering to the moral norm enabled by the moral faculty. As a faculty employed by the moral self, therefore, the moral faculty is differentiated from the moral subjectivity.

As for Habermas, on the one hand, the primary moral faculty that reconstructs the moral norm for the positional self is the "communicative reason." The communicative reason is important for the moral reconstruction of the positional self. Represented through a variety of venues, such as public policy, polls, and public media, the communicative reason can direct, guide, check, or judge the behaviors of the positional self. The communicative reason, however, may become a potential problem to the positional self because the communicative reason can be deeply affected by the group egoism. Unless the aspect of the group egoism is properly checked by a different moral faculty in the appropriation of the communicative reason, the positional self can be greatly delimited in its moral realization. Through the faculty of the communicative reason, the positional self is morally as well as formally connected and plugged into the organizational or corporate world.

As for Niebuhr, on the other hand, the primary moral faculty to reconstruct the moral ideal is "freedom" rather than "reason." Niebuhr does not always differentiate freedom from reason since reason can serve freedom very closely. Rather he generally distinguishes human freedom from reason, and this makes his ethical system unique. By reinvigorating human freedom as the major moral faculty, Niebuhr could effectively cope with the major moral and political issues of his era, such as rationalism and naturalism. Niebuhr's freedom is also deeply related to his identification of agape with self-sacrifice. Since the main function of human freedom lies in self-transcendence, the quintessential role of freedom in the area of morality is mainly characterized in the form of self-sacrifice: the transcendence of one's self-interests.

The positional self's moral identity is not fully established by its mere conformation to the law of society, because it should consider those whose interests are affected by its positional actions beyond the mere adherence to the law. Why does the communicative reason or public reason anticipate the realization of agape (*justitia originalis*)? The answer to this question lies in the limitation of the law. We should realize that even though the law is constituted through the discursive agreement of those affected, it is practically impossible to draw on the whole agreement of all affected. In other words, even though the law is morally appropriated, and thus the positional self can conduct itself morally by abiding by the law, the law itself is always imperfect in terms of realizing the moral principle of communicative reason. Thus there is always a gap between the moral principle of communicative reason and the law established on this principle. This means that the positional self's mere adherence to the law may be lacking in terms of fulfilling the will of its moral faculty, that is, communicative reason. In other words, in order for the positional self to conduct itself according to the will of its moral faculty, it needs to go beyond the mere adherence to the law of society in care of those who are affected by its actions; this is not enforced by the law. This is why the moral faculty of communicative reason is conjoined with the law of freedom. Beyond the mere adherence to the law, there is the realization of universal regard, which is an ideal form of agape.

Why does the law of freedom then necessitate the realization of communicative reason as a requirement? The primary reason for this necessitation is the egoistic nature and human beings. Niebuhr's in-depth analysis of the human nature requires that the positional self should adhere to the law of society because the law is established to check the egoistic tendency of the human nature. Paradoxically, while the law of freedom demands the positional self to go beyond the mere adherence to the law of society, the egoistic nature of the human being necessitates the positional self to abide by the law of society. We can imagine that the law of freedom in the sense of agape is restricted and conditioned by the organizational nature of the position as well as by the egoistic nature of human beings. Since the law of society can check the egoistic nature of human beings, which can turn into a demonic form if it is expressed through the abuse of the organizational power, the adherence to the law of society becomes the necessary measure to curb the immoral aspect of the positional self. The law, however, may not be able to check the group egoism of organizations. This is why the law of freedom is differentiated from the law of society. Established by the exercise of the communicative reason, the law of society can only require the positional self to keep the law, but the law of the freedom offers the higher moral norm to the positional self in the sense of caring for all the affected by its actions. A more detailed discussion on the co-reconstructionism is covered in the final chapter.

This book is composed of six chapters. While the first half of the book is focused on the analyses of the moral predicament of the positional self, the second half is devoted to the constructive development of the moral prospect for the positional self.

The first chapter demonstrates how we can conceptualize three types of the moral self—absolute, intersubjective, and positional—through a reconstructive classification of Kantian autonomy in three relational settings of the autonomous self: the self's immediate relation to oneself, the self's social relation to others, and the self's organizational relation to the world (e.g., markets, stakeholders, constituencies, political parties, legal entities, and so on). Through this classification, I delineate the positional self as a distinctive kind of the moral self. By drawing on Max Weber's sociological concept of the "ideal type,"

I conceptualize the third type of the moral self as the positional self that is conceived in the self's organizational relation to the world. As an ideal type, the positional self is described as an institutional self that finds its moral relevance and significance in organizational and corporate contexts. I will show how the idea of the positional self becomes possible as an ideal type.

The second chapter identifies and analyzes the pervasive moral predicament that a positional self has to face in organizational and corporate contexts. I first clarify the distinctive situation where the positional self is located by using Habermas's sociological terms: the "lifeworld," the "system," and the "colonization of lifeworld by system." More concretely, by describing the positional self as a mediated self between the lifeworld and the system, I formulate the following question: How does the colonization of lifeworld by system morally affect the positional self? In answering this question, I uncover a pathological phenomenon that characterizes the positional self as a mediated self who is increasingly pressured to play the role of "colonizer" at the forefront of the colonization process. Through an analysis of the pervasive moral predicament, we will see how it systemically paralyzes the moral sensibility of the positional self.

The third chapter introduces Habermas's discourse ethics and his legal philosophy. Here I show how Habermas's discourse ethics and its universalizable moral principle can help us construct a moral criterion for the positional self. First, Habermas's discourse ethics and his procedural legal theory provide us with a clear moral guideline to the positional self in the form of a minimal moral imperative: keep the law. Second, Habermas's moral imperative to keep the law is not complete and comprehensive enough to cope with much more complex moral issues that challenge the moral integrity of the positional self in the increasingly globalized social context.

The fourth chapter addresses the methodological shortcomings of the Habermasian procedural approach (keep the law) to the moral issues of the positional self and introduces Niebuhr's insights on human nature and Christian realism. Using a socioexistential analysis of the moral predicaments of the positional self, I situate the positional self in between "moral man" and "immoral society." More concretely, money and power are here depicted as the demoralizing sources over the moral sensibility of the positional self due to their inherent tendency to concentrate: that is, the source of demoralization is the "concentration" of money and power. Yet, how would the positional self deal with the concentrating tendency of money and power as the manager who controls them? In answering this question, I analyze the moral predicament of the positional self as a moral paradox of an organizational self that is controlled by money and power in the name of controlling them.

The fifth chapter deals with the Niebuhrian moral prospect for the positional self by fleshing out Niebuhr's central insight that the political discourse ought to serve a moral purpose beyond the mere balance of power. Here I develop my argument by focusing on Niebuhr's idea of *justitia originalis* that provides a substantive moral norm for the conduct of the positional self. By critically analyzing Niebuhr's concept of the "law of love" and "perfect justice," I demonstrate that for the positional self to become a moral self, it must adhere to the substantive moral nom of perfect justice beyond the formal rule to keep the law.

The last chapter shows how the positional imperative becomes possible as a moral norm for the conduct of the positional self by co-reconstructively integrating Habermas's philosophical reconstructionism and Niebuhr's theological reconstructionism. At the heart of the co-reconstructive method lies the mutual presupposition of each reconstructive enterprise. Habermas's procedural reconstructionism calls for Niebuhr's substantive reconstructionism in that Habermas's universalizable moral principle can only be meaningful by projecting a social construction that is substantiated by Niebuhr's *justitia originalis*. Further, Niebuhr's substantive reconstructionism requires the presupposition of Habermas's procedural reconstructionism because Niebuhr prerequisites constitutional democracy as a basic social arrangement. As a result of this co-reconstructive discussion, we reach the conclusion that the positional moral responsibility of the positional self can be formulated in the form of the positional imperative: Act in such a way that the positional action should not only responsibly meet the standard of law but also anticipatorily receive the approval of all affected. I conclude my argument by saying that in order for us to situate the positional self as a moral self, we have to make sure that the positional self seeks the common benefit for all those affected by its organizational conduct.

1

Delineation of the Positional Self

Introduction

HOW CAN WE DEFINE THE MORAL MEANING OF "HOLDING POSITIONS"? In order to answer this question, we should first differentiate the position holders of organizations and corporations from a generic concept such as job holders or professionals. Position holders are more than employers or employees, because they are all explicit moral subjects who have distinctive moral responsibilities as well as moral predicaments— as free and conscientious beings posited in the organizational environment. Position holders, thus, should not be reduced to a mere category of job holders or professionals. How can we then define the distinctive moral subjectivity of those holding positions? Here I answer the question with the concept of the positional self.

In the introduction, we have already delineated the positional self as an ideal type that exemplifies as a moral subject those who hold positions in political organizations and business corporations. This definition, however, needs further development and clarification when we fully describe the distinctive moral subjectivity of those holding positions. The main purpose of this chapter is therefore to develop the concept of the "positional self" as a distinctive moral subject distinguished from other kinds such as the "absolute self" or the "intersubjective self." While the absolute self and the intersubjective self are each established in the self's absolute relation to oneself and the self's intersubjective relation to others, the positional self finds the self's positional relation to the world of organizations and corporations, including markets, stakeholders, political parties, constituencies, and legal entities.

We should notice here that the fundamental base of this tripartite classification of the moral subjectivity is not the personality, but the relationality of the self. In other words, at the bottom of the tripartite classification lies not the different characters of the same self, but the different relations of the self (the self's relation to oneself, the self's relation to others, and the self's relation to the world of organizations and corporations). The tripartite classification of the moral subjectivity, thus, gives rise to three kinds of subjectivity: the "absolute subjectivity" in the self's absolute relation to oneself, the "intersubjective subjectivity" in the self's intersubjective relation to others, and the "positional subjectivity" in the self's positional relation to organizations and corporations. Although all of these different subjectivities are conditioned by various sets of relations situating the self, there is an important commonality that runs through all of these relations: freedom and its responsibility.

Freedom is what ultimately constitutes moral subjectivity in the self. Without freedom, there is no moral subjectivity. This, however, should not mean that freedom as such guarantees our moral subjectivity. With regard to the moral subjectivity, the true significance of freedom lies, rather, in the aspect that freedom is always accompanied by distinctive responsibility and duty as necessary components. Freedom is not free at all. Moral responsibility and duty are in fact what make possible the self as the moral subjectivity. Along with these two necessary qualifications of the realization of freedom, what we also need to see is that the responsibility and duty of freedom vary according to the relation surrounding the self. Thus what renders the tripartite moral subjectivity possible is not merely the relationality of the self but the distinctive responsibility and duty that are deeply inscribed in the freedom of the self. For example, the moral subjectivity of the positional self is established by the positional freedom and its responsibility in the context of the self's positional relation to the world of organizations and corporations. In the same manner, the moral subjectivity of the intersubjective self is established by the intersubjective freedom and its responsibility in the context of the self's intersubjective relation to others. Likewise, the moral subjectivity of the absolute self is established by the absolute freedom and its responsibility in the context of the self's relation to oneself (as a rational being).

Before we attempt to delineate each type of the moral self, though, we should keep in mind that the tripartite classification of the moral self is in fact the multiple facets of the moral subjectivity of an individual self. Thus, we should abstain from misunderstanding that the tripartite classification of the moral self is the tripartite categorization of all individuals. The tripartite classification of the moral self is useful as long as it enables us to have a clear and critical understanding of the positional self as a distinctive kind by differentiating itself from other possible types. By reviewing each one of the tripartite moral self, we can provide an answer to our quest for the moral meaning of holding positions in the world of organizations and corporations. In defining the tripartite classification of the moral self, we begin with the first of its kinds: the absolute moral self.

The Absolute Self: Kant and the Categorical Imperative

For Immanuel Kant (1724–1804), the major philosophical subject is to study the nature of pure reason, both speculative and practical, rather than to define the characteristic of the individual self as such. Kant's philosophical work on the pure practical reason, however, still provides us with important theoretical ground on which we can constructively develop the first type of a moral self, that is, the absolute moral self. As is well known, for Kant, what renders a human being a moral agent ultimately depends on the exposition of apodictic moral law, represented by the categorical imperative, which must be both absolute and necessary. The concept of the absolute moral self is, then, primarily enabled by the categorical imperative. In order to outline Kant's idea of moral law, we first need to answer the following questions: What is moral law? And, how could it be possible?

In his book *Critique of Practical Reason*, Kant claims that the moral law is the fact of reason: "The moral law is given, as an apodictically certain fact, as it were, or pure reason, a fact of which we are *a priori* conscious, even if it be granted that no example could be found in which it has been followed exactly."[1] According to Kant, since the moral law is apodictically constituted as a fact of reason, we cannot prove its objective reality either out of deduction or out of exertion of theoretical, speculative, or empirically supported reason.[2] Just as moral law cannot be proved or confirmed by any experience *a posteriori*, its apodictic

1. Kant, *Critique of Practical Reason*, 48.
2. Ibid., 49.

certainty cannot be renounced by *a posteriori* endeavors such as scientific experience or speculative argument. Kant observes that morality begins with the acknowledgement of freedom.[3] Since the ideas of freedom, autonomy, and moral law are deeply interconnected with one another, and the concept of freedom becomes the fundamental beginning point in Kant's moral philosophy, we need to first define his idea of freedom.

Kant arrives in his *Critique of Pure Reason* at a philosophical conundrum that although the possibility of human freedom is to be logically presupposed, the epistemological certainty of human freedom is impossible. Reminiscent of Plato,[4] Kant divides the world into two realms: *noumena* and phenomena. Because possible knowledge of objects is limited to objects in the phenomenal realm, those metaphysical objects that belong to the *noumenal* realm, such as God, freedom, and immortality, cannot be known.[5] However, for Kant, this does not necessarily mean that an idea of freedom cannot be presupposed. In the chapter in his *Critique of Pure Reason* dealing with the problem of the antinomy of pure reason, Kant presents the idea that there could be two kinds of causality. He writes, "Causality in accordance with laws of nature is not the only one from which all the appearances of the world can be derived. It is also necessary to assume another causality through freedom in order to explain them."[6] Kant goes further by perceiving that the causality of transcendental freedom, which has the character of "an absolute causal spontaneity beginning from itself," is a logical necessity without which the series of natural appearances can never be complete in the course of nature. For Kant, while the causal law of nature is possible as pure theoretical reason's *a priori* knowledge,

---

3. Paton, *The Categorical Imperative*, 207. According to Paton, "In the discussion of freedom Kant's work is that of pioneer. The Greeks never really came to grips with the subject and did little to carry it beyond limited questions of legal responsibility. In mediaeval philosophy there was a real advance, but the problem was considered in theological terms: how was human freedom to be reconciled with divine omnipotence and omniscience? Kant separated the problem of freedom from its legal and theological setting and asked simply how freedom can be compatible with the causal law which prevails throughout nature?"

4. For Plato's division of the world, see his *Republic*, particularly book 6.

5. While the term *phenomena* includes the objects that appear to the senses, *noumena* has the objects as they really are (things-in-themselves).

6. Kant, *Critique of Pure Reason*, 484.

another law of freedom must be possible as pure practical reason's *a priori* knowledge. Thus, we can say that although the *Critique of Pure Reason* shows that freedom is not incompatible with natural necessity and therefore is a possible concept, an examination of theoretical and speculative reason would not give us any certain knowledge of the idea of freedom as such.

For Kant, freedom is a practical concept of pure reason rather than a theoretical concept, because practical use of reason deals with the grounds determining the will, and Kant considers freedom a property of the will of rational beings: "Now I affirm that we must attribute to every rational being which has a will that it has also the idea of freedom and acts entirely under this idea."[7] Concerning the practical use of pure reason, what Kant tries to uncover is that human free will has its own causality. For Kant, the assumption is logically necessary that a causality characterized not by necessity but by freedom must accord with unchanging laws of a special kind. If we deny an assumption that there is a special kind of causality in human free will, then we will fall into an absurdity because the arbitrary use of will itself eventually becomes a moral law: always choose ends among ends arbitrarily. In this regard, H. J. Paton asserts that a lawless free will would be an absurdity because a lawless free will would be governed merely by chance and so could not properly be described as free.[8] Thus a causality characterized by freedom cannot be lawless; it must accord with unchanging laws of a special kind.

Kant differentiates this unchanging law of free will from the causal laws of nature. According to Kant, the crucial difference between the two lies in the fact that while the law governing causal action in nature is imposed by something else, the laws of freedom are self-imposed. In other words, all rational beings who have free will have self-imposed laws on themselves, which provide them with the grounding of autonomy.

Kant calls the self-imposed law of free will a moral law. Before jumping to the formulation of moral law, however, we need to pay attention to another characteristic of the self-imposed law of free will. Kant's *Fundamental Principles of the Metaphysics of Morals* begins with the following remarks: "Nothing can possibly be conceived in the world,

---

7. Kant, *Fundamental Principles*, 65.
8. Paton, *Categorical Imperative*, 211.

or even out of it, which can be called good without qualification, except a *good will*."[9] When Kant here talks about *good*, he means this in a different way from *good* in Aristotelian use.[10] For Kant, "A good will is good not because of what it performs or effects, not by its aptness for the attainment of some proposed end, but simply by virtue of the volition."[11] A good will is good in itself because it is not defined or shaped by the capacities of feelings, senses, or any other inclinations. The origin and the source of good belong to the volition itself. For Kant, unlike the states of pleasantness or unpleasantness, or of enjoyment or pain, which are related to our sensibility and feelings, good or evil always indicates a relation to the will insofar as it is determined by the law of practical reason.[12] Thus, not the sensory states of the person but the actions conducted by the will are related to good or evil.

As a result of the above discussion, we arrive at a conclusion that, first, freedom is to be presupposed; second, freedom has a law of its own causality; third, the law of free will is self-imposed; and fourth, the self-imposed law of free will is good in itself. According to Kant, the self-imposed law of free will is the moral law, and the moral law is the sole fact of pure practical reason. However, the moral law is not an analytic concept that can be drawn from the direct knowledge of freedom, because freedom is something that belongs to *noumena* as a conceivable but unknowable concept. Thus, the moral law itself cannot be constituted as a set of analytic propositions of freedom. Rather, the moral law is a synthetic proposition *a priori* based on no pure or empirical intuition.[13]

9. Kant, *Fundamental Principles*, 11.

10. The Aristotelian concept of good differs from Kant's view in that it is largely conditioned by our senses and desires.

11. Ibid., 12.

12. Kant, *Critique of Pure Reason*, 62.

13. This sentence can be disputed because in *Fundamental Principles*, especially in sections I and II, Kant proceeds analytically from common knowledge to the supreme principle of morality—the categorical imperative. However, in section III, he proceeds synthetically from the examination of this principle and its sources—the sources in practical reason itself—to the common knowledge in which the principle of morality is employed. In section III, Kant argues that coupled with the idea of freedom, the categorical *ought*, which we become aware of as a member of the world of sense, implies a synthetic *a priori* proposition. Thus we can say that although the principle of morality analytically proceeds from the common knowledge, since the knowledge itself is synthetic *a priori* knowledge, the analytically construed principles of morality are

Kant, however, demonstrates in *Fundamental Principles* that the categorical imperative is the moral law that is an analytically construed *a priori* synthetic proposition.[14] Kant's categorical imperative shows us that the project of positing each individual rational being as an autonomous moral being becomes possible.[15] Kant's argument about the relation between maxim and moral law clarifies how an individual rational being becomes an autonomous moral being. For Kant, while a maxim is the subjective principle of volition, a moral law is an objective practical principle for all rational beings. Since a categorical imperative cannot be established without a necessary formal condition that the maxims which serve as our principles of volition should conform to universal law, the first categorical imperative is generally construed as follows: "Act as if the maxim of your action were to become through your will a universal law of nature."[16]

According to Kant, meanwhile, since the authentic constitutive choice is always morally good as an end in itself, the rational being necessarily conceives his or her own existence as being so. Moreover, since every other rational being regards its existence similarly, an objective principle follows up: "So act as to treat humanity, whether in thine own person or in that of any other, in every case as an end withal, never as means only."[17] Every agent is morally bound to respect the will of all other rational beings. Based on these concepts, Kant also develops the idea of a "kingdom of ends."[18] His categorical imperative shows us that each and every individual rational being is entitled to become an authentic moral self as long as the individual rational beings regard the categorical imperative as their subjective, but universal and necessary, moral law.

---

ultimately synthetic *a priori* propositions rather than analytic *a priori* ones. See Paton, *Categorical Imperative*, 29; and Kant, *Fundamental Principles*, 71.

14. Kant, *Fundamental Principles*, 61.

15. It is important to differentiate the categorical imperative from the hypothetical imperative in Kant's moral philosophy. While only the former for Kant can be called "practical law," the latter is to be called a "principle of will" because the hypothetical imperative depends on desires. In its most famous formulation, the categorical imperative requires that the "maxim" implied by a proposed action must be such that one can will that it become a universal law of nature.

16. Kant, *Fundamental Principles*, 38.

17. Ibid., 46.

18. Ibid., 50.

The discovery that each rational being is not only the carrier of the moral law but also its actual legislator makes it even more evident that each individual rational being is the legitimate moral self. On both subjective and objective grounds, each rational being becomes an authentic moral self in Kant's moral philosophy. Indeed, for Kant, we are legislative members of a moral world, which is possible through freedom; in addition, freedom is presented to us as an object of respect by practical reason.[19] This, however, does not mean that we are the sovereigns in moral realm; in fact, we are only subjects in it.[20]

Morality for Kant involves not only the law—the categorical imperative—and the autonomy of the will; it also includes an object, that is, an ultimate end at which all action is supposed to be directed. In book II of *Critique of Practical Reason*, Kant claims that this object is defined as the "highest good," consisting of the perfect combination of morality and happiness. He also says that this combination is known as *a priori* and thus as practically necessary, and not derivable from experience. Kant, however, holds that although the highest good may be the entire object of pure practical reason, that is, of a pure will, it is still not to be taken as the motive of the pure will.[21] According to Kant, what shapes the rational being as moral self is not the highest good but, rather, the moral law of pure will because it is the foundation for rendering the highest good. But Kant could not give an answer to the question of how a moral law in itself can be the direct motive of the will. Thus, "We shall not have to show *a priori* the source from which the moral law supplies a drive but rather what it effects (or better, must effect) in the mind, so far as it is a drive."[22]

By defining the moral life as a life characterized by the realization of the highest good as well as the morality, Kant shows that an

---

19. Indeed, respect for the moral law is an important concept because it makes it clear that our action becomes moral not because our moral action is prompted by inclination "according to duty" but because it occurs from duty, that is, "merely for the sake of the law." Since practical law absolutely commands a dutiful action and also actually produces it, it has a very special name: respect. See Kant, *Critique of Practical Reason*, 84.

20. Duty is the proof of this. Kant defines duty as the "action which is objectively practical according to the moral law excluding any inclination from its determining grounds" (*Critique of Practical Reason*, 84).

21. Ibid., 115.

22. Ibid., 75–76.

autonomous moral life is practically possible solely based on the idea of moral law. For Kant, moral law and moral life cannot be disconnected. However, by consolidating the moral law and moral life on a transcendental level, Kant makes it absolute and necessary that the moral life is impossible without the moral law.

Kant's moral philosophy enables us to constitute the first paradigm of moral self: the absolute model. Kant's individual moral self is most distinctively characterized by his argument that each rational being who has freedom as pure will is the legislator of his or her own moral law. Since each and every rational being is entitled to live an authentic moral life solely according to his or her own self-legislated moral law, each one becomes the moral subject of his or her own. The same subject views himself or herself as the determinable moral self only by laws that he or she gives to himself or herself through reason. Since the life according to the moral law is also the happy life because the realization of moral law itself is the highest good, Kant's moral self is supposed to live a happy life.

However, Kant's moral self is not supposed to be an "isolated" individual because he or she is not only a moral subject to himself or herself but also a member of the kingdom of ends. According to Kant, the human being as a rational being who gives laws to himself or herself must not be treated solely as means because the human being is the final end itself. Each rational being as a member of the kingdom of ends is to live in a condition that people treat each other as ends not as means only. Virtue is none other than treating people as an end, and in this regard a moral life is a virtuous life for Kant. Indeed, each one of us is entitled to receive the respect of others as an end itself since everyone and each individual is an absolute moral self enabled by the reality of the universal moral law that lies in all human beings. Thus, we arrive at the conclusion that Kant's moral self can be typified as an absolute moral self that is characterized by its universality and autonomy.

The Intersubjective Self: Hegel's Critique and Habermas's Linguistic Intersubjectivity

For all its remarkably coherent and systematic construction, Kant's moral philosophy was constructed on an unquestioned presupposition. It is ironic that the master of apodictic and analytic logic has established his magnificent moral philosophy on an unqualified moral presupposition. If I am not mistaken, this problem seems to originate in his fundamental project itself: to set up an *a priori* moral philosophy that only regards pure reason as an ultimate source of morality against Aristotelian *a posteriori* moral philosophy, which recognizes desire as a rudimentary element of moral life.

In *Fundamental Principles*, Kant claims, "Now we cannot possibly conceive a reason consciously receiving a bias from any other quarter with respect to its judgments, for then the subject would ascribe the determination of its judgment not to its own reason, but to an impulse."[23] As this key sentence implies, Kant presupposes that when it comes to the matter of moral judgment, there are no other alternatives between the pure practical reason and impulses. Indeed, Kant does not pay enough attention to the possibility that many moral judgments can be derived from the communal process, that is, discourse or dialogue among the individuated moral beings.

G. W. F. Hegel (1770–1831) is probably the first major critic who recognized this problem in Kant's moral philosophy. Although Hegel does not specifically deal with the idea of the intersubjective moral self as such in his ethical theory, we can learn some important insights and methodologies from his moral philosophy as a preparatory step into a full-fledged Habermasian idea of an intersubjective moral self.

Hegel's critique of Kant's moral philosophy begins with his critical engagement with Kant's idea of the categorical imperative.[24] In his famous *Natural Law*, Hegel points out that Kant's moral philosophy does not give us any substantive universal moral law because it only tells us a formalistic concept.[25] Hegel first makes it clear that while the maxim of

---

23. Kant, *Fundamental Principles*, 65.

24. According to Seyla Benhabib, Hegel's critique of Kantian moral philosophy can be grouped around three major points: the procedural critique, the critique of the institutional deficiency, and the critique of Kantian moral psychology. Hegel's critique of categorical imperative can be understood as a procedural critique. See Benhabib, *Critique, Norm, and Utopia*, 72.

25. For Hegel, the lack of concrete universal law in Kant's moral philosophy is not just a contingent matter in the field of his moral philosophy. It is, rather, a logical and necessary result of Kant's basic epistemological scheme. According to Kant, we think of objects not as conforming to a realm of objects but as conforming to our ways of knowing, which is usually called a Copernican revolution in philosophy. Objects are given to the mind in sensory experience, and pure concepts or categories, through which they are thought. Since objects must appear to us in accordance with these sensible forms in

the arbitrary will (*Willkühr*) has contents and includes specific actions in exerting its own intentions, the pure will (*Wille*) of the moral law is free from specification. The absolute law of practical reason is to elevate that specification into the form of pure unity, and the expression of this specification taken up into this form is the law as Hegel interprets Kant.[26] But, according to Hegel, the problem is how we could legitimately and justifiably affirm that a certain specification is to be taken up into the form of the pure concept.

Hegel's argument is that since Kant's categorical imperative ("So act that a maxim of thy will shall count at the same time as a principle of universal legislation") is a formal concept in contrast to the specified and singularized maxim, the universality conferred on it by its reception into the form is thus a merely analytic unity.[27] The lack of any substantial criterion within the categorical imperative itself hinders the individual moral self from verifying or justifying one's own maxim to be a universal moral law. According to Hegel, thus, "When the unity conferred on it [maxim] is expressed in a sentence purely as it is, that sentence is *analytic* and *tautological*."[28] Indeed, the conundrum that overcasts Kant's categorical imperative is deeply related to his epistemological impasse that the concrete knowledge of pure practical reason is impossible. If there is any knowledge that we can call a substantive practical criterion by which we can verify a certain maxim's unity with a universal law, then since it will be nothing other than the pure knowledge of pure practical reason, Kant's moral philosophy contradicts with its own basic epistemological position.

Hegel's critique of Kant's categorical imperative goes even further by criticizing it as the principle of immorality. "But the analytic unity and tautology of practical reason is not only superfluous but, in its expression or exercise it is false and must be recognized as the principle of immorality."[29] According to Hegel, Kant's moral formalism is ulti-

---

order to be known, it follows that we can know them only as they appear, not as they may be in themselves. Accordingly, for Kant human knowledge is limited to appearances or phenomena, whereas things-in-themselves, or *noumena*, are thinkable but not actually knowable. Kant terms this doctrine "transcendental idealism."

26. Hegel, *Natural Law*, 75.
27. Ibid., 76.
28. Ibid., emphasis added.
29. Ibid., 78.

mately a principle of immorality, since all sorts of rules of wickedness could be adopted and justified on the grounds that they are not self-contradictory. Hegel writes, "In this way anything specific can be made into a duty."[30]

Although Hegel denies Kantian ethics as formalistic, according to Seyla Benhabib, Hegel himself provides no substantive or material theory of ethics. In addition, Hegel himself accepts universalism as a normative principle while rejecting Kantian universalizability procedures at best as empty and at worst as dogmatic and arbitrary.[31] Most important, Hegel does not reject the principle of autonomy regarding the status of moral agent vis-à-vis moral judgment and verification of norms.[32] For all the limitations, however, Hegel successfully points out that Kant's morality cannot be established without conjuring an overly abstract, formalistic, individualistic, disengaged, and ahistorical model of the moral agent. Thus, Hegel tries to develop a new concept of the moral self, which particularizes itself in diverse historical, ethical, practical, and institutional contexts. Hegel's idea of the *Sittlichkeit* (ethical life) could be his most quoted concept, which represents Hegel's basic understanding of moral philosophy as well as the moral self contra Kant's *Moralität* and the independent moral subject.[33]

In section 142 of his book *Philosophy of Right*, Hegel claims that the ethical life is the idea of freedom. By this he means that the ethical life is not only the good endowed in self-consciousness with knowing and willing and actualized by self-conscious action; it is also the ethical realm in which self-consciousness has its absolute foundation and actuates its effort. Thus, for Hegel, the "ethical life is the concept of freedom developed into the existing world and the nature of self-consciousness."[34]

Without doubt, the idea of the ethical life is important for our discussion because the idea of the ethical life provides us with a foundation for and through which the intersubjective moral self evolves.

30. Ibid., 79.
31. Benhabib, *Critique, Norm, and Utopia*, 72.
32. Ibid.
33. According to Habermas, Hegel criticizes Kant by stipulating that moral commands must be internally related to the life-plans and lifestyles of affected persons in a way they can grasp for themselves. See Habermas, *Inclusion of the Other*, 100.
34. Hegel, *Philosophy of Right*, 105.

However, this should not mean that the ethical life is exhausted by the ethical activity of intersubjective moral selves. The ethical life has a much more broad meaning in Hegel's *Philosophy of Right* and other works. Suffice it to say that the ethical life enables Hegel to develop not only a political philosophy by interpreting the ethical life as the spirit of a people but also a philosophy of history by introducing the idea that the ethical life as the reality of freedom takes on different form developmentally during the course of historical process. In the following, I will limit the scope of the ethical life to the world of "self-consciousness" in Hegel's *Phenomenology of Spirit* because only within this boundary can we discuss the idea of the intersubjective moral self. In the latter part of *Phenomenology of Spirit*, Hegel's intersubjective self develops into a transsubjective self characterized by "absolute knowledge," which subsumes the freedom of each individual.

In my view, the idea of freedom takes a crucial position in Hegel's moral philosophy just as we have seen in Kant's system. Their different understandings of freedom are quite apparent, of course. While for Kant, freedom is best revealed as a principle of rational choice in the realm of independent pure reason, Hegel's freedom is best delineated as an ontological concept, which realizes itself through the intersubjective and dialectical movements in the realm of various human relations, life-plans, and history.

In the chapter "Self Consciousness" in *Phenomenology of Spirit*, we can discover how Hegel develops his distinctive understanding of the self as an intersubjective self by showing how the development of freedom is materialized on the intersubjective level. We can have a clear picture of this through his famous analysis of the "master-slave relation." According to Hegel, the "lord" (master) is at first the consciousness that exists for itself. The lord, however, soon recognizes that his consciousness is mediated through another consciousness, that is, of the "bondsman" (slave). In Hegel's analysis, the bondsman becomes consciousness of what he truly is through his work. Since the work forms and shapes the thing, the bondsman acquires an element of permanence through his formative activity (work). Therefore, consciousness, qua worker, comes to see in the independent things its own independence.[35] Hegel, however, says that there needs to be the moment of fear. Fear is important

---

35. Hegel, *Phenomenology of Spirit*, 118.

because it gives the bondsman a moment through which he becomes aware of negativity of freedom, which eventually enables the bondsman to recognize the thing not as alien being but as his own being-for-self (self-consciousness). The bondsman posits himself as a negative in the permanent order of things, and thereby becomes for himself someone existing on his own account.[36] Hegel calls this process of the bondsman's acquiring being-for-self "rediscovery."

As for the lord, ironically, as the lord succeeds, he fails. Hegel explains, "What now really confronts him is not an independent consciousness but a dependent one. He is, therefore, not certain of being-for-self as the truth of himself. On the contrary, his truth is in reality the unessential consciousness and its unessential action."[37] As the lord attempts to become an independent self-consciousness, a true lord, he actually enslaves himself by making himself dependent on the bondsman for his own existence qua lord. Hegel puts this ironical relation between the lord and bondman as follows: "But just as lordship showed that its essential nature is the reverse of what it wants to be, so too servitude in its consummation will really turn into the opposite of what it immediately is."[38]

Hegel's dialectical account of self-consciousness is important because it exemplifies a paradigm of an intersubjective selfhood in contrast to Kant's ahistorical conception of an epistemic and individuated self. Hegel's idea of the self evidently incorporates such dimensions as the dialectical relation between the self and others, and through negativity, the development of freedom within selfhood. For all this achievement, however, Hegel's self at the stage of self-consciousness is yet inceptive, and far from being regarded as a fully established paradigm of the intersubjective self. First, Hegel's intersubjective self is characterized by a dialectical relation between different individual self-consciousnesses rather than by a reciprocal relation between the self-conscious subjects. By the "dialectical relation," I mean a constant struggle between self-consciousnesses to overcome the other to exist in its own right and on its own account (*an und für sich*). And by the "reciprocal relation," I mean a dialogical relation between equal sub-

---

36. Ibid.
37. Ibid., 117.
38. Ibid.

jects to attain their common interests as well as to enhance their mutual recognition. Second, Hegel's idea of the intersubjective self is still vague because it is not clear whether the dialectic of master and slave evolves exhaustively between the two parties or just within a single unfulfilled consciousness. Regarding this, Richard J. Bernstein states, "As the subsequent sections in the *Phenomenology* ("Stoicism, Skepticism, and the Unhappy Consciousness") show, the dialectic of master and slave is not exclusively a dialectic that takes place between different individual self-consciousnesses or even between classes of men; it repeats itself within a single 'Unhappy Consciousness.'"[39] In sum, it would not be wrong to say that for all its limitations, we can find an inceptive idea of the intersubjective self in Hegel's moral philosophy.

We can find in Jürgen Habermas a full-fledged idea of the intersubjective self. For Habermas, Hegel's understanding of the self is still another self-thematization because Hegel's absolute subject is willing to disrupt all differences and distinctions of small selves by reverting them to itself. Habermas finds the incipient form of intersubjectivity in Johann G. Fichte (1762–1814). It was not until Fichte dealt with the issue of intersubjectivity even in its incipient form that we came to a philosophical ground on which we could overcome the problem of self-thematization, which occurs whenever one confines oneself within one's own domain.

Fichte's concept of intersubjectivity is best exemplified in his *The Science of Ethics*, which was originally published in 1798.[40] In this work, particularly in book 4, Fichte emphasizes repeatedly that a rational being does not become rational in an isolated condition. He perceives clearly that our selfhood cannot be established without considering the freedom of others: "Namely, my Egohood and self-sufficiency generally is conditioned through the freedom of the other individual; hence my *craving after self-determination* cannot possibly have for its object to annihilate the *condition of its own possibility*; namely, the freedom of the other."[41] Indeed, Fichte understands correctly that the identity of a selfhood or individuality can only be attained through the mutual in-

---

39. Bernstein, *Praxis and Action*, 28.

40. The original German edition of *Das System der Sittenlehre nach den Principien der Wissenschaftslehre* was translated into English by A. E. Kroeger and published in 1897.

41. Fichte, *Science of Ethics*, 233, emphasis in original.

terconnection with other selfhoods. "The *first* condition, which might be called the root of my individuality, is not determined through my freedom, but through my connection with another rational being."[42]

In Habermas's account, Fichte's individuality exists by reciprocally limiting the relations of spontaneous individualities. Thus, the development of freedom and the confrontation between subjects are necessarily interconnected. However, the mode of this interconnection is not something truly intersubjective because in Fichte's philosophy subjects can only be objects for one another. For this reason, Habermas says, "their individuality does not reach beyond the objectivistic determinations of the strategic freedom of choice whose paradigm is the arbitrary will of privately autonomous legal subjects."[43] According to Habermas, although Fichte portrays the relation between individual subjects as mutual, objectivistic determination, Fichte is still important in that he lays claim to language as a medium through which one is able to connect with the other. But his understanding of language is in much need of reshaping and reconstruction.[44] For all the limitations, however, Fichte enables us to step forward to a new horizon in understanding the concept of the intersubjective self.

Wilhelm von Humboldt (1767–1835), Habermas argues, plays an important role in developing further the concept of the intersubjective self beyond Fichte, because Humboldt develops Fichte's intersubjective self by incorporating the role of language. Language becomes an important concept, which opens up a new horizon of the intersubjectivity between subjects. Humboldt's philosophy of language is masterfully displayed in his *On Language*, published posthumously in 1836.[45] With regard to the concept of the intersubjective self, Humboldt's philosophy of language is best outlined in section 9 ("Nature and Constitution of Languages as Such"), and his main thesis is that as a socially constituted institution, language should not be understood as the exclusive posses-

---

42. Ibid., 234.

43. Habermas, *Postmetaphysical Thinking*, 161.

44. Habermas points out that like all philosophers of consciousness, Fichte still takes language as if it were a glassy medium without properties. See Habermas, *Postmetaphysical Thinking*, 161.

45. The original German title is *Über die Verschiedenheit des menschlichen Sprachbaues und ihren Einfluss auf die geistige Entwickelung des Menshengeschlechts*. This book was translated by Peter Heath and published in English in 1988.

sion of a single subject. He emphasizes the social nature of language by saying, "In appearance, however, language develops only *socially*, and man understands himself only once he has tested the intelligibility of his words by trial upon others."[46] Humboldt also argues that the picture of language as mere object is a dire misunderstanding because language should be seen as something that produces itself eternally: "For language cannot indeed be regarded as a material that sits there, surveyable in its totality, or communicable little by little, but must be seen as something that eternally produces itself, where the laws of production are determined, but the scope and even to some extent the nature of the product remain totally unspecified."[47]

For Habermas, then, Humboldt understands that although language itself is subjectless, it makes possible the linguistic practice among subjects who belong to a linguistic community.[48] Belonging to a certain linguistic community thus becomes an essential factor in developing intersubjectivity among subjects. For Habermas, Humboldt's interest in a synthetic force in the process of linguistic communication is particularly important because it distinguishes the concept of unforced agreement in conversation from Kant's constructivistic concept of synthesis. Language, for Habermas, at last enables us to free ourselves from the gravity of solitary subjectivity. Speakers and hearers come to intersect one another not at the focal point of subjectivity centered in itself but at the focal point of language, through which each conversant exchanges ideas and feelings reciprocally. According to Habermas, since Humboldt opens up a linguistic communication, the paradigm of the subject-object relation changes into the subject-subject relation.

George Herbert Mead (1863–1931) develops this understanding of language into a more nuanced theory of intersubjectivity, enabling a new paradigm for dealing with the matter of subjectivity. According to Habermas, Mead first makes use of the performative attitude of the first person toward the second person as the key for his critique of the mirror model of the self-objectifying subjects.[49] By the "self-

46. Humboldt, *On Language*, 56.

47. Ibid., 58.

48. Habermas, *Postmetaphysical Thinking*, 162.

49. A performative act realizes this between the speaker and the hearer, by requiring the differentiation between "you," as the alter ego on my level with whom I seek to reach an understanding, and the "something" about which I want to reach an understanding with "you." See Habermas, *Postmetaphysical Thinking*, 163, 172.

objectifying subjects," Mead means a subject who establishes its individual identity without realizing itself in social process. In this sense, Mead distinguishes the self of the practical relation-to-self from the self of the epistemic relation-to-self. While the former means a self who finds an alter ego from others in social relation, the latter is a self who finds a co-acting alter ego from oneself. The self of the epistemic relation-to-self is a self-thematizing self that fails to appreciate the self's being in social situatedness. In *Mind, Self & Society*, Mead writes, "The social act is not explained by building it up out of stimulus plus response; it must be taken as a dynamic whole no part of which can be considered or understood by itself."[50] For Mead, since society is prior to individuals, the self arises only within social experience. Without social experience and activity, no self can be conceived. Thus, "it is the social process itself that is responsible for the appearance of the self."[51]

According to Mead, the process of social individualization is inevitable in modern societies, which transit from the conventional to the postconventional, and it has two different aspects. On the one hand, each individual has to meet with the burdens of the moral decisions of one's own and of one's life planning based on one's own ethical self-understanding (individuation). As Mead perceives, in modern civilized society, individuality is constituted rather by the individual's departure from any given social type than by his or her conformity to it. On the other hand, each individual is increasingly expected to constitute one's own self socially (socialization). It is impossible for an individuated self to step outside of society altogether and settle down in a space of abstract isolation and freedom. Mead further argues in *Mind, Self & Society* that as modern society becomes decentralized from the conventional way of life and values, the transition to a postconventional morality becomes unavoidable. The postconventional morality becomes possible only through an idealized form of communication, which preserves a moment of unconditionality for the discursive procedure of the formation of the will. As Habermas points out, we can find in Mead a Peircean concept of a consensus achieved in an unlimited communication community.[52]

50. Mead, *Mind, Self & Society*, 7.
51. Ibid., 142.
52. Habermas, *Postmetaphysical Thinking*, 184. The Peircean concept of consensus—the pragmatic way of arriving at truth—is later dealt with in chapter 6.

Developing Mead's insight on the social construction of self, Habermas holds that the nonconventional ego-identity can only be found along a detour by way of others, by way of counterfactually supposed universal discourse. Thus, the process of social individuation means nothing other than the postconventional ego's discovering its own identity through the performative speech act with other alter egos. "The self of the practical relation-to-self can only assure itself of itself if it is able to return to itself from the perspective of others as their alter ego."[53] By "returning to itself from the perspective of others," Habermas means the other's recognition of my claim to uniqueness and irreplaceability rather than the agreement with my judgment.[54]

Habermas's development of the intersubjective self is deeply indebted to Mead's social psychology in that Mead exposes the intersubjective core of the ego by successfully demonstrating that moral and existential self-reflection is not possible without taking up the perspective of the other. Following Mead, Habermas holds that the development and the formation of the intersubjective self become possible as the society has evolved from the traditional and conventional stage into a postconventional and decentered world. Although detachment from the conventional social forms and the loss of the traditional certainties have brought the moment of disenchantment and the state of anomie, Habermas sees that the crisis itself provides the people with the impetus not only for the singularization of individuals but also for "a new kind of social integration."[55]

Here, however, we need to examine how Habermas reconstructs a new kind of social integration in the postconventional society with regard to the intersubjective self. In order to delineate Habermas's distinctive idea of social integration, we need to analyze his ideas such of "the concept of three worlds" and the "universal pragmatics." First, taking the cue from Jean Piaget's cognitive-developmental theory, Habermas demarcates the concept of the world into three different worlds: the objective world (as the totality of all entities about which true statements are possible), the social world (as the totality of all legitimately regulated interpersonal relations), and the subjective world (as the totality of the

---

53. Ibid., 187.
54. Ibid., 186.
55. Ibid., 197.

experiences of the speaker to which he or she has privileged access).⁵⁶ Habermas also indicates that the demarcation of the three worlds is matched by three kinds of validity claims, through which the three worlds can be consolidated by the reciprocal interlocutors: "The concepts of the three worlds serve here as the commonly supposed system of coordinates in which the situation contexts can be ordered in such a way that agreement will be reached about what the participants may treat as a fact, or as a valid norm, or as a subjective experience."⁵⁷

Among the three worlds and the correspondent validity claims, the concepts of the social world and the claim to rightness are particularly important because Habermas's intersubjective moral self is explicitly developed in this domain as a moral self. Habermas constructs his account of the intersubjective self by portraying individuals as those who arise in the linguistically mediated complementary processes of individuation and socialization. In *Postmetaphysical Thinking*, Habermas makes it clear that the individual self in the modern world can only be pictured through a linguistically mediated process of socialization and the simultaneous constitution of a life history that is conscious of self. "Individuality forms itself in relations of intersubjective acknowledgement and of intersubjectively mediated self-understanding."⁵⁸ By "intersubjective acknowledgement" and "self-understanding," Habermas means each individual's constructing of one's own individuality through linguistic intersubjectivity.

Habermas's theory of "universal pragmatics" helps us have a better understanding of his concept of the self as an intersubjective self. According to Habermas, both fundamental meaning and the binding character of obligations to others can be discerned in the presuppositions of using language communicatively, that is, in using language in a sincere attempt to come to a mutual understanding with one's interlocutors on the basis of better reasons.⁵⁹ He holds that the universal-

---

56. About the demarcation of the three world concepts, see Habermas, *Theory of Communicative Action*, 1:68-70. Habermas reasons that what Piaget notices to be the case in the cognitive development in individuals may have some parallel in the cognitive development of the culture as a whole.

57. Habermas, *Theory of Communicative Action*, 1:70.

58. Habermas, *Postmetaphysical Thinking*, 153.

59. Concurring with Wittgenstein's central insight on the theory of meaning, Habermas writes, "[One] can understand the 'meaning' of communicative acts only

ity of validity claims lies inherently in the structure of the speech act, which is composed of what J. L. Austin calls the "illocutionary force of utterance."[60] Habermas writes, "Institutionally unbound speech acts owe their illocutionary force to a cluster of validity claims that speakers and hearers have to raise and recognize as justified if grammatical (and thus comprehensible) sentences are to be employed in such a way as to result in successful communication."[61]

For Habermas, then, language is not only the medium through which speakers and hearers realize certain fundamental demarcations (the external world, our social world, a particular inner world); it is also the linking mechanism through which the three worlds are interrelated. According to Habermas's theory of universal pragmatics, anyone engaging in communications, by performing a speech act, raises validity claims and presupposes that he or she can be vindicated or justified when challenged. Seyla Benhabib explains that as a "meta-norm," the "ideal speech situation" specifies the formal properties that discursive argumentations would have to possess in distinction from a mere compromise or an agreement of convenience.[62] Any validated consensus or norm attained through the ideal speech situation then would satisfy the formal conditions such as symmetry and reciprocity between participants in a discourse.

Indeed it was Habermas's ingenious insight to see something innovative in the dissolution of the premodern world, which brought forth the legitimation crisis. As Habermas argues, the dissolution of the premodern world makes it possible for us to build up a new social integration because it becomes available now that each cognitively developed participant comes to a mutual understanding with one another on the basis of better reasons (the force of the better argument alone) rather than on the basis of asymmetries of power or potential threats.[63]

---

because they are embedded in contexts of action oriented to reaching understanding." (Habermas, *Theory of Communicative Action*, 1:115) Based on this insight, Habermas perceives that because communication involves claims to validity, we can analyze the structure of communicative acts through analyzing the structure of argumentation.

60. As for Austin's speech-act theory, see his *How to Do Things with Words*, lectures 8, 9, and 10 (94–132).

61. Habermas, *Communication and the Evolution of Society*, 65.

62. Benhabib, *Critique, Norm, and Utopia*, 284.

63. Habermas's discourse ethics is basically grounded on this fundamental perspective.

Habermas accordingly proposes that communicative action is the most rational choice for all humanity because it enables a new kind of social integration in a situation, where all the traditional or the preconventional kinds of social integration are no longer available. Based on this fundamental insight, Habermas develops a new kind of moral selfhood, one that is deeply rooted in a universal feature of human life, that is, linguistic intersubjectivity.

Habermas's intersubjective moral self, however, cannot be fully conceptualized until we pay heed to Lawrence Kohlberg's influence on Habermas. In his book *The Philosophy of Moral Development*, Kohlberg holds that the ontogenetic form of rational moral thinking can occur universally in all cultures in the same sequence.[64] By incorporating empirical research studies using his famous "Heinz dilemma," Kohlberg theorizes cognitivistic moral development within a six-step categorization. The significance of Kohlberg's study is that the development of the autonomous and the principled self provides us with the formalistic criterion of understanding of the individual moral self. Kohlberg equates the criterion with the idea of the universal principles of justice, the reciprocity and equality of human rights, and the respect for the dignity of human beings as individual persons.[65] For Kohlberg, justice becomes the basic moral principle; this principle, however, is to be completely content free.[66] Habermas later incorporates and develops Kohlberg's formalistic understanding of justice into "discourse ethics." What we have to discover from this discussion is that the ontogenetic development of the autonomous self is critically related to the formulation of Habermas's intersubjective moral self.

Thus we can conclude our discussion by saying that the concrete form of the intersubjective self is realized through the participants' social integration, which can only be attained through the medium of language, and each participant's cognitive moral development. Without combining these two aspects, we cannot fully conceptualize the idea of the intersubjective self. In sum, we can define the idea of the intersubjective self as the linguistically construed social self, which is universal since language is a universal phenomenon, yet conditional because a

---

64. Chapter 4, "From Is to Ought," is particularly important. For viewing Habermas's reading of Kohlberg, see Habermas, *Justification and Application*, 113–32.

65. Habermas, *Communication and the Evolution of Society*, 80.

66. Kohlberg, *Philosophy of Moral Development*, 177.

certain level of cognitive development is required, thereby signifying the decentralization of an egocentric understanding of the world.

The Positional Self: Weber's Ideal Type and the Position-Mediated Self

For all its theoretical ingenuity and comprehensive research, however, we still find some questionable aspects in Habermas's linguistic intersubjectivity. We first need to verify Habermas's tripartite world concept, which purports to encompass the entire domains of our social life. We begin our discussion by raising the following questions: Is Habermas's delineation of the tripartite world concept (the objective, the social, and the subjective worlds) comprehensive enough to account for all the possible domains of our social life? Is it inclusive enough to cover all the domains of social reality? Of course, the tripartite categorization of the domains of social reality is not arbitrarily drawn. When Habermas delineates the tripartite world, he takes a cue not only from Piaget's ontogenetically construed cognitive-developmental psychology but also from J. L. Austin's speech-act theory, originally introduced in 1962 in his posthumously published book, *How to Do Things with Words*.

Habermas's tripartite world concept, however, is not comprehensive enough to cover all the possible domains of social reality for the following reason. We need first to point out that the demarcation of the tripartite world is fundamentally an ontogenetically constituted world concept, which takes a cue from Piaget's cognitive-developmental psychology. Indeed, according to the ontogenetic perspective, institutional domains such as political organizations and business corporations, that is, the phylogenetically constituted world concept, are excluded from the domains of social reality. Political organizations and business corporations cannot be appropriated or subsumed either by Habermas's ontogenetically constituted objective world or by his ontogenetically constituted social world. In my view, the fundamental reason Habermas fails to appropriate the institutional domains such as organizations and corporations as one of the social domains lies not in the disqualification of such worlds but rather in the limitation and incomprehensiveness of his ontogenetically constituted world concept itself.

The significance of this argument is that the moral subjectivity of those who find their positions in the world of organizations and corporations as administrators or organizers cannot be subsumed by the category of the intersubjective self. With the concept of the intersubjective self we cannot explain the moral identity of position holders, because the world of organizations and corporations cannot be appropriated by the ontogenetic world concept, which is analogized in light of cognitive developmental psychology. This means that the moral subjectivity of position holders cannot be captured by the paradigm of the intersubjective self whose moral domain is limited to the ontogenetically constituted world concept. How can we develop the moral subjectivity of those who find themselves in the phylogenetically constituted world concept, such as organizations and corporations? We try to answer this question with the concept of the positional self. The positional self, in this sense, has nothing to do with the psychological analogy; instead, it now has something to do with the sociological prospect because it finds its place in the phylogenetically constituted world concept.

Thus, the purpose of this section is to develop a conceptual scheme to identify a new type of the social self, which would represent and distinguish those posited in the world of organizations and corporations with a view to characterizing them as moral selves later in this book. In the following, then, we will see how the delineation of the third paradigm of the moral self, that is, the positional self, is possible, and why it should not be reduced to either Kant's absolute and autonomous type or to Habermas's intersubjective type. Since the following chapters of this book are devoted to an in-depth analysis of the moral predicaments of the positional self as well as the reconstructive exploration of the possible moral norm for the positional self, I limit the scope of the present section to two specific questions: How is the concept of the positional self possible? And, how can we define it? Distinguished from Kant's absolute self and Habermas's intersubjective self, the paradigm of the positional self is sociologically portrayed as an ideal type. By introducing the "ideal type" of Max Weber (1864–1920), we exemplify how the mere descriptive idea (position holders) develops into a theoretical concept (the positional self) so that it becomes a sociologically constituted moral subjectivity discovered in the world of organizations and corporations.

Since the basic idea of a positional self is here presented as an ideal type based on Weber's sociological methodology, we need first to delineate Weber's basic understanding of the ideal type. He developed the concept of the ideal type in order to analyze social behavior, because it helps us to create certain typical, ideal behavior patterns for purposes of comparison with actual examples of behavior, which we observe in our investigations. With the concept of the ideal type, Weber contributes to the causal explanation of some historically and culturally important phenomena. Weber sees that the ideal type enables us to have increased precision of concepts, which eventually become the objective point of view. Thus, "only on the basis of such ideal types is theoretical analysis possible in the field of sociology."[67] For Weber, however, the formulation of an ideal type is not only for the sake of establishing the objective point of view, because the application of the ideal type to subjective processes is an important part of such an ideal type as well: "Yet the ideal-typical constructs of sociology derive their character not only from the objective point of view but also from their application to subjective processes"[68]

Weber makes it clear that an ideal type should be closely connected with empirical approximation. Thus in order to formulate an ideal type, social researchers should not only analyze empirical facts but also classify possible types of subjective meaning under the probability of a recurrence of a phenomenon in social relations. For this, Weber differentiates the interpretation merely adequate at the level of meaning from the interpretation that is also causally adequate. While the former enables us to have some single sufficient reason for a certain type of behavior, the latter is achieved through the observation that under the same circumstance the probability of a recurrence of a phenomenon is empirically determined.

Thus, when Weber creates the concept of the ideal type, he proposes that it is to be in the realm of probability. However, since the probable classification is not established like a mechanical rule, Weber says, "the resulting divergence from concrete facts must be kept continually in view, whenever it is a question of this level of concreteness, and it must be carefully studied with reference both to degree and kind."[69] For

---

67. Weber, *Basic Concepts in Sociology*, 52.

68. By "subjective process," Weber does not mean all the behaviors of all individuals. He perceives that most of human behavior is governed by habit or instinct. Truly conscious and clearly meaningful behavior is in reality always a marginal case. See Weber, *Basic Concepts in Sociology*, 54.

69. Ibid., 55.

Weber, an ideal type is more likely a logically construed pure concept rather than an exemplary one. Although one may formulate an ideal type through observation of empirical facts in the social realm, one cannot find the ideal type as such empirically anywhere in reality.[70]

According to Anthony Giddens, a common misconception concerning the ideal type is the attempt to understand it as a normative concept: "An ideal type is not, of course, ideal in a normative sense: it does not carry the connotation that its realization is desirable."[71] Another misunderstanding comes from the lack of distinction between "ideal types" and "descriptive concepts." While an ideal type involves "the one-sided emphasis and intensification of one or several aspects of a given event and represents a uniform mental structure," the descriptive type involves "the abstract synthesis of those traits which are *common* to numerous concrete phenomena."[72] The distinction of the ideal type from the descriptive type, however, should not be understood as an opposite relation, because any descriptive concept can be transformed into an ideal type through the abstraction and recombination of certain elements. As Giddens points out, Weber acknowledges that in practical terms this is what is often done.[73]

Although Weber concentrates his discussion on the formulation of objective ideal types, according to Giddens, he recognizes various kinds of ideal types that, without being simple descriptive concepts, are nevertheless generic in character. Giddens also claims that the transition from descriptive to ideal types is possible, and it actually takes place "when we move from the descriptive classification of phenomena towards the explanatory or theoretical analysis of those phenomena."[74] In the following, then, based on Giddens's interpretation, as a first step to illuminate the "positional self" as a meaningful ideal type, we will begin with the exposition of the descriptive type, which portrays the general idea of what the positional self would be like.

In 1956 William H. Whyte Jr. published a book titled *The Organization Man,* which was the first complete study of a way of life that

---

70. Giddens, *Capitalism and Modern Social Theory*, 142.
71. Ibid.
72. Ibid.
73. Ibid.
74. Ibid., 143.

today we call "corporate America." In *Organization Man* Whyte describes the life of a certain group of people—a life characterized by big organizations such as the corporation, the government and possibly the university, charitable organization, or labor union. These people usually believe that their jobs in such organizations promise security and a high standard of living. Whyte's book triggered important discussions on everything from their lifestyle to their role in the American public realm. Many other publications dealing with the topic have since been written.[75] Currently, Christian ethicists have also begun to address the issues of possible moral problems about the life and the role of the organization man and the organization woman.[76] Whyte describes organizational men and women as follows:

> They are not the workers, nor are they the white-collar people in the usual, clerk sense of the word. These people only work for The Organization ... They are the ones of our middle class who have left home, spiritually as well as physically, to take the vows of organization life, and it is they who are the mind and soul of our great self-perpetuating institutions. Only a few are top managers or ever will be ... [T]hey are of the staff as much as the line, and most are destined to live poised in a middle area that still awaits a satisfactory euphemism ... [I]t is from their ranks that are coming most of the first and second echelons of our leadership, and it is their values which will set the American temper.[77]

Whyte presents the corporate man and woman, or managerial people, as the most conspicuous example of the organization man, and he claims that the organization man is in need of a "social ethic," which he also calls an organization ethic or a bureaucratic ethic. By "social ethic," he means the contemporary body of thought that makes morally legitimate the pressures of society against the individual. Whyte, however, does not equate the social ethic with conformity. By creating this descriptive term "the organization man," Whyte shows that there

75. To name a few works worthy of note, see Hennig and Jardim, *Managerial Woman*; Kanter, *Men and Women of the Corporation*; Leinberger and Tucker, *New Individualists*; and Bennett, *Death of the Organization Man*.

76. For example, the Abingdon Press's series in Christian ethics and economic life, such as Roels et al., *Organization Man and Organization Woman*, addresses this particular issue.

77. Whyte, *Organization Man*, 3.

are dilemmas in the life of the organization man. On the one hand, the organization man is likely to assume that the ends of organization and morality coincide; on the other hand, the organization man needs to speak of his individualism within organization life.[78] Whyte's main thesis lies in his claim that since the organization has been made by people, it can be changed by them. "It has not been the immutable course of history that has produced such constrictions on the individual as personality tests. It is organization man who has brought them to pass and it is he who can stop them."[79]

Although Whyte's *Organization Man* gives us a glimpse of what the positional self is like as managerial people in corporations, we can only view his ideas as descriptive concepts that still need to be developed further into an ideal type. Indeed, Whyte's description of the organization man is more exemplary than explanatory or theoretical. Whyte created the term "the organization man" by observing and drawing common traits that involve many concrete people who find themselves in various organizations.[80] Instead of relying on analytic investigation and theoretic exploration but rather drawing out common traits from numerous interviews and observations, Whyte develops a descriptive concept of a certain group of people. For all its limitations, however, Whyte's work provides us with an important notion that we are going to develop into an ideal type of the positional self.

In order to move from the mere description or exemplary classification (the organization man or woman) toward the explanatory or theoretical categorization and conceptualization (the positional self), we need to go back to Weber again, particularly to his idea of "bureaucracy," because the positional self can only be found in bureaucratic institutional structure.[81] Our discussion, therefore, will focus on the

78. Ibid., 12.
79. Ibid., 14.
80. Whyte says that he coined the term "organization man" because he can think of no other way to describe the people with whom he deals. Indeed, the main purpose of creating the term lies not in analyzing or comparing but in designating and exemplifying a certain group of people. See Whyte, *Organization Man*, 3–15.
81. According to Martin Albrow, the origin of the term *bureaucracy* can be credited to de Gournay in the eighteenth century. Throughout the nineteenth century, the idea became widely popularized both in England and on the Continent. In the nineteenth century, however, the idea itself became distinguished into three major concepts. The first view saw bureaucracy as a major form of government, to be compared and contrast-

following question: How does the development of modern bureaucracy contribute to the conceptualization of the positional self as an ideal type in the context of the increasingly diversified and pluralized sociocultural milieu?

Although Weber never defines *bureaucracy* specifically, by "bureaucracy" he roughly means an administrative body of appointed officials.[82] Among the types of bureaucracy, Weber considers rational bureaucracy to be a major element in the rationalization of the modern world.[83] According to Giddens, the advance of rational bureaucracy in the modern world is directly associated with the expansion of the division of labor in various spheres of social life. Indeed, it was Karl Marx who first saw that the separation of labor from the control of the means of production was the most distinctive feature of modern capitalism. However, Weber perceives that such separation extends throughout the polity, the army, and other sectors of the society in which large-scale organizations become prominent.[84] Giddens holds that the pure type of bureaucratic organization shows the following characteristics:

> The activities of the administrative staff are carried out on a regular basis, and thus constitute well-defined official "duties." The spheres of competence of the officials are clearly demarcated, and levels of authority are delimited in the form of a hierarchy of offices. The rules governing conduct of the staff, their authority and responsibilities, are recorded in written form. Recruitment is based upon demonstration of specialized competence via competitive examinations or the possession of diplomas or degrees giving evidence of appropriate qualifications. Office property is not owned by the official, and a separation is

---

ed with monarchy, democracy, or aristocracy (Mill). The second group concentrated on the particular form that nineteenth-century German administrative arrangement took (Heinzen). The third saw the essence of bureaucracy in the officiousness of the paid civil servant (Von Mohl and Olszewski). Although Gaetano Mosca and Robert Michels were influential in the early twentieth century, Albrow says that it was Max Weber who took on the huge task of advancing the sociological account of Mosca and Michels to a high degree of refinement. See Albrow, *Bureaucracy*, 13–37.

82. Ibid., 42.

83. Ancient patrimonial bureaucracy is the counterpart of modern rational bureaucracy. Bureaucracies of ancient Egypt, China, and the later Roman principate are distinctive examples of the patrimonial bureaucracy.

84. Giddens, *Capitalism and Modern Social Theory*, 158.

maintained between the official and the office, such that under no conditions is the office "owned" by its incumbent.[85]

Weber observes clearly that the bureaucratic organization has distinctive consequences for the position of the official. First, although the modern official always strives for and usually enjoys social esteem, his or her position is guaranteed by the prescriptive rules of rank order and by special definitions of the legal code. An abstract conception of duty governs the position of the official. Second, the official obtains his or her position through being appointed rather than through being elected. Weber holds that popular elections of the administrative chief usually endanger the expert qualification of the official as well as the precise functioning of the bureaucratic mechanism. Third, the official's position normally is a tenured position. Fourth, the official receives the fixed and regular salary and has the pension plan. Last, the occupational position of the official is set for a career within the hierarchical order involving movement up the hierarchy of authority. Manifest ability or seniority, or the combination of the two, determines the degree of progression in the hierarchical order.[86]

Although Weber's ideal type of the official provides us with an important conceptual perspective and direction concerning our question (how to conceptualize the positional self as an ideal type), we need further exploration beyond Weber. As we will now see, the major criticism raised against Weber originates in the view that the administrative rationality cannot be assessed out of the context of the culture in which an organization is situated.

According to Martin Albrow, Rudolf Smend, a distinguished German jurist, made one of the earliest criticisms of Weber. Smend complained that Weber mistakenly conceived of administration as a rational machine and of officials as mere technical functionaries. It is worthwhile to quote Smend's critique here because it allows us to develop an ideal type of the positional self: "The judge and the administrative official are not *etres inanimes*. They are cultured (*geistig*), social beings, whose activity has a function within a cultural whole. It is defined by that whole, is oriented towards it, and in return helps to define the

---

85. Ibid.
86. Weber, *From Max Weber*, 198–204.

nature of that whole."[87] In the same vein, Reinhard Bendix also argues that it is not possible to adhere to a rule without the intrusion of the general social and political values. For this reason, Albrow says that since the rules (the letter) cannot be complete guides to action, social scientists must take into account the factors outside the rules (the spirit) when they interpret the action of the officials.[88]

Another critique posed against Weber is that he appears to ignore the problem of responsibility, which involves the actions of the officials. Criticizing Weber on this matter, Carl Friedrich holds that Weber's emphasis on authority vibrates with something of the Prussian enthusiasm for the military type of organization, and the way seems barred to any kind of consultative, let alone cooperative, pattern.[89] O. D. Corpuz also makes a similar critique by arguing that responsibility stems from adherence to attitudes and values that are outside the administrative apparatus.[90] The essence of these critiques lies in the belief that the rationality of bureaucracy depends on the cultural context, and the problem of responsibility should be involved with the acts of the officials.

The responsibility issue requires that we deal with the problem of bureaucracy in relation to democracy because in modern constitutional, democratic society, officials are responsible not only to their chief executive in the bureaucratic system but also to the people at large, to pressure groups, to the legislature, to political parties, to the courts, and to the profession itself.[91] Since the ideal type of the positional self cannot be established without paying attention to the matter of responsibility, which originates in the correlating context between bureaucracy and democracy, we need to look more closely at how we are going to characterize the relation between bureaucracy and democracy.

Our discussion regarding the complex relation between bureaucracy and democracy eventually leads us to criticize Weber's classical view, which is that "while the extension of democratic rights in the contemporary state cannot be achieved without the formulation of new bureaucratic regulations, there is a basic opposition between democ-

87. Albrow, *Bureaucracy*, 57.
88. Ibid.
89. Ibid.
90. Ibid.
91. See Maass and Radway, "Gauging Administrative Respon-sibility" in *Democracy, Bureaucracy, and the Study of Administration*.

racy and bureaucracy."[92] According to Weber, it is inevitable that modern mass democracy is accompanied by bureaucracy. Since one of the most important characteristic principles of bureaucracy is the abstract regularity of the execution of authority, which democracy also tries to realize in the name of equality before the law, democracy promotes bureaucratization. Thus, Weber says, "The progress of bureaucratization in the state administration itself is a parallel phenomenon of democracy, as is quite obvious in France, North America, and now in England."[93]

For all the necessary yet unintended parallels between democracy and bureaucracy, however, Weber perceives that under certain conditions democracy creates obvious ruptures and blockages to the bureaucratic organization. According to Weber, the political concept of democracy, deduced from the equal rights of the governed, includes two important postulates that inevitably come into conflict with the bureaucratic tendencies. That is, democracy not only prevents the development of a closed-status group of officials in the interest of universal accessibility of office but also minimizes the authority of officialdom in the interest of expanding the sphere of influence of public opinion as far as is practicable.[94]

Regarding democracy and bureaucracy in modern times, Weber claims that whereas the extension of democratic rights demands the expansion of bureaucracy, the reverse (that expanding bureaucracy leads to extended democratic rights) does not follow. As a result of this, Weber predicts that more and more the material fate of the masses depends on the steady and correct functioning of the increasingly bureaucratic organizations of private capitalism, and the idea of eliminating these organizations becomes more and more utopian.[95] Anthony Giddens describes Weber's pessimism as follows: "The rationalization of modern life, especially as manifest in organizational form in bureaucracy, brings into being the 'cage' within which men are increasingly confined."[96]

Weber's classical view is problematic because it does not show as much critical and comprehensive attention to democracy and its poten-

---

92. Giddens, *Capitalism and Modern Social Theory*, 180.
93. Weber, *From Max Weber*, 225.
94. Ibid., 226.
95. Ibid., 229.
96. Giddens, *Capitalism and Modern Social Theory*, 184.

tial role in the modern and postmodern state as it does to bureaucracy and its already-dominating role in early modern society. Habermas's critical-social theory begins at this point by pointing out the shortcomings of Weber's analysis and prediction. While Weber falls into despair over the "iron cage" in his discourse of the process of modernization from traditional society to capitalistic modern society, Habermas captures a hidden possibility of enhancing humanity characterized by "communicative reason," "intersubjectivity," and "social individualization." Weber does not show as much attention to who the citizen is as he does to who the bureaucrats are. As opposed to the officials, the executive leaders, and the administrators, Weber describes the citizens as a "*demos* . . . in the sense of an inarticulate mass," "the governed," and "the ruled" when he discusses the relation between bureaucracy and democracy.[97] Thus instead of establishing a cohesive and integrating view, Weber develops a more polarized or bifurcated understanding of the relation between bureaucracy and democracy.

Therefore when I claim that the positional self can only be found in the correlating context of bureaucracy and democracy, I regard the context as a cohesively and integrally connected framework through which various position holders are supposed to responsibly realize not only administrative goals but also public values and personal meanings. For example, Arthur A. Maass and Laurence I. Radway hold that bureaucracy is the very core of constitutional democracy in the sense that no modern government can survive long without an efficient administrative organization. Thus, "It is . . . not a question of *either* democracy *or* bureaucracy, of *either* constitutionalism *or* efficient administration," but of "a combination of the two, of a working balance between them, in short, of a responsible bureaucracy."[98] They go further by saying, "Politics (the making of policy) and administration (the execution of policy) are not two mutually exclusive processes; they are, rather, two closely linked aspects of the same process."[99]

The positional self is therefore a mediated self as an ideal type that emerges in the correlating context between bureaucracy and democracy because the context itself necessarily requires not only competent

---

97. Weber, *From Max Weber*, 225–29.
98. Maass and Radway, "Gauging Administrative Responsibility," 164.
99. Ibid., 165.

but also responsible individuals who take the positions established in the context. The positional self is supposed to realize itself in the world of organizations and corporations. Various organizations and corporations affect the quality of people's lives—that is, not only those who find themselves in the organizations and corporations as the positional holders, but also those who are affected by the acts of those position holders. We will see the specific features of the mediation itself in the following chapters. Suffice it to say here that the positional self is mediated by both bureaucracy and democracy, administrative structure and cultural orientation, Habermasian "system" and "lifeworld," with which we will extensively deal shortly.

For further clarification, the concept of the positional self should be differentiated from that of the bureaucrats. In contrast to Weber, who does not count popularly elected presidents or constitutional monarchs or rulers as bureaucrats, these individuals would each be considered here to be a positional self. While Weber's individual bureaucrats cannot squirm out of the apparatus in which they are harnessed as "single cogs in an ever-moving mechanism" that prescribes to them an essentially fixed marching route,[100] the positional self understands itself as a responsible subject who has a will of its own in the choice of means for accomplishing its work. The positional self is not and ought not to be a mere passive instrument. The positional self also enjoys a degree of autonomy in decision making by virtue of its specialized knowledge and skill, but it is to be restrained by responsibility.

Further, the positional self should be differentiated from the ordinary citizens of the democratic society. While relations between the citizens are largely characterized as reciprocal and mutual, the same kind of reciprocity or mutuality cannot be expected in relations among positional selves or between the positional self and the non–position holders. There is indeed a great power discrepancy between the affecting agents (the positional self) and the affected subjects (the ordinary citizens or the non–position holders) with regard to the capacity to affect others' lives, because positional selves are not ordinary citizens, but rather public administrators, corporate managers, professional executives, or citizen-administrators entrusted with great powers and responsibilities.

---

100. Weber, *From Max Weber*, 228.

Conclusion

I have reviewed the three types of a moral self—"absolute," "intersubjective," and "positional"—related to three different kinds of freedom. The absolute model claims that each individual is entitled to be moral because each person has a moral norm (categorical imperative) as a rational being—a norm applicable to all rational beings universally. Since the moral norm can be drawn through transcendental deduction without actual or practical relation to others, it is grounded on an individualistic stance.

The intersubjective model demonstrates that a linguistically characterized intersubjective relation itself becomes the ground in which the universal moral norm is embedded, and thus the intersubjective relation enables us to be moral. The intersubjective model indeed gives us a new paradigm because it overcomes the Kantian individualistic orientation by enabling us to have a dialogical and communicative moral perspective.

The positional model shows that the position-mediated relation itself should also be morally construed, because the positional self affects the quality of many others' lives through its position-mediated actions as an organizational self who has freedom to access strategic positions and sources of political and economic power. The position-mediated relation is mostly characterized by nonreciprocity or nonmutuality in terms of power and authority, in contrast to the language-mediated, intersubjective relation. A position-mediated relation, however, can and ought to be morally appropriated because position holders in modern democratic society are not just cogs of a huge mechanical machine, but, rather, they are morally responsible individuals whose positional authority needs to be legitimized by all who are affected by their positional acts.

The positional model also claims that just as in the cases of the absolute moral self and the intersubjective moral self, the positional self is regulated by its distinctive moral norms, which not only entitle it to be moral but also hold its actions to be accountable. In the constructive part of this book (chapter 6), we will discuss this further. Suffice it to say here that as an ideal type, the positional self is construed as a new paradigm for representing those who find their selfhood in the systemic world of organizations and corporations.

2

The Moral Predicament of the Positional Self
Habermasian Analysis

Introduction

In the previous chapter, we developed the concept of the positional self as an ideal type in contrast to other types: Kant's absolute self and Habermas's intersubjective self. While Kant's absolute self and Habermas's intersubjective self are respectively construed philosophically (as transcendental deduction) and linguistically (as formal pragmatics), the paradigm of the positional self is sociologically conceptualized as an ideal type. Through a critical reading of Max Weber, particularly of his sociological method, we have examined how the mere descriptive idea (of the position holders) develops into a theoretical concept (of the positional self). As a result of this study, we can characterize the subjectivity of the positional self as a sociologically constituted moral subjectivity realized in the world of organizations and corporations.

To be more specific, through Weber's sociological analyses, we have conceptualized the positional self as a mediated self whose membership resides both in democracy and bureaucracy. Weber's sociological typology is partly helpful in terms of delineating the general background in which the positional self is initially construed. Weber's theory of rationalization, however, is inadequate to portray the full aspect of the positional self, in that it fails to accommodate a more sophisticated social and linguistic framework that has evolved as a result of the rationalization process. It is in fact one of Habermas's central complaints about Weber's theory of rationalization that Weber fails to distinguish between the "lifeworld" and the "system." According to Habermas, since Weber regards as rationalizable only the means-ends relation of teleologically conceived, monological action, Weber reduces the possibilities of rationalization to "truth" claims about the facts or the objective world, and thus confines practical reason to instrumental, purposive rationality.[1] In this sense, Habermas points out the limitation of Weber's idea of rationality, which eventually leads one to "loss of meaning" and "loss of freedom." For Habermas, Weber's social theory is insufficient because it does not capture a hidden possibility of the rationalized society characterized by "communicative reason," "intersubjectivity," and "social individualization." Habermas thus not only observes the social pathologies of modernity through Weber's sociological analyses, but he also perceives the possibility of social reconstruction through his "discourse ethics." This is why we should reconfigure the sociological background of the positional self from Weber's paradigm to Habermas's. In a new paradigm, the primary social milieu for the positional self is the lifeworld and the system rather than democracy and bureaucracy.

Habermas is crucial in identifying the moral prospects as well as the moral predicaments of the positional self. Critically appropriating Weber's sociological analysis of the rationalization process and Karl Marx's critique of the political economy,[2] Habermas reconstructs a new social philosophy in which we discover new conceptual tools to delineate the positional self. Although Habermas does not specifically mention or theorize about the concept of the positional self, his critical-theoretical views and methods are helpful in defining not only the pervasive moral predicament that paralyzes the moral aspect of the positional self but also the reconstructive moral prospectus that resuscitates the moral vision of the positional self.

In this chapter, we first examine the moral predicament of the positional self by critically analyzing Habermas's sociological concepts, particularly his lifeworld and system. The purpose of this study is to derive a theoretical perspective in developing the concept of the positional self. We begin with a review of the theoretical background about how Habermas's sociological concepts have evolved through a critical reading of Marx. In his book *Communication and the Evolution of Society*, Habermas formulates a daring question: Does the development

---

1. Habermas, *Theory of Communicative Action*, 1:281.

2. Using Habermas's terms, while Weber's major sociological concern was the emergence of subsystems in the lifeworld, Marx's econopolitical agenda was how to solve the problem of the subsystem's encroachment on the lifeworld.

of productive forces primarily determine the evolutionary advances of the human species as Marx claims? The purpose of raising this question is to argue that the development of productive forces does not necessarily lead to an evolutionary challenge.[3] According to Habermas, the evolutionary stages of Marx's historical materialism are one sided because they only mark linear progress along the axis of the development of productive forces, without paying attention to the development of moral-practical elements. For Habermas, what supports social movements such as the revolutionizing of bourgeois society is not cognitive potential but rather moral-practical consciousness.

Unlike Marx, Habermas envisions his own view of the evolution of society by focusing on a new capacity of the human species, that is, the capacity to learn in both technical and moral fields.[4] He writes, "The species learns not only in the dimension of technically useful knowledge decisive for the development of productive forces but also in the dimension of moral-practical consciousness decisive for structures of interaction."[5] Since Habermas proposes that the learning process takes place not only in the dimension of technically useful knowledge but also in the dimension of moral-practical consciousness, he tries to portray the existence of developmental stages for both productive forces and forms of social integration. For Habermas, while forces of production incorporate technical and organizational knowledge, which can be analyzed in terms of cognitive structures, forms of social integration incorporate practical knowledge, which can be analyzed in terms of structures of interaction and forms of moral consciousness. In this respect, it would not be wrong to say that Habermas's concepts, particularly the lifeworld and the system, are the theoretical extension and the conceptual revision to lay out the complex interconnection between Marx's two developmental spheres: productive forces and the forms of social integration.

Without attempting to develop an overarching scheme that synthesizes the two types of development views, Habermas maintains two

---

3. "But the great endogenous, evolutionary advances that led to the first civilizations or to the rise of European capitalism were not conditioned but followed by significant development of productive forces" (Habermas, *Communication and the Evolution of Society*, 146).

4. See Ibid., 163.

5. Ibid., 148.

dimensions in the learning process. "The development of productive forces, in conjunction with the maturity of the forms of social integration, means progress of learning ability in both dimensions: progress in objectivating knowledge and in moral-practical insight."⁶ On the basis of the distinction between technical progress and social interaction, Habermas perceives that the development of the human species can be reconstructed as a historical process of technological, (and interdependently) institutional, and cultural development.

By analyzing Habermas's study on the "legitimation crisis," which transpires in an advanced capitalist society, we will see more extensively how the two developmental paradigms interact with each other. Through this analysis, we examine a significant example that demonstrates Habermas's main point that the development of the human species can be reconstructed as an interdependent historical process between technical progress and social interaction. As a result of this study, we also develop a new perspective of the positional self as a historical-practical reality that evolves in the development process of the human species.

The Legitimation Crisis

In the part 2 of his book *Legitimation Crisis*, "Crisis Tendencies in Advanced Capitalism," Habermas distinguishes four types of "possible crisis tendencies" detected in advanced capitalism: "economic crisis," "rationality crisis," "legitimation crisis," and "motivation crisis."⁷ Unlike Marx, whose critique of political economy is exclusively focused on the relation between the "productive forces of society" and the "relations of production," Habermas presents a new critical perspective in analyzing the crisis of liberal capitalism.⁸ According to Habermas, the crisis that advanced capitalism encounters is not confined to the economic system

---

6. Ibid., 177.
7. Habermas, *Legitimation Crisis*, 44–50.
8. Although Habermas stands in Marxist form in that he accepts the view that "what is morally required is being empirically prepared; the seeds of the new society are being formed in the womb of the old," he differs from Marxist view on two points. First, Habermas locates the crisis tendencies in the sociocultural sphere rather than in the economic sphere. Marxist economic crisis is modified into a legitimation crisis in Habermas's social theory. Second, Habermas is not interested in systematic prediction of the crisis as Marxist critique attempts but rather in laying out the qualified conditional thesis itself. For Habermas, "to say that a crisis could occur is not to say that it *will* occur." See McCarthy, *Critical Theory of Jürgen Habermas*, 359.

per se, because such aspects as the political system and the sociocultural system are deeply interrelated. Instead of arguing the historical determinism (Marx), Habermas now focuses on the interdynamics between the steering mechanism (market and state apparatus) and social integration (sociocultural systems). Let me describe in the following paragraphs how Habermas reinterprets the Marxian theory about the crisis arguments.

First of all, according to Marx, the economic crisis is largely about the output crisis in or the disturbance of liberal capitalism. The relationship of wage labor and capital anchored in the system of bourgeois law becomes problematic insofar as the liberal capitalist state cannot control the naturelike development of anarchical commodity production. In his book *A Contribution to the Critique of Political Economy*, Marx explains this phenomenon as a discrepancy between the productive forces and the relations of production: "At a certain stage of their development, the material productive forces of society come in conflict with the existing relations of production . . . From forms of development of the productive forces these relations turn into their fetters. Then begins an epoch of social revolution."[9] Marx holds that the institutional nucleus of liberal capitalism is not the state; rather it is the market mechanism, because the economic exchange is the dominant steering medium. This mode of organization, however, gradually leads to structurally insoluble problems in the form of tendencies toward a decrease in profit (crises of capital accumulation), reduced powers of consumption, and fewer incentives to invest (crises of capital realization). The typical result is the cycle of prosperity, crisis, and depression that characterizes liberal capitalism.[10] According to Marx, even the interventionist state does not suspend the spontaneous working of the law of value. The interventionist state is, instead, subject to it. Hence, in the long run, the administrative system does not resolve the economic crisis.[11]

9. Marx, *Contribution to the Critique of Political Economy*, 21. This section can also be found in Tucker, *Marx-Engels Reader*, 4–5.

10. McCarthy, *Critical Theory of Jürgen Habermas*, 361.

11. According to McCarthy, Marx's main point is that in liberal capitalism, the conflict potential of class opposition is transposed from the political into the economic sphere as legitimation no longer comes primarily from above (from traditional worldviews) but from below (from the inherent justice of the market). In Marx's analysis, conflicts of interest are displaced from the political arena to the economic sphere, resulting in structurally insoluble problems that themselves bring to light the latent class antagonism (McCarthy, *Critical Theory of Jürgen Habermas*, 362–63).

To this Marxian analysis, Habermas holds that Marx's critique of the political economy can no longer be applied to organized capitalism. While providing multiple reasons for this, Habermas argues primarily that the economy no longer has the degree of autonomy that justified the exclusivity of Marx's focus. Habermas writes, "This movement [of capital] is no longer realized through a market mechanism that can be comprehended in the theory of value, but is a result of the still effective economic driving forces and a political countercontrol in which a *displacement of the relations of production* finds expression."[12] Habermas enumerates four categories of governmental activity that prove the state's role in displacing the imperatives of the economic system.[13]

According to Habermas, the state's changing role in advanced capitalism reveals the state's need to legitimate the political system. This need arises because the power that government administrators wield must be legitimate power. Habermas states, "Functions that have accrued to the state apparatus in advanced capitalism and extension of administratively processed social matters increase the need for legitimation."[14] As an administrative system steps into functional gaps in the market, the need for legitimation increases.[15]

Before Habermas outlines the legitimation crisis, he states that there is a rationality crisis between the economic crisis and the legitimation crisis. The concept of the rationality crisis is modeled on the concept of the economic crisis: The purposive-rational actions, not of market-participants but of members of the administration, manifest themselves in their contradictory steering imperatives. According to Habermas, as the government budget bears such common costs as infrastructural costs,

---

12. Habermas, *Legitimation Crisis*, 52–53 (emphasis original).

13. According to Habermas, governmental activity of advanced capitalism relates to imperatives of the economic system through the following four categories: securing the system of civil law; regulating new forms of business organization, competition, financing, and so forth; creating new economic states of affairs; and compensating for dysfunctional consequences of the accumulation process (Habermas, *Legitimation Crisis*, 53–54).

14. Ibid., 58.

15. By "legitimacy," Habermas means that "there are good arguments for a political order's claim to be recognized as right and just; a legitimate order deserves recognition." By this definition, Habermas emphasizes that legitimacy is a contestable validity claim, which is at least de facto recognized through dispute among the contestants. Habermas, *Communication and the Evolution of Society*, 178–79.

costs of social welfare, and costs of environmental strain, the state apparatus faces two tasks simultaneously: raising the requisite amount of taxes and legitimating this increase. Habermas says, "If the state fails in the former task, there is a deficit in administrative rationality. If it fails in the latter task, a deficit in legitimation results."[16] Contradictory steering imperatives that arise in economic crisis are then operative within the administrative system. The state apparatus vacillates between expected intervention and forced renunciation of intervention, resulting in a deficit of rationality in the advanced capitalist state. In Habermas's analysis, the steering imperatives of administrations directly threaten system integration and thus endanger social integration.[17]

To this point we have examined that crisis tendencies shift from the economic into the administrative system. Although the liberal-capitalist economic system is broken, the naturelike development of economic processes can still reestablish itself in the political system in a purposive-rational way. Thus according to Habermas, in order for the governmental activity not to fall back on economic crisis, it is required to find a necessary limit only in available legitimations.[18]

Habermas first distinguishes the administrative system (instrumental functions of the administration) from the legitimating system (meaningful symbols that release an unspecific readiness to follow). In order to understand the legitimating system, we should understand cultural traditions, because the latter provide the former with interpretive systems that guarantee continuity and identity. According to Habermas, there is a structural dissimilarity between areas of administrative action and areas of cultural tradition, and the state cannot simply take over the cultural system. Below we will examine this dissimilarity by contrasting the purposive-strategic rationality and the practical-moral rationality.

As the state apparatus expands its administrative areas, according to Habermas's analysis, cultural matters that have been taken for granted become problematic. State planning and its administrative force encroach upon the traditional resources that guarantee meaning. Meaning becomes ever scarcer. As a result, expectations conditioned by success arise in the general public, and the rising level of demand is pro-

---

16. Habermas, *Legitimation Crisis*, 62.
17. Ibid., 68.
18. Ibid., 69.

portional to the growing need for legitimation. As Habermas points out, the ever-scanty resource of "social meaning" is increasingly substituted by the "fiscally siphoned-off resource value." Rewards conforming to the system are thus expected to counterbalance culturally provided legitimation. After all, "a legitimation crisis arises as soon as the demands for such rewards rise faster than the available quantity of value, or when expectations arise that cannot be satisfied with such rewards."[19]

Habermas then claims that the legitimation crisis must be based on the motivation crisis, which is a discrepancy between the need for motives declared by the systemic devices, on the one hand, and the motivation supplied by the sociocultural system, on the other hand. Habermas understands that a motivation crisis arises "when the socio-cultural system changes in such a way that its output becomes dysfunctional for the state and for the system of social labor."[20] In advanced capitalist societies, according to Habermas, there are two kinds of privatism in the sociocultural system: civil and familial-vocational. These compose the most important motivational factor. Whereas civil privatism denotes an interest in steering and maintaining the performances of the administrative system with little participation in the institutionally provided legitimizing process, familial-vocational privatism consists in a family orientation with developed interests in consumption, leisure, and a career orientation. Whereas civil privatism corresponds to the structures of a depoliticized public realm, familial-vocational privatism corresponds to the structures of educational and occupational systems.[21]

Thus we see in Habermas's diagnosis that both civil and familial-vocational privatisms have been traditionally coordinated with cultural patterns represented and determined by bourgeois ideologies, religious traditions, and value orientations.[22] As religious traditions (dominant traditional worldviews) retreat into the regions of subjective belief, however, they can no longer provide normative structures, resulting in the

19. Ibid., 73.
20. Ibid., 75.
21. Ibid., 75–76.

22. By "bourgeois ideologies," Habermas means an empiricist or rationalist theory of knowledge, the new physics, and the universalistic value systems of modern natural law and utilitarianism, whereas by "religious traditions," he means Protestant ethics, and by "value orientations" he means possessive individualism and Benthamite utilitarianism.

destroyed motivational patterns of privatism. Habermas explains this result as a necessary outcome of bourgeois rationalization. However, he finds a hopeful alternative to counterbalance the thinning source of meaning and legitimation in bourgeois art and moral universalism.[23] Below we will see that through his theory of universal pragmatics and reconstruction of communicative competence, Habermas provides an adequate basis for a historically relevant critique and for the exploration of developmental possibilities in the moral-practical sphere.

In supplying his diagnosis and analysis of the legitimation crisis, Habermas gives us an inceptive perspective of how his ideas of the system and the lifeworld have evolved. For Habermas, crisis cannot be resolved without discovering legitimate social resources, which he locates reconstructively in the theory of universal pragmatics and communicative competencies. Habermas calls these resources the rationalized lifeworld. Thus by capturing the moral significance of the lifeworld and its necessity, Habermas shows us that we can overcome the perils and predicaments of modern society, which he attributes to the legitimation crisis. Before we discuss Habermas's ideas of the lifeworld and the system, however, we need to examine his basic understanding of rationality, because he reconstructs the concepts of the lifeworld and the system on the basis of different kinds of rationality.

Habermas divides rationality into two kinds: the purposive (cognitive-instrumental) rationality and the communicative rationality. These two different rationalities allow the "cumulative processes." According to David Held, Habermas holds that human beings' capacity for freedom is dependent on cumulative learning in theoretical and practical activity.[24] Through such learning, the technical mastery of the natural and social worlds and the organization and alteration of social relations become possible. The human praxis is therefore composed of two key elements: work and interaction. By "work," Habermas means instrumental action or purposive-rational action, and by "interaction," he means communicative interaction. While work is oriented to technical control over objectified processes, interaction is oriented to mutual

---

23. Unlike the other members of the Institute of Social Research, Habermas is not much concerned with aesthetics. He instead explores the acquisition of communicative competence in ontogenesis and phylogenesis. We will see more on this when we discuss his discourse ethics.

24. Held, *Introduction to Critical Theory*, 257.

understanding. Habermas also alludes to a third type of action: strategic action, which is oriented to the calculated pursuit of individual interests. Although strategic action is instrumental insofar as it involves reflection on the relationships between means and ends, it is nevertheless bound to a context of social interaction. Thomas McCarthy argues that it is misleading to present strategic action as a wholly distinct type of action.[25] Part of the confusion originates in Habermas's using Weber's concept of social action, which refers to both strategic and purposive-rational action without distinguishing between the two: taking account of and being oriented to others' behaviors and the success-oriented pursuit of rationally considered ends. In the following discussion, we will distinguish Habermas's basic action categories as two kinds: purposive-rational action and communicative action.

According to Habermas's basic contention, the human species evolves in two separate but interrelated dimensions through the development of the forces of production and the development of normative structures of interaction. At the heart of these two types of development reside Habermas's different rationalities: cognitive-instrumental rationality and communicative rationality.

The concept of cognitive-instrumental rationality (or purposive rationality) is characterized by its noncommunicative, objectifying, monological, and purposeful use of reason in teleological action. Habermas writes, "It carries with it connotations of successful self-maintenance made possible by informed disposition over, and intelligent adaptation to, conditions of a contingent environment."[26] Through cognitive-instrumental rationality, we can apply technical knowledge to the control of human behavior as well as inanimate objects. The concept of communicative rationality, however, is marked by the mutual and communicative employment of propositional knowledge in assertions. Habermas says, "This concept of communicative rationality carries with it connotations based ultimately on the central experience of the

25. McCarthy argues that it is misleading to present the distinction as one between two types of action (strategic and instrumental) because rational decision and the application of technically appropriate means appear rather to be two moments of purposive-rational action. McCarthy, thus, distinguishes broader and narrower meanings of purposive-rational action in its relation to social action by including or excluding strategic action. Unless otherwise stated, Habermas's basic action categories are narrowly employed. See McCarthy, *Critical Theory of Jürgen Habermas*, 16–40.

26. Habermas, *Theory of Communicative Action*, 1:10.

unconstrained, unifying, consensus bringing force of argumentative speech, in which different participants overcome their merely subjective views and, owing to the mutuality of rationally motivated conviction, assure themselves of both the unity of the objective world and the intersubjectivity of their lifeworld."[27]

According to Habermas, different sets of criteria legitimize the two kinds of rationality. In cognitive-instrumental rationality, a goal-directed action can be rational only if the actor satisfies the conditions necessary for realizing his or her intention to intervene successfully in the world. By contrast, in communicative rationality, an assertion can be called rational only if the speaker satisfies the conditions necessary to achieve the illocutionary goal of reaching an understanding about something in the world with at least one other participant in the communicative interaction.

The two kinds of rationality differ from each other also in the way they use knowledge. While in cognitive-instrumental rationality, knowledge is used for the purpose of instrumental mastery; in communicative rationality, it is used for the purpose of communicative understanding. Furthermore, the two rationalities require different conceptualizations of the world. Whereas cognitive-instrumental rationality presupposes an ontological concept of the world, as the sum total of what is the case, communicative rationality enables those who behave rationally to presuppose necessarily an abstract concept of the world. Habermas calls the former stance "realistic," whereas he calls the latter "phenomenological."[28] This differentiation of the two world concepts that arise out of different kinds of rationality develops much further into complex conceptualizations, such as the conception of the system as objective and realistic, as well as the conception of the lifeworld as an intersubjective and phenomenological idea. However, it is not clear whether Habermas maintains a strict stipulation that the system is organized solely by cognitive-instrumental rationality, whereas the lifeworld is organized solely by communicative rationality.

---

27. Ibid.

28. While the realist envisions the world of existing states of affairs, the phenomenologist does not simply begin with the ontological presupposition of an objective world. Unlike the realist, the phenomenologist inquires about the conditions under which the unity of an objective world is constituted for the members of a community. See Habermas, *Theory of Communicative Action*, 1:12.

The Lifeworld

Above we have seen that the learning capacity of humankind in advanced capitalist society has been cumulatively developed in two dimensions: technological-instrumental and moral-practical. The differentiation of these two dimensions is critical for Habermas, particularly with regard to his attempt not only to overcome Marx's theoretical weakness but also to amend Weber's rationalization, which stops short of distinguishing between action oriented to mutual understanding and action oriented to success. Indeed, Weber was not able to distinguish critically between "the communicative rationalization of everyday action and the formation of subsystems of purposive-rational economic and administrative action as complementary developments."[29]

In Habermas's revision of critical theory, social conflict in late modern society lies not in the struggle between reason and unreason or between the working class and the ruling class. Rather it lies in the contest between the mechanisms of coordinating and integrating people's actions.[30] On the one hand, mechanisms of linguistic communication, by aiming at mutual understanding, harmonize the action orientations of individuals; on the other hand, delinguistified steering media, such as power and money, functionally stabilize the unintended interconnections of decision that have not been subjectively coordinated. Habermas says, "In the one case, the integration of an action system is established by a normatively secured or communicatively achieved consensus, in the other case, by a non-normative regulation of individual decisions that extends beyond the actors' consciousnesses."[31] According to Habermas, while social integration of society takes effect in action orientations, systemic integration reaches through and beyond action orientations.

---

29. Ibid., 341.

30. In distinguishing the two kinds of actions, as McCarthy argues, we have a difficulty in that instrumental or purposive-rational action would seem to be not governed by social norms, not grounded in intersubjectivity, not sanctioned by convention, in short, not social. However, this cannot be true because "the activity of scientists and technicians, of producers and planners, is manifestly subject to consensual norms, based on reciprocal expectations, grounded in intersubjectivity, and sanctioned by convention" (McCarthy, *Critical Theory of Jürgen Habermas*, 26–27). Cognitive-instrumental or purposive-rational action is normally embedded in communicative action.

31. Habermas, *Theory of Communicative Action*, 2:117.

This distinction, Habermas claims, calls for a corresponding differentiation in the concept of society itself. Habermas writes:

> No matter whether one starts with Mead from basic concepts of social interaction or with Durkheim from basic concepts of collective representations, in either case society is conceived from the perspective of acting subjects as the lifeworld of a social group. In contrast, from the observer's perspective of someone not involved, society can be conceived only as a system of actions such that each action has a functional significance according to its contribution to the maintenance of the system.[32]

In distinguishing between the lifeworld and the system, we need to see that the distinction itself should not be interpreted as a mere separation of the two worlds, which would imply a total disconnection between the two. Habermas is more interested in the relational dynamics between the differentiated processes of social and system integration rather than in the distinction itself. In Habermas's view, the reproduction of the "inner logic" of the symbolic structures of the lifeworld and the systemic maintenance of its material substratum are both indispensable for the evolution of the society. Habermas explains that the pathologies of the posttraditional society lie in the pathological relation between the two differentiated processes of social and system integration rather than in either of the processes itself. In order to understand more clearly the relational dynamics between the lifeworld and the system, and its meaning in reconstructing the idea of the positional self, we need to understand Habermas's concept of the lifeworld.

According to Habermas, the concept of the lifeworld should be first introduced from the perspective of reconstructive research as complement to the concept of communicative action. Since social action is possible in general by virtue of the rationally binding force that results from the actors' readiness to make good the claims raised in their actions, and since these claims must be validated by a notion of mutual or common knowledge, Habermas develops the idea of the lifeworld. For Habermas, social action is impossible without social order, and social order must be presupposed. If this social order or commonality cannot be presupposed, the actors have to draw on the means of strategic ac-

---

32. Ibid. The original German phrases for the "lifeworld of a social group" and a "system of actions" are *Lebenswelt einer sozialen Gruppe* and *System von Handlungen*, respectively (Habermas, *Theorie des kommunikativen Handelns*, 2:179).

tion with a view to bringing about a common definition or to negotiating directly between them.[33]

Habermas understands the concept of the lifeworld as the place in which the social action is realized. Habermas writes, "Subjects acting communicatively always come to an understanding in the horizon of a lifeworld. Their lifeworld is formed from more or less diffuse, always unproblematic, background convictions. This lifeworld background serves as a source of situation definitions that are presupposed by participants as unproblematic."[34]

In order to explicate the concept of the lifeworld as the horizon, we need to go to Edmund Husserl (1859–1938), because Habermas adopts the term from Husserl's phenomenology, particularly from his *The Crisis of European Sciences and Transcendental Phenomenology*. Husserl initially understands the lifeworld as an ontic meaning of the pregiven totality: the world as world for all, which is valid as existing for us and to which we, together, belong.[35] Husserl differentiates the concept of the lifeworld (as a pregiven world) from the objective-true world. While the former provides us with a realm of original self-evidence that can be perceivable, the latter provides the scientists with the object of scientific exploration, which is not experienceable in its own proper being.[36]

Husserl consistently claims that the two realms should be differentiated, but he perceives that there is a certain relevance that connects the two realms. He holds that the lifeworld ultimately grounds the theoretical-logical, ontic validity for all objective verification (mathematical, natural-scientific, positive-scientific insights) as the source of self-evidence and the source of verification.[37] The objective theory (science) has its hidden sources of grounding itself in the lifeworld, in which the prescientific, ontic meaning as the primal self-evidence resides.[38] Thus all the conceivable verification leads from objective-logical

33. Habermas, *Theory of Communicative Action*, 2:121.
34. Ibid., 70.
35. Husserl, *Crisis of European Sciences*, 109.
36. Ibid., 127.
37. Ibid., 126.
38. According to Husserl, a self-evidence taking place purely in the lifeworld is the source of self-evidence for what is objectively established in the sciences; but echoing Kant, Husserl claims that the objective is precisely never experienceable as itself. See Husserl, *Crisis of European Sciences*, 129.

self-evidence back to the primal self-evidence in which the lifeworld is ever pregiven. In Husserl's argument, we can discover Habermas's main idea of the lifeworld as the source of knowledge. However, while Husserl regards this source as something that can be drawn through the intuition and phenomenological "epoché" that can arise in subjective-relative consciousness, Habermas considers this a resource that is drawn upon through communicative action in the intersubjective relation.

Since Husserl argues that the lifeworld is the source of self-evidently prescientific, ontic meaning, he raises the following question: How can the pregivenness of the lifeworld become a universal subject of investigation in its own right? Husserl humbly admits the limitation in answering the question. He says, "To be sure, we do not yet know how the lifeworld is to become an independent, totally self-sufficient subject of investigation, how it is supposed to make possible scientific statements—which as such, after all, must have their own 'objectivity,' even if it is in a manner different from that of our sciences."[39] Despite the limitation Husserl acknowledges, we need to investigate how he tries to give an answer to the question, because Habermas develops his own view of the lifeworld by critically responding to Husserl's proposal.[40]

Husserl first develops an idea of the epoché as a method of access to the new science's field of work, in which we explicate the source of prescientific, ontic meaning. By "epoché," Husserl means "a withholding of natural, naïve validities and in general of validities already in effect."[41] Through the epoché, thus, one brackets the cognitions of the objective sciences, resulting in an epoché of any critical position-taking that is interested in their truth or falsity, even any position on the sciences' guiding idea of an objective knowledge of the world. Through the phenomenological method of the epoché, Husserl argues, we can distinguish between the objective-logical *a priori* and the *a priori* of the lifeworld. This distinction provides us with the fundamental insight that the universal *a priori* of the objective-logical level is grounded in a universal *a priori* that is in itself the lifeworld.[42]

39. Ibid., 133.

40. Answering this question is essential in developing his idea of the lifeworld, because if he could not provide a method, then the concept of the lifeworld cannot be self-sufficiently established.

41. Husserl, *Crisis of European Sciences*, 135.

42. Ibid., 141.

According to Husserl, the genuine transcendental epochē makes possible the transcendental reduction through which one can discover and investigate the transcendental correlation between the lifeworld and world-consciousness. Husserl states that the epochē is not a meaningless, habitual abstention; rather, it is an abstention that is a kind of liberation, enabling us to discover the "universal, absolutely self-enclosed and absolutely self-sufficient correlation between the world itself and world-consciousness."[43] By "world-consciousness," Husserl means the conscious life of the subjectivity that effects the validity of the world. For him, subjectivity not only always has the world but also continues actively to shape it anew, thereby constituting its meaning and ontic validity. Husserl claims:

> Through the epochē a new way of experiencing, of thinking, of theorizing, is opened to the philosopher; here, situated *above* his own natural being and *above* the natural world, he loses nothing of their being and their objective truths and likewise nothing at all of the spiritual acquisitions of his world-life or those of the whole historical communal life; he simply forbids himself—as a philosopher, in the uniqueness of his direction of interest—to continue the whole natural performance of his world-life; that is, he forbids himself to ask questions which rest upon the ground of the world at hand, questions of being, questions of value, practical questions, questions about being or not-being, about being valuable, being useful, being beautiful, being good, etc. All natural interests are put out of play.[44]

This explanation helps us see that Husserl approaches the question of the lifeworld through the transcendental reduction of subjective consciousness, that is, as a philosopher. Of course, Husserl argues that the world concept is not a view or an interpretation bestowed on the world. It is rather about the pregiven world that is validated through the epochē. But even though he develops a universal *a priori* concept of the lifeworld that has a universal *a priori* quality in contrast to the objective-logical world, he still needs to answer the question, how can the lifeworld of a philosopher become that of humankind? Husserl tries to solve this problem by reducing the concept of humankind to the phenomenon of mankind, which becomes the self-objectification

---

43. Ibid., 151.
44. Ibid., 152.

of transcendental subjectivity. He asks, "How can we make it more concretely understandable that the reduction of humankind to the phenomenon 'mankind,' which is included as part of the reduction of the world, makes it possible to recognize mankind as a self-objectification of transcendental subjectivity which is always functioning ultimately and is thus 'absolute'?"[45]

Here we can rephrase Husserl's question as, how can a subjectively verified ontic meaning become an intersubjectively verified meaning? Paul Ricoeur discerns this problem by asking, "How the primacy of the ego, sole *originary* principle of transcendental phenomenology, can be maintained throughout this progression toward the Other, toward the world of Others, and toward the Others as world."[46] Husserl perceives that the difficulty of this problem resides in the fact that between the requirement of reduction and the requirement of description, between ontic meaning and phenomenal meaning, and between the transcendental epochē and the objective-logical investigation, the other is no longer a thing but another ego, someone other than I. Fully aware of this problem, Husserl tries to conceptualize the "intersubjective constitution" of the world, which means the total system of manners of givenness and also of modes of validity for egos.[47] Although Husserl claims that the ego constitutes transcendental intersubjectivity "through a particular constitutive accomplishment of its own," his method still remains in the philosophy of transcendental subjectivism.[48]

---

45. Ibid., 153.
46. Ricoeur, *Husserl*, 116.
47. Ibid., 166.

48. Husserl states that there is an analogue between the self-temporalization through depresentation of the past *I*, and my self-alienation as depresentation of my primal presence into (for example) a merely presentified empathy. Thus, he claims, "in me, 'another I' achieves ontic validity as co-present with his own ways of being self-evidently verified, which are obviously quite different from those of a 'sense'—perception" (Ibid., 185). In my view, Husserl's argument renders him more bound to the philosophy of transcendental subjectivism. Indeed, being rooted in the subjectivism, he tries to incorporate the objective phenomena of others and their world as transcendental phenomena. At least, as Ricoeur puts it, Husserl does mark out the shape of the true problem: "How can one escape from the solipsism of a Descartes seen through Hume, ... How at the same time can one avoid the Hegelian trap of an absolute history elevated to equal an external God?" (Ibid.,174). Although Husserl deals with the philosophical problem of others in the "fifth meditation" in his *Cartesian Meditations*, we stop short of discussing it here. Suffice it to say that Husserl's concept of the transcendental lifeworld

Husserl's main concept of the lifeworld as a pregiven horizon, which provides the constant ground of validity, is critically incorporated and developed by Habermas from a different methodological stance. First of all, Habermas accepts Husserl's image of the horizon regarding the concept of the lifeworld, in that the horizon shifts according to one's position, by expanding and shrinking as one moves through the situation.[49] Habermas also concurs with Husserl by saying that the category of the lifeworld has a different status from normal world-concepts. Just as the *a priori*, pregiven lifeworld and the objective-logical world are differentiated in Husserl's transcendental phenomenology, so the concept of lifeworld is differentiated from the normal concept of world in Habermas's thought. However, unlike Husserl, Habermas understands the lifeworld not only as a resource drawn upon in communicative action but also as a topic about which communicative actors seek to reach agreement. By "the lifeworld as a topic," Habermas means the segments of the lifeworld (that is, elements of the lifeworld such as traditional rules or cultural norms), and not the lifeworld as such. Habermas writes, "Whereas *a fronte* the segment of the lifeworld relevant to a situation presses upon the actor as a problem he has to resolve on his own, *a tergo* he is sustained by the background of a lifeworld that does not consist only of cultural certainties."[50]

The concept of the reproduction of the lifeworld (i.e., the lifeworld as a topic) fleshes this out more clearly. For Habermas, the lifeworld is reproduced through the interpretive accomplishments of its members, and the process of interpretation requires the segments of the lifeworld to be tested as a topic. Indeed, actors are not products of the lifeworld, in that the lifeworld can be viewed as a self-generating process that has a life of its own, because individuals and groups reproduce the lifeworld through their communicative actions and with reference to the formal world-concepts.[51]

---

needs to be further developed, although we now find it in Habermas's theory of the lifeworld and the system.

49. Husserl holds that every horizon is flexible in that once opened, it awakens new horizons, and yet the endless whole, in its infinity of flowing movement, is oriented toward the unity of one meaning. See Husserl, *Crisis of European Sciences*, 170.

50. Habermas, *Theory of Communicative Action*, 2:135.

51. Baynes, *Normative Grounds of Social Criticism*, 83.

Perhaps the most important distinction between the lifeworld of Husserl's transcendental phenomenology and the lifeworld of Habermas's communicative action lies in Habermas's attempt to correct the culturalistic abridgment of the transcendental concept of the lifeworld through his communicative-theoretical concept of the lifeworld. Habermas articulates this point by distinguishing "the perspective of participants" based on communication theory from "the perspective of narrators" originated in the philosophy of consciousness. For Habermas, the concept of the lifeworld according to the perspective of narrators is necessarily limited to a "culturalistic" concept of the lifeworld, because the structural components of the lifeworld (i.e., culture, society, and personality) are not yet differentiated in this view. Hence by identifying the lifeworld with culturally transmitted background knowledge as such, the narrators cannot incorporate the institutional orders (society) or personality structures as elements of a situation. From the perspective of narrators, thus, the idea of the lifeworld can only be abridged as a culturalistic concept. Habermas claims that such limitation can be overcome if we begin to understand the concept of the lifeworld from the communicative-theoretical perspective.

The communicative-theoretical perspective, unlike the narrators' perspective, holds that the participating actors owe their mutual understanding to their own interpretative performances. Language is no longer understood as a conduit that reports total states of the everyday world. Rather, language becomes a medium through which the lifeworld is reproduced as the horizon-forming context of an action situation. Communicative actions serve three functions under three structural components of the lifeworld: culture, society, and personality.[52] "Under the functional aspect of *mutual understanding*, communicative action serves to transmit and renew cultural knowledge; under the aspect of *coordinating action*, it serves social integration and the establishment of solidarity; finally, under the aspect of *socialization*, communicative action serves the formation of personal identities."[53]

The lifeworld is reproduced through three corresponding processes: cultural reproduction, social integration, and socialization. Thus, symbolic structures of the lifeworld are reproduced through the

---

52. Habermas uses the term "culture" for the stock of knowledge, "society" for the legitimate orders, and "personality" for the competences.

53. Habermas, *Theory of Communicative Action*, 2:137 (emphasis in original).

continuation of valid knowledge, stabilization of group solidarity, and socialization of responsible actors.[54] According to Kenneth Baynes, individuals (as communicators, not as narrators) draw on the lifeworld as a resource in the forms of "cultural knowledge," "legitimate social orders," and "acquired individual competencies" in their social interactions.[55] As a result of the above discussion, we come to an understanding that the communicative-theoretical perspective enables us to develop a new concept of the lifeworld that transforms the culturalistically abridged concept of the lifeworld that originated in the phenomenological tradition stemming from Husserl.

According to Habermas, the reconstruction of the communicative-theoretical perspective of the lifeworld is not at all trivial, because the validity of the lifeworld concept purports to be universal—"a validity reaching across cultures and epochs."[56] This does not mean that there is only one lifeworld in the world. Habermas argues that as long as there is communicative action in any society, the concept of the lifeworld is entailed. He also develops an idea that there should be a developmental logic with the concept of the lifeworld, "if the structures of historical lifeworlds vary within the scope defined by the structural constraints of communicative action . . . in dependence on learning processes."[57] For Habermas, then, the description of structural differentiation between culture, society, and personality becomes a definite example of a "directional variation of lifeworld structures." Habermas holds that this direction means an increase in rationality, and we can find the historical evidence in Western society's development from its conventional to its postconventional level since the eighteenth century. At the center of this development Habermas discovers the rationalization of the lifeworld. The development of communicative reason, the structural differentiation of the lifeworld, the linguistification of the sacred, and the evolution of society from its conventionality to postconventionality are

---

54. Ibid.

55. Baynes, *Normative Grounds of Social Criticism*, 82. The rationality of knowledge, the solidarity of members, and the responsibility of the adult personality become the standard in evaluating the individual reproduction processes.

56. Habermas, *Theory of Communicative Action*, 2:44.

57. Ibid., 145.

all practically and historically interconnected in Habermas's theory of rationalization of the lifeworld.[58]

The System

The material maintenance of the lifeworld and the reproduction of the symbolic structures of the lifeworld should be, according to Habermas, distinguished from each other. While the symbolic structures of the lifeworld are reproduced through the continuation of valid knowledge, stabilization of group solidarity, and socialization of responsible actors, material reproduction takes place through the medium of the purposive activity with which associated individuals intervene in the world to realize their aims.[59] By "system," Habermas means the formal structure that makes possible the maintenance of the material substratum of the lifeworld. Since the reproduction of the symbolic structures of the lifeworld cannot be guaranteed without it maintaining its own material substratum, the maintenance of the material substratum of the lifeworld becomes necessary. For Habermas, the linguistification of the sacred in the domain of symbolic reproduction (i.e., in the family and the public sphere) accompanies delinguistified forms of material reproduction that include economy and state administration. It is Habermas's ingenious point that the two diametrically opposed concepts (the lifeworld and the system) compose together the course of modernization.

In order to delineate Habermas's concept of the system, we first need to see Talcott Parsons's understanding of systems theory, because Habermas develops his own view by critiquing the Parsonian understanding of systems theory. Habermas categorizes Parsons's theoretical development into three periods: the early period (*The Structure of Social Action*, 1937), the early-middle period (*The Social System*, 1951, and *Toward a General Theory of Action*, with Edward A. Shils, 1951), and the middle-late period (*Working Papers in the Theory of Action*, 1953, and *Social Systems and the Evolution of Action Theory*, 1977).

---

58. Habermas argues that historical reference points of which Mead and Durkheim are in support are a rationalization of the lifeworld in their own terms, and we can systematize rationalization of the lifeworld under three perspectives: structural differentiation of the lifeworld, separation of form and content, and growing reflexivity of symbolic reproduction (a functional specification). See Habermas, *Theory of Communicative Action*, 2:146–47.

59. Ibid., 138.

During the first (early) period, Parsons develops a theory of action with the concept of the "unit act" and the "action system." While the unit act is the most elementary form of human action, the action system refers to the interconnected chains of action. Although Parsons is largely concerned with examining the properties of the action system, the concept of the unit act holds an essential position in his *Structure of Social Action*.[60] According to Parsons, two fundamental "frames of reference" define an action: time and purpose.[61] Action is not only organized over time; it is also involved with the purposive use of means to achieve goals. The concept of the unit act also shows that Parsons has a subjectivistic view of an action formulated as a process of attaining goals. By "subjectivistic point of view," Parsons means that the social scientist is concerned with things and events as they appear from the standpoint of the actor, not from anyone else's point of view. It is important to see here that Parsons takes into account the normative standard in developing the concept of the unit act because he believes that the actions of an actor need to be in accord with certain norms. Among the action types (rational, ritual, and expressive), Parsons gives greatest attention to rational action, which he derives from Weber's concept of social action, which in this case is purposive-rational action. As Parsons argues, central to rational action is a normative principle that connects means to ends according to the "logico-experimental point of view."[62] Thus, the concept of action is largely considered under two aspects: with respect to goal attainment and appropriation of the normative standard.

According to Habermas, however, although Parsons tries to formulate the concept of an action as a process of attaining goals and taking into account the normative standards, Parsons's theory of action cannot ultimately coordinate the concept of a normative action

---

60. According to Parsons, the unit act comprises five elements: actor, end, means, situations, and norms. Among these elements, end and norms are particularly important. Parsons believes that the unit act is the sociological equivalent of the concept of the particle in classical mechanics. He thus writes, "Just as the units of a mechanical system in the classical sense, particles, can be defined only in terms of their properties, mass, velocity, location in space, direction of motion, etc., so the units of action systems also have certain basic properties without which it is not possible to conceive of the unit as 'existing'" (Parsons, *Structure of Social Action*, 43). For Parsons's explanation of the five elements, see Parsons, *Structure of Social Action*, 44.

61. Ibid., 732–33.

62. Ibid., 210.

orientation with an action-theoretical framework. Habermas argues that Parsons's theory of the action system ultimately reflects only isolated actors. Lacking in "intersubjectively harmonized" value standards, Parsons cannot but hold on to "the core of the utilitarian concept of action," which reflects a voluntaristic notion of a contingent freedom of choice between alternative means for given ends.[63] For this reason, Habermas claims that Parsons fails to provide theoretical grounds to integrate the monadic concept of action (the idea of the unit act) with the intersubjective concept of order (values and norms). In this sense, Habermas writes, "Although he [Parsons] views purposive activity as bounded by value standards and corresponding value orientations, the individualistic approach of a theory oriented to the teleology of action comes through inasmuch as the singular actions of solitary actors remain the ultimately decisive point of reference."[64]

Aware of this shortcoming, Parsons—in what Habermas terms Parsons's second ("early-middle") period—begins to conceive of the action orientation itself as a product of the combined operations of culture, society, and personality.[65] Instead of orienting a conceptual scheme around the unit act, he now develops a new model in which he analyzes action orientation in terms of how a concrete action occurs in relation to those three components. Parsons thus writes, "The theory of social systems is, in the sense of the present work, an integral part of the larger conceptual scheme which we have called the theory of action. As such, it is one of the three main differentiated sub-systems of the larger conceptual scheme, the other two being the theory of personality and the theory of culture."[66] In this new approach, for example, individual actors no longer claim value standards as their subjective properties; instead they orient their action according to cultural standards of value. Parsons calls this orientation "pattern-consistency."[67] According to this

63. Habermas, *Theory of Communicative Action*, 2:214.
64. Ibid.
65. See Parsons, *Social System*, 3–23; and Parsons and Shils, *Toward a General Theory of Action*, 3–25, 53–109.
66. Parsons, *Social System*, 537.
67. Ibid., 17. According to Parsons, a cultural system only "functions" as part of a concrete action system. So do the social system and the personality system. Each of these three is considered to be an independent focus in the organization of the elements of the action system.

new paradigm, the elementary units of actions are no longer considered to be unit acts, but instead they are regarded as patterns or symbolic meanings.

Habermas recognizes a theoretical development from 1937 to 1951 in Parsons's sociological study; that is, Parsons develops his conceptual scheme in delineating the action orientation from a subjective to an intersubjective mode. Habermas, however, points out that Parsons is not rigorous enough in laying out the methodological roadmap. For instance, Parsons answers too simplistically the question of what it means for an actor to orient his or her action in the context of tradition. According to Habermas, the idea behind Parsons's conceptual scheme is that "an actor acts within the framework of his culture by orienting himself to *cultural objects*."[68] Contrary to Parsons, though, Habermas regards the objectification of transmissible cultural contents to be "reification." Although Parsons's revision of social action overcomes the problem that he cannot resolve in his first work, Habermas determines that Parsons fails to differentiate clearly between spatiotemporally individuated objects and symbolic meanings of culture.[69] Ultimately, Parsons's problem lies in his incapacity to conceive the symbolic meanings of culture from the perspective of the speaking and acting subjects (the participant's view), rather than the viewpoint of the knowing subjects (the observer's view).

According to Habermas, Parsons's reification of culture hinders him from developing a conceptual model that enables us to get a clear picture of how culture, society, and personality hang together as components of a symbolically structured lifeworld. Habermas thus argues that without the concept of the lifeworld reproduced by communicative action, we cannot have a fruitful analysis of the interconnections among culture, society, and personality.[70] In this sense, Parsons's revision of action orientation is incomplete for two reasons: first, it still portrays a concept of action as a kind of purposive activity; second, it

---

68. Habermas, *Theory of Communicative Action*, 2:218. Although Parsons is aware that language is a medium for cultural transmission, he does not fully incorporate this aspect into his theory of action. As a result of this, in Habermas's account, Parsons regards the orientation to values not as an action oriented to mutual understanding but as an action oriented to cultural objects.

69. Ibid., 219.

70. Ibid., 222.

entails a concept of social structure and thus does not yield the complementary concept of an intersubjectively shared world. As a result, Parsons treats the three orders—society, culture, and personality—as autonomous systems or sectors that directly act on and partially interpenetrate one another.[71] Parsons's mature idea of systems theory emerges in this context.

After failing to make a conceptual transition from the unit act to the context of action, Parsons shifts his theoretical direction from the primacy of action theory to that of systems theory. Parsons articulates social action starting with problems of social structure and moves from there to the level of the individual actor in the system. The concept of structural functionalism becomes the central framework in which roles and institutions are analyzed in terms of their contribution to the internal integrity of a system or in terms of their contribution to the relationship of the system to its environment. Parsons argues that functional processes in any system can be classified into four categories, which he labels A, G, I, and L.[72] For example, action systems such as behavioral organism (the A subsystem of action), the personality (the G subsystem of action), the social system (the I subsystem of action), and the cultural system (the L subsystem of action) exhibit these four functional processes. Parsons not only divides into four the functions in the general action system, but he also sets up a hierarchy among the social systems in terms of cybernetic relations. Cybernetic hierarchy is developed to sort out the causal relations that exist between the various

71. Habermas writes, "Parsons gave up the attempt to provide an *action-theoretical* account of the idea that cultural values are incorporated into society and personality via the channels of institutionalization and internalization. Instead, he moved the model of *the interpenetration of analytically separate systems* into the foreground" (Ibid., 225, emphasis original).

72. See Parsons et al., "Phase Movement in Relation to Motivation, Symbol Formation, and Role Structure," in Parsons et al., *Working Papers in the Theory of Action* (chap. 5). With the AGIL scheme, Parsons outlines the basic classification of the functional problem of social systems into four main categories: the adaptive mechanisms (A), which concern allocation of resources to cope with the environment; goal attainment (G), which refers to the mechanisms of the direct process of goal implementation; the integrative mechanisms (I), which link the structure of the organization with the structure of the society as a whole; and pattern maintenance (L), which defines and legitimizes the goals of the organization. In 1953, Parsons specified the function of allocation with the conceptions of adaptation and goal attainment, while he subsumed cultural reproduction and socialization under pattern maintenance. With integration, he covered both functional and social integration.

systems and subsystems. For instance, Parsons argues that the cultural subsystem stands at the top of the hierarchy as a governing control-value, followed in an ordered way by social (norms), personality (goals), and behavioral (means, facilities) subsystems.[73]

According to Habermas, once Parsons has given up the primacy of action theory in light of systems theory, it is no longer a question of the cultural determination of action orientations, but it is, rather, a question of how actors' choices issue directly from processes of system formation.[74] In Habermas's analysis, the most important change in Parsons's systems theory is the leveling of the central disparity between functional and social integration. These two aspects are brought together under "integration." As a result of this, "Parsons makes the important—but nowhere explicitly acknowledged—decision to drop the concept of a social integration established via values and norms and to speak from now on only of 'integration' in general."[75] By "integration," Habermas means the cybernetic hierarchy, which lacks in intersubjective linguistic relations.

In particular, Habermas criticizes Parsons's systems theory for its overgeneralization. In particular, Habermas argues that Parsons's systems theory reduces the structures of linguistically generated intersubjectivity to mechanisms such as exchange and organization. Parsons's systems theory renders the linguistically generated intersubjectivity unduly eclipsed by the mechanisms of the system. For instance, Parsons's later work stipulates money, power, and influence as the three principal media of interchange between differentiated structures.[76] Language is not fully incorporated as a medium in Parsons's systems theory.

Habermas disagrees with the systems theorists' assumption that any steering medium whatsoever can be differentiated out of language. Against systems theorists, Habermas states, "The only functional do-

---

73. According to Parsons, while those processes that are high in "information" are especially important in controlling the overall development of a system, those that are high in "energy" are able to limit or condition this development.

74. Habermas, *Theory of Communicative Action*, 2:242.

75. According to Habermas, the leveling of the distinction between functional and social integration "*makes unrecognizable* the seams that resulted from joining the two paradigms of 'action' and 'system'" (ibid., 241).

76. The societal community generates influence as a circulating medium, while the interchanges between differentiated economic and political structures are mediated by money and power.

mains that can be differentiated out of the lifeworld by steering media are those of material reproduction."[77] This functional domain of material production is what Habermas means by "system." In contrast to the lifeworld, which is reproduced only via the basic medium of communicative action keyed to cultural reproduction, social integration, and socialization, the system remains in effect through the maintenance of the material substratum of the lifeworld. Unlike the lifeworld, which is rationalized through communicative action, the system is sustained through the medium of the purposive activity with which individuals intervene in the world to pursue their goals.

According to Habermas, in order for the lifeworld to be reproduced, the maintenance of the system must be affirmed. It is inaccurate, however, to portray from a hierarchical perspective the system as a subordinate entity to the lifeworld. Indeed, differing from Parsons, particularly his idea of cybernetic relation among action systems, Habermas deals with the system and the lifeworld without presupposing any hierarchical order. Focusing rather on the reciprocal dynamic between the two, Habermas conceives the basic feature of the uncoupling of the system and the lifeworld as a second-order differentiation.[78] He refuses to view the uncoupling process either from the system perspective or from the lifeworld perspective. Instead, he claims that we need to analyze the connections in a way that critically coordinates the increasing complexity of the system with the rationalization of the lifeworld.

Habermas thus describes the system through the lens of an uncoupling process of the system and the lifeworld, which he also portrays as a historical process. He starts with the archaic societies characterized by kinship systems and the mythical structures of consciousness. According to Habermas, although the lifeworld concept finds its stron-

---

77. Habermas, *Theory of Communicative Action*, 2:261. By distinguishing the functional domain from the communicative lifeworld, Habermas uncouples the system from the lifeworld.

78. By "second-order" differentiation, Habermas means that the stages of social evolution (from tribal societies to modern societies) are not distinguished exclusively either by the system differentiation or by the lifeworld differentiation. The system and the lifeworld are differentiated from each other at the same time, as the complexity of the system and the rationality of the lifeworld grow. According to Habermas, if we overlook this, then the uncoupling of the system and the lifeworld is depicted in such a way that while the lifeworld gets cut down more and more to one subsystem among others, the system gets disconnected from norms and values.

gest empirical foothold in archaic societies, kinship relations divide the lifeworld into two groups—those who are kin and those who are not. In contrast, mythical worldviews blur the categorical distinctions between the objective, social, and subjective worlds.[79] The archaic societies evolve as they gain complexity in terms of "segmental differentiation" and "stratification." The exchange of women, normed by the rules of marriage in tribal societies makes possible segmental differentiation of society insofar as it horizontally strings together similarly structured groups into a larger organism. Stratification is realized in the form of a status system based on prestige, because tribal societies do not yet take the form of political power. The most conspicuous feature of tribal societies lies in the fact that social integration and system integration still operate within the dimensions set by the kinship system: sex, generation, descent.[80]

The power mechanism of tribal societies changes as their political power begins to derive their authority from a disposition over judicial means of sanction rather than from the prestige of leading descent groups. The power mechanism and kinship structure are differentiated from each other. As tribal societies turn into forms of state organization, markets steered by the medium of money also arise. Habermas claims, however, that money as a steering medium is able to have a structure-forming effect for the social system as a whole only when the economy is separated from the political order.[81] According to Habermas's historical analysis, European societies experienced this differentiation process during the early modern period. Since the capital economy necessitated a reorganization of the state in Europe, Habermas defines the relationship between the subsystems of the market economy and the modern administration as "complementary." Both the market economy and the state administration become the mechanisms of the steering media in modern societies. These media are what Parsons refers to as "symbolically generalized media of communication" in connection to "adaptation" and "goal-attainment."[82] Money and power thus become the major

79. Ibid., 157–59.

80. Ibid., 163. Habermas also writes, "Systemic mechanisms remain tightly intermeshed with mechanisms of social integration only so long as they attach to pregiven social structures, that is, to the kinship system" (ibid., 165).

81. Ibid., 165.

82. Ibid.

steering media that compose the system through which the maintenance of the material substratum of the lifeworld is attained. According to Habermas's analysis, the increasing systemic complexity of modern societies is also what comprises the evolution of the society along with the rationalization of the lifeworld.

We can understand Habermas's concept of the system more fully by investigating the relational dynamic between the lifeworld and the system, which Habermas has already assessed to be complementary. Here we can see Habermas's view on what this complementary relation is like.

> Both are conceivable: the institutions that anchor steering mechanisms such as power and money in the lifeworld could serve as a channel either for the influence of the lifeworld on formally organized domains of action or, conversely, for the influence of the system on communicatively structured contexts of action. In the one case, they function as an institutional framework that subjects system maintenance to the normative restrictions of the lifeworld, in the other, as a base that subordinates the lifeworld to the systemic constraints of material reproduction and thereby "mediatizes" it.[83]

In my view, Habermas, at least in his *Theory of Communicative Action*, is more concerned about the latter case, that is, the system's mediatization of the lifeworld through its subsystems—the market economy and state administration. Concerning the former case, we can discover a more promising vision in his later work *Between Facts and Norms*, to which we turn in the next chapter.

According to Habermas, systemic complexity increases only through the introduction of a new system mechanism, and every new mechanism of the system differentiation must be anchored in the lifeworld.[84] Habermas explains the systems' "anchoring" in the lifeworld as a necessary condition because the evolutionary innovations of systemic

---

83. Ibid., 185.

84. "It must be *institutionalized* there via family status, the authority of office, or bourgeois private law" (Ibid., 173). Habermas differentiates morality and law in light of Lawrence Kohlberg's tripartite distinction of moral consciousness keyed to ontogenesis. While morality is anchored only in the personality system, law develops into an external force sanctioned by the state as an institution detached from the ethical motivations of the legal person and dependent on abstract obedience to the law. See Habermas, *Theory of Communicative Action*, 2:174.

institution depend on the sufficient rationalization of the lifeworld, particularly regarding the development of law and morality: "The institutionalization of a new level of system differentiation requires reconstruction in the core institutional domain of the moral-legal (consensual) regulation of conflicts."[85] Since morality and law secure the next level of consensus to which we have recourse when the normal coordination of actions does not come to pass and thus violent confrontation is in order, Habermas regards moral and legal norms as "second-order norms of action." After all, without being anchored in moral and legal order, innovations of the systemic institution cannot be legitimate.

Habermas holds, however, that the system's anchoring in the lifeworld should not be simplistically understood, because law as a second-order norm and meta-institution has become interconnected not only with the lifeworld but also with the system, especially its economic and bureaucratic subsystems. The legal sphere is particularly polarized as the uncoupling process of the system and the lifeworld takes place. Habermas perceives that the legal sphere becomes situated in a unique but complex position. The legal sphere not only has an essential relation to the rationalization of the lifeworld by implying and evoking the problems of the basic principles of legitimation, but it also increases the separation of the system from the lifeworld, rendering itself as a demoralized, positive, compulsory law that exacts a deferment of legitimation.[86] Habermas's differentiation between "law as medium" and "law as legal institution" gives us a clear example of a situation in which the lifeworld and the system are uncoupled in the course of modernization.[87] This, however, should not be interpreted

85. Ibid.
86. Ibid., 180.
87. Habermas classifies legal norms according to the following criteria: whether they can be legitimized only through procedure in the positivist sense, or are amenable to substantive justification. While the former criterion enables us to identify law with "law as medium," the latter allows us to conceptualize law as "law as legal institution." Thus, while "law as medium" is relieved of the problem of justification in that it is connected with the body of law whose substance requires legitimation only through formally correct procedure, "law as legal institution" cannot be sufficiently legitimized through a positivistic reference to procedure. While most areas of economic, commercial, business, and administrative law fit with the law as a medium, such legal institutions as constitutional law, the principles of criminal law and penal procedure, and all regulations (e.g., against murder, abortion, rape, and so forth) are typical of the law as a legal

in such a way that the uncoupling process itself gives birth to the disconnected lifeworld and system. On the contrary, in the uncoupling process we discover not only the "pathologies of modernity" that have been widely detected but also the "remedial vision" that has been developed in the name of discourse ethics.

Colonization of the Lifeworld and the Moral Predicament of the Positional Self

Through Habermas's in-depth analysis of the lifeworld and the system, we realize that there is an ironic and paradoxical aspect in the process of uncoupling the concepts of the lifeworld and the system. Although the rationalization of the lifeworld enables the emergence of the system, the system later encroaches upon the lifeworld: "The rationalization of the lifeworld makes possible a heightening of systemic complexity, which becomes so hypertrophied that it unleashes system imperatives that burst the capacity of the lifeworld they instrumentalize."[88] Since action oriented to mutual understanding could not cope with ever-greater demands made on it after the rationalization of the lifeworld, it gets overloaded in the end and replaced by delinguistified media such as money and power. Then the independent imperatives of subsystems destructively turn back on the lifeworld itself.[89]

As a result of this paradoxical relation in the uncoupling process, the lifeworld is increasingly invaded and colonized by a systemic mode of integration, which Habermas calls the "colonization of lifeworld by system." Habermas, however, shows us that there can also be a promising aspect in this uncoupling process because we can expand the lifeworld principle into subsystems of purposive-rational action. In Habermas's

---

institution. While "law as medium" serves for organizing media-controlled subsystems, "law as legal institution" belongs to the societal components of the lifeworld. While the law as a medium is enacted, the law as a legal institution is justified. Most conspicuously, unlike "law as medium," which remains indifferent in relation to the lifeworld, "law as legal institution" stands in a continuum with moral norms superimposed on communicatively structured areas of action. See Habermas, *Theory of Communicative Action*, 2:365–67.

88. Ibid., 155.

89. Ibid., 186. From Habermas's view, while Weber's major sociological concern was the emergence of subsystems in the lifeworld, Marx's econopolitical agenda was how to solve the problem of the subsystem's encroachment on the lifeworld.

terms, a system is supposed to be anchored in a lifeworld. Although Habermas mentions these two types of potential interconnection in *Theory of Communicative Action*, he is more focused on the critical analysis of the colonization of the lifeworld by the system than he is on the reconstructive element of the other aspect, that is, on the expansion of lifeworld principles into a systemic world.[90]

The two seemingly contradictory directional modes provide us with two important methodological tools with which we are able not only to analyze the moral predicament of the positional self but also to develop a moral prescription to emancipate the positional self from its pathological predicament. In the rest of this chapter, we will deal with the first issue—the analysis of the predicament of the positional self—by introducing Habermas's critical investigation of the pathologies of contemporary society: the colonization of the lifeworld by the system. As a result of this investigation, we will be able to have a clearer view of the positional self's moral situation and its problems. In the next chapter, we will deal extensively with Habermas's theory of morality, law, and democracy. Along with this, we will cover Habermas's reconstructive proposal for the moral establishment of the positional self in the systemic world.

Before we investigate the moral predicament that the positional self faces in contemporary society, we need first to situate the positional self as a mediated self between the lifeworld and the system. By mediating the worlds (the lifeworld and the system), the positional self holds a distinctive position in the organizations of subsystems as an administrator or an executive representative. The positional self at the same time belongs to the private and public spheres of a lifeworld as family member, citizen, and customer in society. In my view, it is implausible for us to connect Habermas and the concept of the positional self because he is not interested in developing an idea similar to the mediated self in his *Theory of Communicative Action*. He does, however, provide us with important clues on how the positional self can be conceptually differentiated from the four types of persons who inhabit both the

---

90. Johannes Berger raises this point in his article "The Linguistification of the Sacred and the Delinguistification of the Economy." According to Berger, "trends toward the humanization of labor or democratization of the economy could be interpreted as the interference of communicative rationality into formally organized subsystems" (Berger, "Linguistification of the Sacred," 178).

lifeworld and the system: the employee, the consumer, the client, and the citizen.

Habermas conceptualizes these types of persons by categorizing two modes of relations between the institutional orders of the lifeworld and the media-steered subsystems. In the first category, relations are defined by organization-dependent roles in the employment or administrative system. The two kinds of systems—the employment system and public administration—regulate their interchanges with the lifeworld respectively via the role of a member (employee) of an organization and the role of the client.[91] According to Habermas, "Actors who assume the roles of employees or of clients of the public administration detach themselves from lifeworld contexts and adapt themselves to formally organized domains of action. Either they make some organization-specific contribution and are compensated for it (normally in the form of wages or salaries), or they are the recipients of organization-specific services and make compensation therefore (normally in the form of taxes)."[92]

For Habermas, although the interchange relations of the second category are also defined with reference to formally organized domains of action, they are not dependent on economic or administrative systems. Unlike the employees and clients who belong to the first category, the consumers and participants (citizens) in an economic system and public sphere compose the second category. According to Habermas, then, the roles of consumers and citizens are not constituted in the same way as are those of employees and clients of the economic and the political systems. While the roles of the employee and the client are constituted by legal fiat, "the roles of consumer and citizen refer to prior self-formative processes in which preferences, value orientations, attitudes, and so forth have taken shape."[93] Since cultural patterns of demand (consumer) and political legitimation (citizen) are tied to lifeworld contexts, the roles of consumer and citizen cannot be taken over by a system via abstract quantities of labor power and taxes. In sum, Habermas uncovers the four types of the social self that can be con-

91. Habermas, *Theory of Communicative Action*, 2:319–21.
92. Ibid., 321.
93. Ibid. Habermas argues that while such orientations for the roles of consumer and citizen are developed in the private and public spheres of the lifeworld, they cannot be "bought" or "collected" like labor power and taxes by private or public organizations.

ceptually distinguished as the interchange relations between the institutional orders of the lifeworld and the media-steered subsystems that develop into a rationalized form. As a result, we see clearly that while the employee and the client are the social selves who posit themselves in the system by detaching themselves from the lifeworld, the consumer and the citizen find their primary space in the lifeworld.

The positional self is different from these four types of the social self in that the positional self belongs not only to the lifeworld but also to the system. Interestingly, Habermas does not mention such groups of people as employers, manufacturers, administrators, and executives of economic corporations or political organizations, whom we could identify as examples of the positional self. Although these people are situated in the subsystem as important position holders, they are not estranged from the institutional orders of the lifeworld. They are the system organizers, but at the same time they are consumers or citizens of the society. Without considering consumers' value orientations or citizens' political preferences, the positional self who is an executive officer or a political leader cannot organize or maintain the system. The positional self needs to understand itself as a mediated self, belonging not only to the system but also to the lifeworld.

The status of dual membership for the positional self is more clearly outlined when we analyze its distinctive positional function or character mediating the lifeworld and the system. We need to understand first that the positional self is different from employees and clients posited in the system. Unlike employees and clients, such position holders as employers, executive directors, and representatives of parties have administrative autonomy in organizing and sustaining the system that they represent.[94] This autonomy is a social reality through which the value orientation comes into realization in organizational and institutional forms. Since both the lifeworld and the system provide the positional self with the sources of value orientation, it is up to each positional self to decide which sources to incorporate and how sources will be incorporated into decisions or policies.

This, however, should not be interpreted in such a simplistic way that the decision making of the positional self comes down to an indi-

---

94. The idea of administrative autonomy will be analyzed again in chapter 4, in which I will deal with the moral predicament of administrative autonomy with the concept of positional freedom by drawing on Niebuhr's conceptual tools and insights.

vidual's choice based on personal preference. The social effects of the positional self's role is sometimes so far reaching that many people who have no relationship with the positional self are affected by the role. Thus, from a moral perspective, we need to distinguish the positional self from non-position holders or individual selves. In this sense, the moral responsibility that the positional self holds should not be reduced to a personal or private kind; rather, it should be regarded as a positional responsibility. Since the positional character includes both personal and organizational aspects (in Habermas's terms, the "life-world perspective" and the "systemic perspective"), the moral aspect of the positional self ought to be understood in a distinctive way that integrates both elements.

Habermas's idea of the colonization of the lifeworld gives us an important perspective in deciphering the moral aspect of the positional self, particularly with regard to the moral predicament of the positional self. In order to uncover the moral predicament of the positional self, we need first to examine a pathological symptom of modern society. For this we begin with Max Weber's diagnosis of the fragmentation of the modern person, which came into being as a result of the rationalization of the society. Weber discovers that the private conduct of life is increasingly polarized between "specialists without spirit" and "sensualists without heart." According to Habermas's interpretation, the notion of specialists without spirit arises as an "adaptation to the objectified milieu of large organizations [that] is combined with a utilitarian calculation of the actor's own interests."[95] Weber sees that the practical-moral character of specialists is eclipsed by cognitive-instrumental attitudes toward themselves and others. "Ethical obligations to one's calling give way to instrumental attitudes toward an occupational role that offers the opportunity for income and advancement, but no longer for ascertaining one's personal salvation or for fulfilling oneself in a secular sense."[96]

Using Habermas's technical terms, we can roughly identify Weber's specialists as the employees and clients who find their places in the subsystem. However, it is not clear whether the idea of the positional

---

95. Habermas, *Theory of Communicative Action*, 2:323.

96. Ibid. According to Weber, although the two lifestyles can be strikingly represented by different personality types, they can also take hold of the same person. Specialists are shaped and occupied by the utilitarian lifestyle, while sensualists by expressive attitudes in private space.

self can be fully covered and characterized by the concept of Weber's specialists. Since Weber's specialist is detached from the lifeworld, there is a significant difference between the concepts of the positional self and the specialist. In my view, Habermas provides a better conceptual scheme, by which we can identify the moral predicament that befalls the positional self.

Habermas identifies the pathologies of modern society differently from those that Weber developed. According to Habermas, the real problem that modern society faces is not the rationalization of the lifeworld or an increasing system complexity. For Habermas, "Neither the secularization of worldviews nor the structural differentiation of society has unavoidable pathological side effects per se."[97] The real problem is rather the pathological dynamics arising between the two modes of progress.

For Habermas, unlike Weber, the neutralization of vocational-ethical attitudes is no longer counted as a sign of social pathology. According to Habermas, pathologies of modern society lie in "a colonization of the lifeworld by system imperatives that drive moral-practical elements out of private and political public spheres of life."[98] As a result of the irresistible inner dynamics, media-steered subsystems not only colonize the lifeworld but also detach themselves from science, morality, and art. Habermas writes,

> It is not the uncoupling of media-steered subsystems and of their organizational forms from the lifeworld that leads to the one-sided rationalization or reification of everyday communicative practice, but only the penetration of forms of economic and administrative rationality into areas of action that resist being converted over to the media of money and power because they are specialized in cultural transmission, social integration, and child rearing, and remain dependent on mutual understanding as a mechanism for coordinating action.[99]

The pathologies of modern society thus can be identified as the monetarization and the bureaucratization of everyday practices both in the private and public spheres.

---

97. Habermas, *Theory of Communicative Action*, 2:330.
98. Ibid., 325.
99. Ibid., 330.

The identification of the pathologies of modern society gives us an important clue concerning the uncovering of the moral predicament that would lead many positional selves of modern society into the state of moral bankruptcy. As Habermas perceives, the more the social systems become complex, the more the lifeworld becomes provincial, and the possibility to draw a promising roadmap for the positional self's moral realization in the organizational world becomes slender. We find in Habermas's theory of law a clearer example of the moral predicament that befalls the positional self.

Concurring with Otto Kirchheimer, Habermas states that modern society is marked by "juridification" (*Verrechtlichung*), which refers to the tendency toward an increase in formal (or positive, written) law. According to Habermas's analysis, as society develops toward the welfare state, which is the last stage in the four epochal juridification processes,[100] an apparent dilemma emerges. "While the welfare-state guarantees are intended to serve the goal of social integration, they nevertheless promote the disintegration of life-relations when these are separated, through legalized social intervention, from the consensual mechanisms that coordinate action and are transferred over to media such as power and money."[101] By "legalized social intervention," Habermas means the enactment of law as a means for organizing media-controlled subsystems.

According to Habermas, then, the emergence of law as a medium becomes available as the uncoupling of the system and the lifeworld fits in with the legal structure. As the society develops into the welfare state, legal positivism crashes into most areas of economic, commercial, business, and administrative law. As a result, the inner dynamics of those action systems, such as capitalist enterprise (the economy) and the bureaucratic apparatus of domination (the state), unfold within the organizational forms of law. They do so, however, "in such a way that law here takes on the role of a steering medium rather than supplementing

---

100. Habermas states that four epochal juridification processes can be distinguished: the first wave led to the bourgeois state, the second wave to the constitutional state (*Rechtsstaat*), the third wave to the democratic constitutional state, and the last stage to the democratic welfare state (*soziale und demokratische Rechtsstaat*). See Habermas, *Theory of Communicative Action*, 2:357.

101. Ibid., 364.

institutional components of the lifeworld."[102] Habermas provides us with some specific examples of how the lifeworld is colonized by the system through juridification in such areas as social welfare, the school, and the family. In Habermas's terms, thanks to social-welfare law and the expansion of legal protection and the enforcement of basic rights in the family and the schools, domains of the lifeworld are increasingly opened up to bureaucratic intervention and judicial control. Indeed, "the subsystems of the economy and state become more and more complex as a consequence of capitalist growth, and penetrate ever deeper into the symbolic reproduction of the lifeworld."[103]

Conclusion

As a result of the above discussion, we understand that the positional self as a position holder in a capitalistic enterprise or in an administrative apparatus is increasingly forced to adapt to the systemic mode of life. Situated at the juncture between the system and the lifeworld, the positional self has to serve the systemic mechanisms exemplified by growing juridification as their agents. Habermas gives us a picture in which it is almost impossible for any positional self to act against the systemic mode of life. From this perspective, paradoxically, the positional self is construed not only as the victim of the colonization process but also as the colonizer of the lifeworld.

In sum, the moral predicament that inevitably befalls the positional self in modern capitalistic society is identified as a social pathology that renders the positional self both as the victim of the colonization and as its proxy. Positional selves are the enemies of the lifeworld, but at the same time they are the hostages held by the system. For this reason, the moral problems that the positional self has to confront are complex and intricate. The moral predicament of the positional self is exemplified by the social condition in which the positional self sometimes cannot choose the good without engendering social evil.[104] For the sake of sur-

102. Ibid., 366.
103. Ibid., 367.
104. Habermas gives an example of this predicament. According to Habermas, "The protection of pupils' and parents' rights against educational measures (such as promotion or nonpromotion, examinations and tests, and so forth), or from acts of the school or the department of education that restrict basic rights (disciplinary penalties), is gained at the cost of a judicialization and bureaucratization that penetrates to the

vival and preservation, the positional self is increasingly pressured to play the role of the colonizer as an agent of the colonization process. From this perspective, it appears to be impossible for the positional self to establish itself as a moral self. In the next chapter, however, we will probe the possibility of constituting the positional self as a moral self through an in-depth analysis of Habermas's discourse ethics. Is there any moral prescription to the moral pathology of the colonizing process?

---

teaching and learning process" (Habermas, *Theory of Communicative Action*, 2:371).

3

Habermas's Philosophical Reconstruction and the Positional Self

Introduction

THE MAIN PURPOSE OF THIS CHAPTER IS TO SEARCH FOR A POSSIBLE solution in reconstructing the moral aspect of the positional self in the organizational and institutional world. In the previous chapter, we examined how the modern social pathologies—the colonization of the lifeworld by the system—bring morally negative effects to the positional self in the uncoupling process of the lifeworld and the system. In particular, we discovered that the positional self as a mediated self between the lifeworld and the system is increasingly pressured to conform to the systemic mode of life, and thus is more likely to play the role of the "colonizer" in the uncoupling process. Paradoxically, the positional self is colonizing itself while playing the role of the colonizer in the system's colonization process of the lifeworld. This, however, should not mean that the positional self is doomed to be immoral just because it is unlikely for a positional self to realize itself as a moral self in Habermas's critical theory.

A careful reading of Habermas enables us to see that he mentions not only the "colonization" of the lifeworld by the system but also the system's "anchoring" in the lifeworld. Without the latter, no positional self could realize its moral sphere in its relation to system. We will see in this chapter how the system's anchoring in the lifeworld has to do with the reconstruction of the moral dimension of the positional self in light of Habermas's discourse ethics. The social phenomenon of the system's anchoring in the lifeworld is crucial in supplying moral guidance to the positional self because without importing moral principles or norms from the lifeworld, the system itself cannot provide any moral norms to the positional self. Nor can we develop any moral insights to situate the positional self as a moral self in political or economic systems. As we have seen, with the advent of the capitalist economic systems and a state apparatus, actions of the positional self are systemically integrated to the structure of a steering medium. Habermas, however, emphasizes that the steering media ought to be anchored in the lifeworld. The significance of this anchoring is that by keeping the laws of society, established through the agency of consensus mechanisms, the positional self can establish itself as a moral self although it appears to be minimalistic and indirect. Thanks to the anchoring, actions of the positional self can be coupled to normative contexts of the lifeworld, although indirectly.[1] This, of course, requires a political condition that the consensus mechanism itself is a democratic process of will formation.

The anchoring of the system in the lifeworld, as Habermas states, "presses for the implementation of lifeworldly imperatives in the form of restrictions imposed on the capitalist mode of operations in the economic system and the bureaucratic mode in the administrative system."[2] The concepts of the law, of the public sphere, and of public reason become important topics with regard to our reconstructive project to establish the positional self as a moral self. Habermas's concept of the public sphere makes possible the procedures and communicative presuppositions of democratic opinion and will formation as the most important channels for the discursive rationalization of the decisions

---

1. Habermas differentiates the lifeworld from the democratic political system. While the lifeworld is conceptually divided into two categories according to its functions and contents: systems like religion, education, and the family and systems like science, morality and art, and the democratic political system are composed of legal regulations, administrative control, or political steering. Between the two lies the distinctive social space called the public sphere. Public spheres such as forums, stages, and arenas must be anchored in the voluntary associations of civil society and embedded in liberal patterns of political culture and socialization. Habermas perceives that although public spheres are anchored in civil society depending on a rationalized lifeworld, the lifeworld meets them halfway. Public spheres also meet with the political system "as a sounding board for problems that must be processed by the political system." (359) In Habermas's proceduralist perspective, the positional self can be morally constituted only in its halfway connection to the lifeworld through public spheres. See Habermas, *Between Facts and Norms*, 358–60.

2. Habermas, "A Reply," 260.

of a government and an administration bound by law and statue. Since morality and law are established on the same principle—the discourse principle of the communicative action—it becomes critical for us to start with the idea of discourse theory by which we can reconstruct the moral identity of the positional self as a self that is responsible to the procedurally constituted legal norms.

We can see now that Habermas's critical theory generally portrays the moral aspect of the positional self as a dialectical concept between two seemingly contradictory social phenomena: the colonization of the lifeworld by the system and the anchoring of the system in the lifeworld. It is my contention that while the system's anchoring in the lifeworld enables the moral character of the positional self as a responsible agent, the colonization process contradictorily makes the positional self a colonizer of the lifeworld. As Habermas writes, the former signifies a strengthening of "the institutional framework that subjects system maintenance to the normative restrictions of the lifeworld," the latter a consolidation of existing class structures and thus of "a base that subordinates the lifeworld to the systemic constraints of material reproduction and thereby 'mediatizes' it."[3] In my view, by correlating the two contradictory concepts of Habermas's critical theory, we come to have a clearer vision of the positional self: its moral predicament and its moral prospect.

The System's Anchoring in the Lifeworld

According to Habermas, the system's anchoring in the lifeworld is realized through the legal institutionalization of steering media: "Through the legal institutionalization of steering media, however, these systems [economy and administration] remain anchored in the society component of the lifeworld."[4] We have to remember that while the lifeworld is characterized by a network composed of communicative actions, the system is operated by the steering media: money and power. As delinguistified media, money and power are initially excluded from the domain of moral discourse. Since the validity claim for rightness is strictly confined to the social world in which practical reason real-

---

3. Ibid., 260-61. It is originally from Habermas, *Theory of Communicative Action*, 2:185.
4. Habermas, *Between Facts and Norms*, 354.

izes itself intersubjectively through communication and discourse, the system becomes irrelevant to the domain of moral discourse. As steering media, money and power attach to empirically motivated ties such as calculable amounts of value, whereas language attaches to forms of rationally motivated trust through criticizable validity claims.

As Habermas posits, unlike money and power, which are disconnected from the domain of morality, the language of law can correlate the disconnected domains: the lifeworld and the system. He writes, "The language of law brings ordinary communication from the public and private spheres [lifeworld] and puts it into a form in which these messages can also be received by the special codes of autopoietic systems—and vice versa."[5] In that the ordinary language of the lifeworld could circulate throughout society through the language of law, Habermas thus describes the law as "transformer." In short, such systems as monetary economy and administrative politics can be anchored in the society component of the lifeworld through legal norms. From the perspective of the system's anchoring in the lifeworld, Habermas claims that "problems of functional coordination, when handled politically, are *intertwined* with the moral and ethical dimensions of social integration."[6]

Although the role of the language of law is critical when it comes to the matter of the system's anchoring in the lifeworld, we should not overlook the important point that, along with the anchoring of the system in the lifeworld, there is another set of anchoring: the anchoring of the legal norm in moral discourse. Since the system is regulated by legal norms, and the lifeworld is reproduced and maintained by communicative action and moral discourse, the system's anchoring in the lifeworld cannot be conceived without the law's anchoring in moral discourse. Thus in order to investigate how the system's anchoring in the lifeworld has to do with the reconstruction of the moral character of the positional self, we have to begin by clarifying the concept of the law's anchoring in moral discourse. For this, we have to go back to Habermas's idea of discourse ethics and his theory of law.

---

5. Ibid.
6. Ibid., 351.

Discourse Ethics

According to Habermas, discourse ethics is not possible unless the traditional society is fully rationalized. By the "rationalization of society," Habermas means the substitution of "posttraditional communication" for "traditional dialogue." He also means the substitution of "rationalized lifeworld" for the "traditional society." In contrast to the traditional, the posttraditional signifies a world concept in which there is no such thing as overarching and substantive value orientation. Habermas's discourse ethics is indeed a theoretical endeavor to show that without relying on any substantive religious or metaphysical traditions, the "cognitivist ethics of responsibility" can be possible.

According to Habermas, Weber's rationalization of society renders the traditional society radically transformed into a posttraditional society in which the world concept is decentered along with the generalization of values. Habermas at first agrees with Weber's argument that the institutionalization of purposive-rational economic action is initially shaped by way of the Protestant vocational culture and subsequently by way of the modern legal system.[7] The role of the Protestant ethic, however, in anchoring the sphere of purposive-rational action in one's calling is ambivalent in Weber's analysis of societal rationalization. Although the Protestant ethic of the calling fulfills necessary conditions for an emerging motivational basis for purposive-rational action in the sphere of social labor, it is not able to secure the conditions for its own stabilization. Habermas thus writes: "In Weber's view, the subsystems of purposive-rational action form an environment that is destructive of the Protestant ethic in the long run."[8]

Weber diagnoses that as the immanent laws of capitalist growth and the reproduction of state power dominate the moral-practical rationality of the ethic of conviction fueled by religious beliefs, the

---

7. Calvinist doctrine affirms that successful activity in one's calling does not count directly as means for attaining salvation but as an outward sign for ascertaining a state of grace. Weber discovers in Calvinism and in the Protestant sects the teachings that singled out the methodological conduct of life as a path to salvation. Success in one's calling is connected with the individual's redemptory fate in such a way that labor in one's calling is ethically charged and dramatized. Habermas calls this the "moral anchoring" of a sphere of purposive-rational testing in one's calling. The sphere itself is set free from traditional morality. Habermas, *Theory of Communicative Action*, 1:223–25.

8. Ibid., 228.

Protestant ethic is later substituted by the ethics of utilitarianism.[9] From Habermas's perspective, Weber's argument contains a serious problem, because Weber's conclusion lacks any empirical and methodological qualification when he presupposes that a moral consciousness guided by principles can survive only in a religious context.[10] Habermas thus claims that Weber's presupposition is groundless because it lacks not only convincing empirical evidence but also strong systematic arguments.[11]

Habermas argues that a cognitivist ethics of responsibility can be established as a result of the ethical rationalization of religious worldviews, enabling the differentiation of a value sphere. In Habermas's analysis, Weber's problem is that he is generally fixated on the relations of tension between religion and the world, and thus he cannot take into account a new ethic that can fill the space once occupied by religious worldviews. Habermas claims that a secularized form of the religious ethic of brotherliness can be established even while it is detached from its foundation in salvation religion.[12] His discourse ethics offers an ultimate proof of this because it provides the most plausible alternative to the religious worldviews in a society that has already undergone value generalization. It is Habermas's ingenious point that the rationalization of the lifeworld has not led society into moral bankruptcy along with the liquidation of the religious worldview, but rather it has actually opened a new possibility of moral reconstruction. In short, whereas Weber sees the seeds of moral destruction in the rationalization of the world, Habermas discovers a hopeful possibility of "higher rationalization" that has been best realized in the form of "discourse ethics."

Habermas's discourse ethics thematizes not the debatable points or contents of communication but the form or act of communication itself from a proceduralist perspective. The universal phenomenon of

9. Ibid., 241.

10. Ibid., 229.

11. For empirical evidence, Habermas draws on Bernard Groethuysen's well-known 1927 study, which demonstrates that the development in the French bourgeoisie of a bourgeois moral consciousness was autonomous in relation to the church. Habermas also argues: "The thesis that a moral consciousness at a posttraditional stage cannot be stabilized without being embedded in religion also lacks systems" (Habermas, *Theory of Communicative Action*, 1:230).

12. Ibid., 242.

language itself becomes an important subject in Habermas's critical theory. In his book *Moral Consciousness and Communicative Action*, Habermas holds two modes of language use. "In one mode of language use, *one says what is or is not the case*. In the other, *one says something to someone else in a way that allows him to understand what is being said.*"[13] According to Habermas, only the second mode of language use satisfies the conditions of posttraditional communication. In order for a communication to be realized, there must be a speech situation in which "a speaker, in communicating *with* a hearer *about* something, gives expression to what *he/[she]* means."[14] Therefore, when language is used for coming to terms or reaching an understanding with someone else, three relations are involved: the expression of one's belief, the communication with another member, and the speech about something in the world.

Habermas calls the second mode of language use the "performative use of language," which is characterized by the perspectives of a speaker and a hearer. In the performative use of language, according to Habermas, the "speaker" refers to something in three different worlds: the objective world as the sum total of what is or could be the case, the social world as the sum total of legitimately ordered interpersonal relations, and the subjective world as the sum total of experiences that can be manifested and to which one has privileged access.[15] He also analyzes the second mode of language from the perspective of the lifeworld (the background of the shared assumptions and practices), wherein he finds that language is serving three functions: that of reproducing culture and keeping traditions alive, that of social integration or the coordination of the plans of different actors in social interaction, and that of socialization or the cultural interpretation of needs. Habermas develops his theory of communicative action in relation to the second function: the use of language for social integration or the coordination of the plans of different actors.[16]

---

13. Habermas, *Moral Consciousness and Communicative Action*, 24 (emphasis original).

14. Ibid.

15. Ibid., 25.

16. Habermas correlates the first function with Hans Georg Gadamer's philosophical hermeneutics, while he identifies the third function with the perspective of George Herbert Mead's social psychology. See Habermas, *Moral Consciousness and Communicative Action*, 25.

Although, as Habermas argues, language has been traditionally conceived in terms of the model of assigning names to objects and viewed as an instrument of communication that remains external to the content of thought, a new understanding of language has been found since the work of Wilhelm von Humboldt. Habermas calls this new transition the "linguistic turn," and he claims that the new, transcendentally characterized conception of language (formal pragmatics) helps us attain methodological advantage over semantics and semiotics.[17] Habermas also claims that with the linguistic turn, it becomes possible to attack the problem that cannot be solved using the basic concepts of metaphysics: the problem of individuality. By providing the intersubjective validity of observation, the linguistic turn enables us to overcome the methodological limitations that all types of the philosophy of the subject have entailed, that is, the introspective access to facts of consciousness.

According to Habermas, "the task of universal pragmatics is to identify and reconstruct universal conditions of possible understanding."[18] Thus, Habermas develops the concept of the communicative rationality reconstructively, by analyzing formal pragmatic conditions of universal discourse. Among the many linguistic and social philosophers, Ludwig Wittgenstein, J. L. Austin, and Karl-Otto Apel are particularly important in developing Habermas's idea of communicative rationality. First, Wittgenstein's central insight provides a key methodological clue to Habermas about the necessary condition for meaningful human understanding. According to Wittgenstein, "one can understand the 'meaning' of communicative acts only because they are embedded in contexts of *action* oriented to reaching understanding."[19] Habermas recognizes the character of all argumentation as being embedded in contexts of action toward reaching understanding in its act of claiming, that is, claiming to be valid. As long as communication involves claims to validity, we can analyze the structure of communicative acts through analyzing the structure of argumentation.

Thus, according to Habermas, formal pragmatics provides us an important ground for the rationalization of society because rational-

---

17. Habermas, *Postmetaphysical Thinking: Philosophical Essays*, 46–47.
18. Habermas, *Communication and the Evolution of Society*, 1.
19. Habermas, *Theory of Communicative Action*, 1:115.

ity depends on a disposition of speaking and acting subjects that is expressed in modes of behavior for which there are good reasons or grounds. This means that rational expressions admit objective evaluation.[20] Any symbolic expressions connected with validity claims require an exacting form of communication satisfying the conditions of argumentation. Thus for Habermas, unlike for Weber, it becomes possible that the normative regulations of human interaction come to be criticizable, so that valid norms and claims receive argumentative grounding.

Following Wittgenstein and Austin, Habermas holds that the discovery of the performative-propositional double structure of linguistic utterances is the first step on the way to bringing pragmatic elements into a formal analysis. The second step is the analysis of universal presuppositions that must be fulfilled if participants are to come to an understanding in their communicative actions.[21] Habermas recognizes the character of all argumentation as embedded in contexts of action toward reaching understanding in its act of claiming validity. Habermas's point is that since communication inevitably involves claims to validity, we can analyze the structure of communicative acts through analyzing the structure of argumentation.

Habermas formulates three kinds of validity claims that match the three different worlds to which the actor takes up relations with his utterance: claims to truth, claims to rightness, and claims to truthfulness.[22] Habermas analyzes the structure of communicative acts in contrast to strategic action. While the strategic action purports to influence the behavior of another through the threat of sanctions or the prospect of gratification in order to cause the interaction to continue as the first actor desires, communicative action seeks rationally to motivate another by relying on the illocutionary binding effect in his or her speech act.[23]

20. Ibid., 22.
21. Habermas, *Postmetaphysical Thinking*, 46.
22. While "claims to truth" matches with objective world, "claims to rightness" and "claims to truthfulness" correlate respectively with the social world and the subjective world.
23. According to Habermas's analysis, Austin develops the three concepts of the speech act—locution, illocution, and perlocution—in order to investigate more closely how language is joined with interactive practice in a form of life. Austin particularly pays attention to the relationship brought out by truth semantics between language and the objective world, between a sentence and a state of affairs. Austin first develops

Habermas further distinguishes between "open" and "concealed" strategic action. We can define the differences as follows: in communicative action, all participants seek to coordinate action through illocutionary aims alone; in strategic action, one or more participants seek to coordinate action through illocutionary aims and threats or rewards (open strategic action) or through deception and perlocutionary aims (concealed strategic action).

Further, Habermas distinguishes communicative action from discourse proper. While communication is conceivable only against the background of broad agreement concerning the basic features of the natural and social worlds within which human life unfolds, discourse arises where consensual interaction is disrupted and factual and normative claims are subjected to critical scrutiny in a process of argumentation freed from the imperatives of action.[24] Habermas holds that communicative action, by its very structure, is oriented to discourse as the mechanism for repairing disruptions in the consensual basis of communicative interaction.

Along the path of this distinction, Habermas also differentiates ethics from morals. For him, even though both ethics and morals are related to practical reason, ethics is concerned with reasoning about the good life, while morality is concerned with justice and rightness. Only moral claims are practical claims subject to universal discourse. In this sense, discourse ethics concerns neither ethics nor good but morality and rightness. "Moral-practical discourse detaches itself from the orientation to personal success and one's own life to which both pragmatic and ethical reflection remain tied."[25] The subject matter of discourse

---

a dualistic conception that opposes illocutionary acts to the representation of facts. For Austin, locutionary acts denote an aspect of speech act in which the speaker is saying something, while illocutionary acts indicate a performance of a social action with linguistic expression. Austin makes the following provisional classification: "Locutionary Act—Assertoric Sentence—Meaning—True/False. Ilocutionary Act—Performative Sentence—Force—Felicitous/Infelicitous" (Habermas, *Postmetaphysical Thinking*, 70) By incorporating Austin's distinction between illocutions and perlocutions, Habermas characterizes locutionary, illocutionary, and perlocutionary acts as follows, respectively: to say something, to act in saying something, and to bring about something through action in saying something. See Habermas, *Moral Consciousness and Communicative Action*, 58, and Habermas, *Postmetaphysical Thinking*, 69–70.

24. Habermas, *Justification and Application*, xv.

25. Ibid., 12.

is, then, about the justification of the impartiality of norms and their application.

For Habermas, the crucial condition for impartiality is to be found in the consensus of all who might be affected by it. Thus, "the moral principle is so conceived as to exclude as invalid any norm that could not meet with the qualified assent of all who are or might be affected by it."[26] Habermas asserts that the moral principle is a bridging principle, which makes consensus possible; this principle ensures that only those norms are accepted as valid that express the general will.[27] Thus every valid norm has to fulfill the condition of the universalizability principle, which Habermas calls "(U)." "All affected can accept the consequences and the side effects its general observance can be anticipated to have for the satisfaction of everyone's interests (and these consequences are preferred to those who know alternative possibilities for regulation)."[28] This principle of universalization is then a "rule of argumentation" for moral-practical discourse. The valid norms are supposed to be "generally observed," not in the sense that norms themselves are equally good for everyone, but in the sense that "general observances" of them are "equally in interest of all" or "equally good for all."[29] For Habermas, since the principle of universalization itself does not contain in it any substantial or material idea of good, it is formal. Habermas also contends that because this bridging principle has been justified, we are able to make the transition to discourse ethics.[30] Habermas emphasizes that since the principle of universalization implies the plurality of participants and the perspective of real-life argumentation, his idea should be differentiated from that of John Rawls, whose perspective, which Habermas criticizes, is "monological."[31]

The justification of the principle of universalization requires Habermas to rely on Karl-Otto Apel's transcendental-pragmatic

26. Habermas, *Moral Consciousness and Communicative Action*, 63.
27. Ibid.
28. Ibid., 65.
29. Habermas, *Justification and Application*, 8.
30. Habermas, *Moral Consciousness and Communicative Action*, 66.
31. John Rawls's "monological" perspective is best represented by his notion of "reflective equilibrium." According to Rawls, reflective equilibrium is a state which is "reached after a person has weighed various proposed conceptions." See Rawls, *A Theory of Justice*, 48.

justification of ethics. Unlike Apel, however, Habermas claims that transcendental-pragmatic justification should be limited to the justification of moral principle in the sense of the rule of argumentation. By this, Habermas means that what is justified by transcendental-pragmatic argument is not the moral principle itself but the necessary condition of discourse. According to Habermas, Apel has succeeded in revealing the buried dimension of the nondeductive justification of basic ethical norms.[32]

Apel begins his argument by saying, "We must not confuse the freedom of practical decisions with the thesis of decisionism, viz. that an ultimate foundation of ethical norms is impossible and hence an ultimate decision has to step in the place of an ultimate foundation."[33] Further, Apel contends that "an ultimate foundation of ethical norms can be provided by *transcendental-pragmatic reflection on the normative pre-conditions of meaningful arguing*."[34] His transcendental-pragmatic approach testifies that argumentation is not based on propositions alone but on the human competence of reflectively proposing propositions by speech acts that may be made explicit by performatives.[35]

According to Apel, the human truth claim is made explicit and reflected upon in a performative phrase like "I hereby assert that p is true." Here the phrase "is true" is a predicate on the level of meta-language. Apel analyzes that the predicate "is true" is redundant as long as the truth claim is not problematized; but as soon as the truth claim is called into question, the predicate "is true" as a predicate on the level of a meta-language, the self-reflective truth claim of our statement can be made on the topic of disputation or confirmation by argumentative discourse.[36]

Apel also holds that there must be another condition for the self-reflection of speech acts to be possible, which Apel calls "the inter-subjective reciprocity of symbolic interaction between men as co-subjects of actions."[37] Apel's argument is based on the logic of necessity. Therefore

32. Habermas, *Moral Consciousness and Communicative Action*, 80.
33. Apel, "The Common Presuppositions of Hermeneutics and Ethics," 49.
34. Ibid. (emphasis original).
35. Ibid., 50.
36. Ibid.
37. Ibid.

he calls the conditions of the possibility of communicative understanding in every argumentative discourse "transcendental-pragmatic" or "transcendental-hermeneutic" rules in a very radical sense, since they cannot be denied without performative self-contradiction.[38] According to Apel, one may sum up the fundamental ethical norms as the norms of an ideal speech situation or an ideal communication community that is necessarily but counterfactually anticipated in any serious argumentative discourse.

An ideal speech situation is also important to Habermas. According to Habermas, "the participants in argumentation cannot avoid the presupposition that the structure of their communication rules out all external or internal coercion other than the force of the better argument and thereby also neutralizes all motive other than that of the cooperative search for truth."[39] By developing the idea of an ideal speech situation, Apel affirms that the norm of reciprocal acknowledgment of "person as equal partners" and hence the norm of "equal rights and duties" in argumentative speech acts for proposing, defending, explicating, and possibly questioning validity claims is rendered to be the fundamental moral norm.[40] Apel calls this norm the "meta-norm" since it must be acknowledged in every serious argumentative discourse.

Drawing on Apel's argument, Habermas develops his position that what is justified by transcendental-pragmatic argument is not the moral principle itself but the necessary conditions of discourse (for example, equality of participation). From these necessary conditions and the fact that discourse is about conflicts in interest, Habermas derives the principle of universalization.[41]

For Habermas, "practical discourse is not a procedure for generating justified norms but a procedure for testing the validity of norms

38. Ibid., 51.
39. Habermas, *Moral Consciousness and Communicative Action*, 88–89.
40. Apel, "The Common Presuppositions of Hermeneutics and Ethics," 51.
41. At this point, we have to note that even though both Habermas and Apel affirm the transcendental-pragmatic justification of the principle of universalization, they have different perspectives concerning the matter of the degree and range of applicability of the justification itself. While Apel insists ultimate justification of the meta-norm itself, Habermas tries to confine the justification to the practical discourse. That is, while Apel insists on the ultimate justification of a metanorm, Habermas tries to confine transcendental-pragmatic justification to the derivation of a rule of practical discourse that is not itself a norm. This difference brings a mutual criticism even though both share a considerable number of common ideas in many aspects.

that are being proposed and hypothetically considered for adoption."[42] This implies that there should be something proposed into practical discourse. In this sense, Habermas contends that "practical discourse depends on content brought to them from outside."[43] He finds the reality of "outside" from the horizon of the lifeworld, rather than from an ideal communication community. Thus, for Habermas, it would be utterly pointless to engage in a practical discourse without real conflicts in a concrete situation in which the actors consider it incumbent upon themselves to reach a consensual means of regulating some controversial social matter. Through discourse the content of "outside" is subjected to a process in which particular values are ultimately discarded as being short of consensus. What must be remembered about this process is that a condition regulates the proper content of discourse. For Habermas, moral-practical discourse properly addresses questions about what is right or just in distinction from questions about what is good.[44]

Both Apel and Habermas agree on important points in developing the theory of discourse ethics. They differ from each other, however, regarding the justification of the supreme moral norm. Most important, while Apel affirms that social action or life practice as such presupposes a supreme moral norm, Habermas denies it. For Habermas, since there is a universal moral principle in the sense of a rule of argumentation in practical moral discourse, the absence of a transcendental norm does not lead one to moral relativism. From Habermas's viewpoint, Apel's ultimate justification fails to differentiate between the epistemic question of how moral judgments are possible and the existential question of what it means to be moral. In his book *Justification and Application*, Habermas says that "justification" of a practical moral norm (an epistemic endeavor) does not guarantee the legitimacy of its immediate "application" in social action or life practice (in one's existence).

42. Habermas, *Moral Consciousness and Communicative Action*, 103.

43. Ibid.

44. Regarding this Habermas states: "The universalization principle acts like a knife that makes razor-sharp cuts between evaluative statements and strictly normative ones, between the good and the just" (ibid., 104). Habermas's "razor-sharp" distinction between the good and the just draws considerable critiques. For example, Franklin I. Gamwell argues that Habermas's such claim contains a self-refuting implication. Without a universal understanding of good, whether it is implicit or explicit, how can we evaluate specific good? See Gamwell, "Habermas and Apel on Communicative Ethics," 32–36.

From Habermas's perspective, Apel is mistaken because he introduces a "teleological" perspective into "deontological" moral theory. Habermas writes: "Apel's auxiliary principle introduces a teleological perspective into deontological moral theory, as he himself remarks: the realization of morality itself is elevated to the highest good. But he thereby explodes the conceptual framework of a deontological ethic."[45]

Apel's ultimate justification implies a fundamental fusion of objective and normative worlds or of theoretical and practical reason. For Habermas, thus, it is essential to distinguish between norm and principle. Unlike the moral norms, for Habermas, moral principle should be formal. In sum, Habermas's main point is that the necessary conditions thereby identified are presuppositions not of life practice as such but rather of the special practice of argumentation of discourse. For Habermas, moral theory is solely a "clarification of conditions under which the participants could find a rational answer for themselves."[46]

Consequently, Habermas's discourse ethics is characterized by three conditions: first, the principle of universalization ought to be thoroughly formal; second, there should be a razor-sharp line between the good and the just; third, the horizon provided by the lifeworld is required in order to settle concrete conflicts. The third condition is important in understanding discourse ethics because it implies that universal discourse is bound up by the horizon of the lifeworld. Depending on the contents and characters of the horizon of the lifeworld, the scope and meanings of practical discourse can vary significantly.

The Discourse Theory of Law

Roughly speaking, Habermas's theory of law is a theoretical extension of the theory of morality to the field of legal discourse. In *Between Facts and Norms*, we find that his procedural understanding of discourse ethics expands its applicable field from the horizon of morality in the lifeworld to the legal institutionalization of society as a whole. Thus Habermas states, "Through a legal system with which it remains internally coupled, however, morality can spread to *all* spheres of action, including those systemically independent spheres of media-steered interactions that unburden actors of all moral expectations other than

---

45. Habermas, *Justification and Application*, 85.
46. Ibid., 24.

that of a general obedience to law."⁴⁷ Habermas acknowledges that moral and legal questions refer to the same problems: "How interpersonal relationships can be legitimately ordered and actions coordinated with one another through justified norms, how action conflicts can be consensually resolved against the background of intersubjectively recognized normative principles and rules."⁴⁸ But they are different in that they refer to these same problems in distinctive ways. While posttraditional morality represents only a form of cultural knowledge, law has additionally a binding character at the institutional level.⁴⁹

Since Habermas's concept of law is based on the discourse principle, which he calls "(D)," we first need to delineate the concept of the discourse principle in Habermas's critical theory. Habermas defines the concept of the discourse principle as follows: "Only those norms can claim to be valid that meet (or could meet) with the approval of all affected in their capacity *as participants in a practical discourse*."⁵⁰ According to Habermas, the discourse principle should be differentiated from the principle of universalization. The universalization principle is conceived as a rule of argumentation and is part of the logic of practical discourse, whereas the principle of discourse ethics stipulates the basic idea of moral theory but does not form part of a logic of argumentation.⁵¹ According to William Rehg, since legal legitimacy involves much more than the approximation of moral idealization, "legal-political structures institutionalize, not (U), but the broader and more abstract discourse principle (D)."⁵² It is important to note that unlike morality, the legitimacy of law is measured not just against the idealization of the moral but also against a range of idealizations, such as the ethical evaluations of goals, the technical-pragmatic assessment

47. Habermas, *Between Facts and Norms*, 118 (emphasis original). According to Habermas, moral contents can spread throughout a society along the channels of legal regulations under conditions of high complexity, whereas in less complex societies, the integral ethical life binds all the components of the lifeworld together, attuning concrete duties to institutions as socially integrating force.

48. Ibid., 106.

49. Ibid., 197. Habermas states that law is more than a symbolic system because it is also an action system.

50. Habermas, *Moral Consciousness and Communicative Action*, 66 (emphasis original).

51. Ibid., 93.

52. Rehg, *Insight and Solidarity*, 219.

of efficient means and strategies, and the nondiscursive ideals of fair compromise formation.[53]

In his book *Between Facts and Norms*, Habermas emphasizes that although moral discourses can be adopted as a model for investigating legal discourses, "the more complex validity dimension of legal norms prohibits one from assimilating the legitimacy of legal decisions to the validity of moral judgments."[54] Unlike moral discourse, legal discourse must incorporate the legislative process that requires the network of argumentation, bargaining, and political communications. In the legislative process, lawmakers also have to take into consideration the pragmatic and ethical dimensions of the sociopolitical order beyond the moral aspect of the lifeworld.

By "pragmatic dimension," on the one hand, Habermas means the process of testing the practicality of strategies under the presupposition that we know what we want. According to Habermas, pragmatic questions require us to position ourselves in the perspective of an actor seeking suitable means for realizing goals and preferences that are already given.[55] As a result of weighing the goals and the purposive-rational choice of means, each actor arrives at certain hypothetical recommendations that optimize the balance between the preferred ends and the selected means. The standpoints of efficiency, expediency, and practicality become the criteria in coming to a best recommendation in interrelating perceived causes and effects to value preferences and chosen ends.

By "ethical dimension," on the other hand, Habermas means ethical-political discourses in which "we reassure ourselves of a configuration of values under the presupposition that we do not yet know what we *really* want."[56] The idea of good must be incorporated in the process of ethical-political discourses, and this becomes a critical point that differentiates universal moral discourse from legal-political deliberation. The idea of good is always incorporated in the form of "good for us," and this makes the legal process much more complex than that of moral discourse. According to Habermas, the way we form who we are and

---

53. Ibid.
54. Habermas, *Between Facts and Norms*, 233.
55. Ibid., 159.
56. Ibid., 161.

would like to be as citizens is based on who we recognize ourselves to be in our cultural transmissions. It is thus inevitable that ethical-political discourse takes into consideration the hermeneutic and critical appropriation of tradition. Through ethical discourse, we attend to the hermeneutic explication of the self-understanding of our historically transmitted form of life that goes beyond the existential level.

According to Habermas, although the legal-political process must incorporate pragmatic and ethical dimensions, lawmakers must consider yet a further aspect, that of justice, which is indispensable for an adequate justification of policies and laws. For Habermas, this aspect derives its original insight from moral discourse. Now the crucial question that we ought to ask in the deliberation process of lawmaking (or legislation) is whether what we are trying to do is equally good for all. Habermas states, "In moral questions, the teleological point of view from which we handle problems through goal-oriented cooperation gives way entirely to the normative point of view from which we examine how we can regulate our common life in the equal interest of all."[57]

Only through moral discourse can the interests embodied in contested norms be unreservedly universalizable, expanding the ethnocentric perspective of a particular collectivity into the comprehensive perspective of an unlimited-communication community.[58] In sum, the judicial constitution of norms cannot be attained if lawmakers do not become involved with a highly complex and abstract discourse process that includes pragmatic issues and compromise formation, ethical discourse, and the clarification of moral questions. For this reason, Habermas claims that in the legislative process, lawmakers have to take into consideration not only the pragmatic and ethical dimensions of the sociopolitical order but also the moral aspect of the lifeworld.

According to Habermas, legal discourse must also pay heed to the procedurally regulated bargaining among politically contested groups. Bargaining is negotiation between success-oriented parties who are willing to cooperate.[59] Habermas posits that bargaining processes are tailored to situations in which, while all the proposed regulations touch on the diverse interests in different ways, no generalizable interest or

57. Ibid.
58. Ibid., 162.
59. Ibid., 165.

priority of value vindicates itself. The purpose of the bargaining process is therefore to reach a balance among conflicting interests through a negotiated agreement. Habermas states accordingly that the bargaining process and rationally motivated consensus are different. "Whereas a rationally motivated consensus (*Einverständnis*) rests on reasons that convince all the parties *in the same way*, a compromise can be accepted by the different parties each for its own *different* reasons."[60]

Since the bargaining process is likely to fall victim to a cunning realization of perlocutionary effects that lack an illocutionary binding force, without procedures that regulate bargaining from the standpoint of fairness, the bargaining process can be easily disrupted by nondiscursive measures. For this reason, from the perspective of the discourse principle, Habermas remarks that "the negotiation of compromises should follow procedures that provide all the interested parties with an equal opportunity for pressure, that is, an equal opportunity to influence one another during the actual bargaining, so that all the affected interests can come into play and have equal chances of prevailing."[61] As long as these conditions are met, negotiated agreements among the parties can be regarded as fair enough. Habermas's main point is that fair bargaining in the sense of compromise formation cannot simply replace moral discourses. He warns against the reduction of political will formation to mere compromise. Just as ethical-political discourse can be compatible with moral principles, the fair bargaining process is to be compatible with the discourse principle. For Habermas, "Fair bargaining, then, does not destroy the discourse principle but rather indirectly presuppose[s] it."[62]

As a result of the above discussion, it becomes clear that legitimate law is generated and derived not by perlocutionary uses of language but by the communicative power of legal discourse based on the discourse principle. The constitution of law is significant to all citizens of society because it represents the medium for transforming their communicative power into administrative power. The enactment of legitimate law provides the political community with an important way through which the communicative power of the people is converted into administra-

---

60. Ibid., 166 (emphasis original).
61. Ibid., 167.
62. Ibid.

tive power. By "administrative power," Habermas means the democratic political system, which he identifies as "deliberative democracy."[63] It now becomes more evident that there is a difference between the processes of legitimating moral norms and enacting legal norms, because political legislation does not rely solely on moral reasons, but on reasons of another kind as well.

Although morality and legality are based on the same principle, that is, the discourse principle, the specification of the discourse principle becomes distinguished with respect to different kinds of action norms. Habermas exemplifies the specification with the principle of morality and the principle of democracy. In a nutshell, "The principle of morality regulates informal and simple face-to-face interactions; the principle of democracy regulates relations among legal persons who understand themselves as bearers of rights."[64] Indeed, in Habermas's critical theory, the discourse principle enables rational discourse, and the latter branches out into two: moral argumentation, on the one hand, and political and legal discourses, on the other hand.

Habermas's theory of law is a strong argument that we can still find a grounding legitimacy for the enacting law in a postmetaphysical era in which religious and metaphysical worldviews have already collapsed. For Habermas, the legitimacy of legal norms can be tested by the discourse principle. In Rehg's account, in order to explain the legitimacy of law, Habermas turns to moral theory "as a means of showing how discourse-ethical idealizations can have some purchase in the real world."[65] The interlocking and interpenetrating relation between morality and legality is enabled because they both share the need of legitimacy for their establishment. Habermas's account of legitimacy is thus crucial in uncovering the inherent interconnection between morality and legality. We can affirm this interlocking relation in the following remarks: "Legitimacy is possible on the basis of legality insofar as the procedures for the production and application of legal norms are also conducted reasonably, in the moral-practical sense of procedural rationality. The legitimacy of legality is due to the interlocking of two types of procedures, namely, of legal processes with processes of moral

---

63. A more in-depth study of Habermas's "deliberative democracy" appears in chapter 6.

64. Habermas, *Between Facts and Norms*, 233.

65. Rehg, *Insight and Solidarity*, 218.

argumentation that obey a procedural rationality of their own."[66] Based on this account, Rehg claims that "the legitimacy of legality" can be described as "the institutional feasibility of morality."[67]

Perhaps legality in the sense of the extension of the moral-practical sense of procedural rationality is best delineated by Habermas's theory of law and politics. In his discussion of law and politics, we can discover the "halfway" interconnection between morality and legality. Although laws in the form of will formation accord with moral insights, they differ from moral norms because they also need to meet with such aspects as ethical or pragmatic ends.

According to Habermas, it is important to understand an internal connection between law and political power. From the discourse-theoretic perspective, Habermas claims that political power is neither externally juxtaposed to law nor implemented by natural or moral rights waiting to be put into effect. It is rather presupposed by law and itself established in the form of law.[68] From Habermas's discourse-theoretic perspective, popular sovereignty and human rights go hand in hand because political power can develop only through a legitimately enacted law. Political power and law presuppose each other mutually; "The principle of discourse can assume the shape of a principle of democracy through the medium of law only insofar as the discourse principle and the legal medium interpenetrate and *develop* into a system of rights that brings private and public autonomy into a relation of mutual presupposition."[69] The law thus receives its full normative sense only through a procedure of lawmaking that begets political legitimacy.

It is crucial to understand that the only law that counts as legitimate in the posttraditional society is a set of legal norms that could be rationally accepted by all citizens in a discursive process of opinion and will formation. Thus from the procedural perspective, politics is more than the matters of popular sovereignty, governmental power, or politi-

---

66. Habermas, "Law and Morality," 230.

67. Rehg, *Insight and Solidarity*, 218. Rehg also states that morality is "ingrained in law," or "penetrates into the core of positive law," while legality is "made pervious" or "open to moral argumentation." According to Rehg, Habermas's favorite metaphor that explains the interconnection between law and morality is "interpenetration" (*Verschränkung*).

68. Habermas, *Between Facts and Norms*, 135.

69. Ibid., 128 (emphasis original).

cal authority over people. Politics becomes the realization of the communicative power of the citizens that regulates governmental power through the democratic rule of law.[70] Habermas's discourse-theoretic perspective enables us to see that a popular sovereignty is internally laced not only with individual liberties of people but also with governmental power. The concept of the circulation of communication is important in understanding the internal connection between law and politics. Habermas thus writes, "Only in this anonymous form can its communicatively fluid power bind the administrative power of the state apparatus to the will of the citizens."[71] Through the democratic rule of law, popular sovereignty becomes effective in the circulation of reasonably structured deliberations and decisions of citizens or their assembled representatives.

Habermas's discourse-theoretic understanding of law is a significant clue for our investigation into what the system's anchoring in the lifeworld has to do with reconstructing the moral aspect of the positional self in the systemic world. Through the study of his idea of law and politics, we come to see more clearly how the communicative power of citizens could turn into administrative power through the medium of the democratic rule of law. The constitution and the enactment of law is a co-original component of politics along with the political power of government. Now politics can be seen as an apparatus through which the will of citizens realizes itself not as a universal moral norm but through the legitimacy of law.

Indeed, Habermas's discussion of law and politics is an important study because it shows us how the discourse principle of the lifeworld can convey the moral insights of the lifeworld and translate them into political will that can regulate the political system through the democratic rule of law. In other words, in his discussion of law and politics, we can discover an effective example that indirect and halfway as it may be, moral insights of the lifeworld can ultimately provide moral guidance to those who have positions in a subsystem (political government) by

---

70. Here we need to distinguish the concept of emergence of political power and the already constituted power. Habermas states, "With the concept of communicative power, we get hold of only the *emergence* of political power, not the administrative employment of *already* constituted power, that is, the process of exercising power" (ibid., 149).

71. Ibid., 136.

helping them attend to the legal norms originally extended from their domain. This aspect is indeed implausible from the perspective of the "colonization of lifeworld by system." Only from the perspective of the system's anchoring in the lifeworld we can reconstruct the moral aspect for the positional self.

Therefore, our original question—what does the system's anchoring in the lifeworld have to do with the reconstruction of the moral norm for the positional self?—now yields one important solution. In short, the positional self can realize its moral aspect by keeping the laws of a society. This, however, should not mean that keeping the laws of a political community exhausts the whole moral aspect of the positional self's various and complex institutional or organizational activities. Without doubt, not all moral insights of the lifeworld translate into legal norms; nor do legal norms extract their legal contents from the moral norms of the lifeworld. Pragmatic and ethical reasoning is deeply involved in the legislative process that covers much more complex and diverse spheres of social life. For all this limitation, however, we need to focus on one key point: from the discourse-theoretic perspective, positional selves are no longer merely system managers or impersonal organizers separated from the moral aspects of the lifeworld. As long as the system is anchored in the lifeworld, the positional self as a mediated self between the lifeworld and the system is to realize its moral aspect in its formal, institutional, or organizational activities. By attending to the law of society, the positional self establishes itself as a moral self.

The Public Sphere and the Reconstruction of a Moral Norm for the Positional Self

In the above discussion, we have reviewed the following subjects: how the system is anchored in the lifeworld; what the procedural understanding of moral and legal norms is; how legality and political power are co-originally related; and what the system's anchoring in the lifeworld has to do with the positional self's moral realization. It is my contention that in order to uncover the moral aspect of the positional self, we ought to have an in-depth understanding of the often hidden, covered, or indirect relation between economic, political, and legal systems of society and various moral insights of the lifeworld. Without this, the reconstruction of moral norms for the positional self is largely restricted.

Regarding the reconstruction of moral norms for the positional self, we have to understand that these norms are not only variant but also flexible depending on how the public sphere has been shaped and developed in civil society. There is no settled set of moral norms for the positional self in Habermas's critical theory. We have to remember that Habermas's critical theory can only give us a procedural perspective concerning the ideas of morality and legal norms. Thus, if we do not discuss the concrete and practical procedures by which we can reconstruct any specific moral insights, ideas, or norms, we will only have an empty and simple rule for the positional self: "keep the law."

Of course "the law" would generally mean the positive law unless we realize that there is more in Habermas's critical theory that develops specific moral norms and insights for the positional self. In order for the positional self to realize its moral aspect, we need to investigate the practical role of the public sphere in civil society, particularly with regard to the constitution of laws. As Habermas perceives, only when citizens participate in the public sphere can the procedural paradigm of law certainly enable law experts and citizens to take into consideration the moral insights of the lifeworld in their making laws. Unless we enliven the public sphere in the project of realizing the system of rights, moral norms for the positional self can only be a statement of moralistic legalism: keep the law.

In Habermas's theory of law, the public sphere is understood as an arena for public communication grounded in civil society. Only through the public sphere can the political system be anchored in the lifeworld, which is shaped by a liberal political culture and corresponding socialization patterns. Habermas states that in how the public sphere is operated, a specific and parallel paradigm of law and politics should be present. He identifies three paradigms of law in his *Between Facts and Norms*: liberal, social-welfare, and procedural. He also interconnects three paradigms of law with the ideal-typical forms of government, respectively—the security state (*Sicherheitsstaat*), the social-welfare state (*Sozialstaat*), and the constitutional state (*Rechtsstaat*).[72] Among these three paradigms of law and politics, Habermas declares that the

---

72. Ibid., 435.

concept of the public sphere is associated with the procedural model of law and the constitutional state.

According to Habermas, both the social-welfare and liberal paradigms of law are inadequate in providing the political ground for the public sphere. While the social-welfare paradigm of law misses the freedom-guaranteeing meaning of legitimate rights by reducing justice to distributive justice, the liberal paradigm assimilates rights to goods by reducing justice to an equal distribution of rights.[73] From Habermas's perspective of procedural justice, both paradigms mistakenly regard the legal "constitution" of freedom as something that we can distribute and assimilate according to the model of equal distribution of goods.[74]

Unlike the two previous paradigms, in Habermas's procedural paradigm of law we can find the points of reference regarding the matters of the "legitimacy of law" and the "realization of the system of rights." It is Habermas's main point that in relying only on money (the market economy) and power (the public administration), we cannot fully derive the sources of social solidarity. Habermas argues that the sources of social solidarity can only be available through the communicative practices of autonomous citizens: "The forces of social solidarity can be regenerated in complex societies only in the forms of communicative practices of self-determination."[75] These sources of social solidarity cannot be discussed without referring to the idea of the political, public sphere. This is the reason why the concept of the public sphere becomes an integral part of our discussion that can allow us points of reference and sources of social solidarity. According to Habermas, in bypassing the communicative power of public citizens, the integration of a highly complex society cannot be attained.

73. Ibid., 418–19.

74. Ibid. Against the social-welfare paradigm, Habermas argues that the normative key should be autonomy, not well-being, because "the distribution of compensations only follows from an equal distribution of rights, which in turn results from the mutuality of recognizing all as free and equal members." Against the liberal model, Habermas argues that rights are not collective goods that one consumes in common. Since rights should be derived from legitimately produced norms, Habermas claims that "the equal distribution of rights cannot be detached from the public autonomy that enfranchised citizens can exercise only in common, by taking part in the practice of legislation" (ibid., 419). This becomes the reason why the idea of the public sphere becomes such a key concept that connects the procedural paradigm of law and its corresponding concept of political system: constitutional state (*Rechtsstaat*).

75. Ibid., 445.

Regarding the concept of the public sphere, we first need to define its relation to the lifeworld. Is the public sphere identical to the lifeworld? If not, what kind of relationship is there between the public sphere and the lifeworld? According to Habermas, first of all, the public sphere and the rationalized lifeworld meet each other halfway. By "halfway," Habermas means not only convergent elements but also distinguishing parts between the two. Habermas signifies that the lifeworld and the public sphere are similar in that they are reproduced through communicative action. The lifeworld and the public sphere do not require specialized language for their reproduction. Only a mastery of natural language suffices, which makes possible the general comprehension of everyday communicative practice.

According to Habermas, however, the public sphere is distinguished from the lifeworld. Unlike the public sphere, the lifeworld is specialized in two ways: categories like religion, education, and the family that are associated with general reproductive "functions" of the lifeworld; and systems like science, morality, and art that take up different validity aspects of everyday communicative action on a "contents" basis.[76] The public sphere is specialized in neither of these two ways. Instead, it is specialized in relation to the third feature of communicative action that refers to the "social space" generated in communicative action.

This space, according to Habermas, is a linguistically constituted space that "stands open, in principle, for potential dialogue partners who are present as bystanders or could come on the scene and join those present."[77] Spaces such as forums, stages, arenas, and the like are examples of the public space, which here clings to the concrete locales where an audience is physically gathered. There is also an abstract form of public space, such as the public media for a larger public of present persons. Habermas claims that as soon as the public space has expanded beyond the context of simple interactions, then a differentiation sets in among organizers, speakers, and hearers, rendering unequal the actors' roles for exerting influence. Habermas argues that from a principle of deliberative democracy, however, the political influence should

---

76. Ibid., 360. While the general reproductive functions of the lifeworld are specified in three forms: cultural reproduction, social integration, or socialization, verifying aspects of communicative action are exemplified by truth, rightness, or veracity (truthfulness).

77. Ibid., 361.

ultimately rely on the approval of a lay public: "The political influence that the actors gain through public communication must ultimately rest on the resonance and indeed the approval of a lay public whose composition is egalitarian."[78] Indeed, the public of citizens possesses a final authority that is constitutive for the internal structure and reproduction of the public sphere.

In order to understand the concept of the public sphere more clearly, we also need to clarify the relation between the private and the public spheres. According to Habermas, the private sphere is distinguished from the public sphere by "different conditions of communication." Whereas the private sphere of the lifeworld is characterized by intimacy and thus by protection from publicity, the public sphere strives to defend its publicity. Encounters between relatives, friends, neighbors, and acquaintances at the level of face-to-face interactions establish the character of the private sphere. Regarding the relation between the private and the public spheres, we need to see that the different conditions of communication do not seal off the private from the public sphere. Rather, they channel the flow of topics from the one sphere into the other. For example, the public sphere draws its impulses from the private handling of social problems resonating in life histories.[79] For this reason, Habermas claims that the public sphere has a complementary relation to the private sphere.[80] Indeed, the public sphere does not simply establish itself without any connection to the private sphere.

Perhaps the most critical function that takes place in the public sphere is the formulation of public opinion. Public opinion is not simply a matter of statistics in Habermas's discourse-theoretic understanding of law and politics. So he warns that public opinion should not be confused with survey results: "Political opinion polls provide a certain reflection [such as survey results] of 'public opinion' only if they have been preceded by a focused public debate and a corresponding opinion-formation in a mobilized public sphere."[81] The formulation of public opinion via the public sphere is critical because it can legitimately influence the political system. Habermas relies on Parsons's

78. Ibid., 364.
79. Ibid., 366.
80. Ibid., 354.
81. Ibid., 362.

idea of "influence" to explain the effect that public opinion has on the political system. However, Habermas distinguishes public opinion from the proceduralist perspective. The most significant point regarding the influence of public opinion is that it feeds on the resource of mutual understanding. This becomes the reason why Habermas repeatedly emphasizes the importance of the quality of public opinion. By "quality," however, he does not mean the content-based, substantive quality of each opinion but rather the procedural, formal quality determined and measured by the procedural properties of its process of generation. Public opinion is in fact discursively induced agreement among people about social problems. Public opinion is, in other words, the result of the public processes of communication as a shared practice of communication.[82] Thus, qualified public opinion cannot be formulated in a power-ridden, oppressive public sphere.

Public opinion formulated in the public sphere is critical in that it represents the general moral insights of the lifeworld. Of course, this should not mean that all public opinions are moral ideas as such. What makes public opinion the representation of moral insights of the lifeworld is not the opinions themselves but rather the process through which they are formulated. When public opinion satisfies the condition of the principle of universalization, it can be viewed from the moral perspective. The following sentence reminds us of Habermas's principle of universalization as a rule of argumentation for moral-practical discourse: "The political public sphere can fulfill its function of perceiving and thematizing encompassing social problems only insofar as it develops out of the communication taking place among *those who are potentially affected*."[83] As long as the affected draw public opinion communicatively and are willing to accept the consequences and the side effects of their agreed opinion, it can be regarded morally from a proceduralist perspective. For Habermas, the quality of public opinion determines its moral aspects, because the quality of public opinion is measured by procedural properties such as equal opportunity in participating in public discourse with no discrimination and oppression. Since the success of public communication is measured by the formal crite-

---

82. Ibid.
83. Ibid., 365 (emphasis original).

ria governing how a qualified public opinion comes about, Habermas claims that the quality of public opinion is an empirical variable.[84]

According to Habermas, the public sphere as a communication structure rooted in the lifeworld can convert public opinion into political power through institutionalized procedures such as enacting law: "Naturally, political *influence* supported by public opinion is converted into political *power*—into a potential for rendering binding decisions—only when it affects the beliefs and decisions of *authorized* members of the political system and determines the behavior of voters, legislators, officials, and so fourth."[85] This explanation is critical because it shows us how the moral insights of the lifeworld can ultimately transform the systemic world by way of influencing the will formation in parliamentary bodies, administrative agencies, and courts. Habermas states, "Just like social power, political influence based on public opinion can be transformed into political power only through institutionalized procedures."[86] Among these institutionalized procedures, Habermas particularly pays attention to the constitution of law in his *Between Facts and Norms*. After all, the lifeworld meets with the political system halfway through the public sphere. And the public sphere can have the interplay with opinion and will formation institutionalized in parliamentary bodies and courts. The communication structures of the public sphere are not only linked with the private life spheres of the lifeworld but also with the institutionalized political center.[87]

In Habermas's critical theory, the most important role of the public sphere is to create and cultivate normative reasons in regard to all parts of the political system with no intention to conquer it. Since in the proceduralist paradigm, public opinion is converted into a communicative power legitimatizing regulatory agencies as well as authorizing the legislature, we can come to have an idea that moral insights of the lifeworld can be converted into legitimate laws that regulate all the institutionalized activities of the system. As Habermas argues, through the legal institutionalization of steering media legitimated in the public sphere, economic and administrative systems remain anchored in the

84. Ibid.
85. Ibid., 363 (emphasis original).
86. Ibid.
87. Ibid., 381.

society component of the lifeworld, allowing ordinary language to circulate through society.[88] This is how the moral insight of the lifeworld can provide a limited level of moral guidance or insight to those who posit themselves in the systemic world.

The public sphere is important because it provides us with a legitimate foundation on which the law is enacted not in a positivistic way but rather in a procedural way in regard to the moral insights of the lifeworld that can be affirmed by communicative participation of all citizens. Habermas's idea of the public sphere needs to be further clarified in regard to his idea of deliberative politics and the public use of reason developed by John Rawls. First, according to Habermas, the new type of democracy, named "deliberative democracy," is established along with the concept of an ideal procedure based on discourse theory. Steering between the alternatives of liberalism and republicanism, deliberative democracy integrates elements from both sides into the concept of an ideal procedure based on discourse theory. Habermas understands that discourse theory makes it possible to realize deliberative democracy, in that it brings a third idea into play: the procedures and communicative presuppositions of democratic opinion and will formation.[89] Discursive rationalization makes deliberative politics possible not only through the institutionalization of the higher-level intersubjectivity of communication processes in parliamentary bodies but also through the informal networks of the public sphere. Through the discursive procedure, deliberative democracy makes possible the integration of both the exclusive function of legitimating the exercise of political power (the liberal view) and the function of constituting society as a political community (the republican view).

Therefore, for Habermas, "the success of deliberative politics depends not on a collectively acting citizenry but on the institutionalization of the corresponding procedures and conditions of communication, as well as on the interplay of institutionalized deliberative processes with informally constituted public opinions."[90] The idea of the public sphere is thus important because the interplay of institutionalized deliberative processes with informally constituted public

---

88. Ibid., 354.
89. Habermas, *Between Facts and Norms*, 249–50.
90. Ibid., 298.

opinions takes place within it. Habermas's "public sphere" can be better understood in comparison with Rawls's "public reason." According to Rawls, "the idea of public reason is not a view about specific political institutions or policies. Rather, it is a view about the kind of reasons on which citizens are to rest their political cases in making their political justifications to one another when they support laws and policies that invoke the coercive powers of government concerning fundamental political questions."[91] In other words, the primary aim of public reason is to give reasonable justification to others so that we are trying to see if we can give reasons that other people can reasonably accept. There is a reasonable expectation among those who participate in public reason that others might accept them on the basis of justification. Rawls uses the concept of public reason mainly as a political conception that satisfies the criterion of reciprocity. Like Habermas, Rawls refers to public discourse as a venue through which public reason comes into realization. Rawls, however, emphasizes that his idea is different from that of Habermas: "He [Habermas] understands a public sphere as any public speech of this kind, in all kinds of environments; whereas by public discourse I mean primarily the discourse of judges, presidents, legislators and ordinary citizens when they are engaged in political campaigns."[92]

According to Habermas, Rawls's concept of engaging in political campaigns must be understood to mean that the procedure of the public use of reason remains the final court of appeal for normative statements. From this perspective, the predicate "reasonable" ultimately points to the discursive redemption of a validity claim. Thus, from Habermas's discourse-theoretic perspective, "the normative substance of basic liberal rights is already contained in the indispensable medium for the legal institutionalization of the public use of reason of sovereign citizens."[93] Indeed what Habermas tries to achieve in *Between Facts and Norms* is that since the public use of reason is manifested in the communicative presuppositions and procedures of a discursive process of opinion and will formation, discourse-theoretic perspective can provide us with an adequate model for moral reconstruction even in the systemic world.

91. Rawls, *Law of Peoples*, 164.
92. Thiemann, "Political Liberalism," 7.
93. Habermas, "Reconciliation through the Public Use of Reason," 130.

Conclusion

Habermas's *Between Facts and Norms* has enabled us to have a constructive vision for the intersubjectively validated use of money and power.[94] This is a significant point because it gives us an important clue for how to situate the positional self as a moral self in the systemic world, although it may not provide a full account in terms of its scope and efficacy. Since many position holders are more likely accountable for the use of money and power in the system, and the procedural understanding of law regulates the use of money and power from the discourse-theoretic perspective, we can develop a conceptual scheme that the positional self becomes subject to the moral insights of the lifeworld under certain restrictions.

Considering Habermas's initial supposition that the system is to be anchored in the lifeworld, in conjunction with his elaboration of the theory of discourse ethics, we can now develop the perspective that the fundamental moral norms of the lifeworld can serve as a channel for influencing the formally organized domains of action, that is, the system. In other words, the institutions that anchor steering mechanisms such as power and money in the lifeworld function as an institutional framework that subjects system maintenance to the normative restrictions of the lifeworld. As Habermas envisions, this institutional framework should be established through communication and discourse.[95]

Indeed, in *Between Facts and Norms*, Habermas exhibits a more affirming view of the system and its media—money and power—for integrating society because legal discourse as a "background" for the integrating source provides legitimacy for the justified use of money and power.[96] Habermas provocatively claims, "Both media of systemic

---

94. Of course, his earlier book *The Theory of Communicative Action* has already forecasted this vision because he writes, "Both are conceivable: the institutions that anchor steering mechanisms such as power and money in the lifeworld could serve as a channel either for the influence of the lifeworld on formally organized domains of action or, conversely, for the influence of the system on communicatively structured contexts of action" (Habermas, *Theory of Communicative Action*, 2:186). We can roughly say that while *Theory of Communicative Action* focuses on the later phenomenon, *Between Facts and Norms* more intensely deals with the former possibility.

95. Habermas, *Theory of Communicative Action*, 2:185.

96. In this sense, Kenneth Baynes states that "the new book assigns to law and legal community generally a more positive and prominent role in the legitimation process" ("Democracy and Rechtsstaat," 201).

integration, money and power, are anchored via legal institutionalization in orders of the lifeworld, which is in turn socially integrated through communicative action."[97] Habermas's procedural understanding of discourse ethics expands its applicable field from the horizon of morality in the lifeworld to that of the legal institutionalization of society as a whole. Habermas thus states, "Through a legal system with which it remains internally coupled, however, morality can spread to *all* spheres of action, including those systemically independent spheres of media-steered interactions that unburden actors of all moral expectations other than that of a general obedience to law."[98]

Moreover, Habermas does not separate law and morality as two unconnected social institutions. For the sake of regulation, political legislators need to incorporate moral aspects in establishing the legal code: "For the simple reason that the will-formation of the political legislator has to include the moral aspects of the matter in need of regulation ... in complex societies, morality can become effective beyond the local level only by being translated into the legal code."[99] Based on this possibility of translation, we have hitherto tried to situate the positional self as a moral self.

Above we have examined how Habermas's discourse ethics can provide us with a conceptual scheme with which we could reconstruct the positional self as a moral self against the backdrop of the constitutional democratic society regulated by law and public reason. Habermas's insight, however, is incomplete in that it stops short of providing us with a comprehensive moral criterion that regulates the moral conduct of the positional self. For example, Habermas's rigorous procedural approach to moral reconstructionism, which sharply distinguishes "ethics" (the domain of good) from "morality" (the domain of right), renders the reconstructed moral criterion ("keep the law") for the positional self "minimalistic" if not irrelevant with regard to the organizational behaviors of the positional self. Why is Habermasian reconstruction of the moral criterion for the conduct of the positional self "minimalistic"?

As is evident, corporations and political organizations are operated and maneuvered by their economic or political agendas such as

---

97. Habermas, *Between Facts and Norms*, 40.
98. Ibid., 118 (emphasis original).
99. Ibid., 110.

maximizing corporate profits or concentrating organizational power. These agendas are in fact what constitute the concept of good as the strategic goals of corporations and political organizations. Since, however, the moral criterion reconstructed by discourse ethics is based on the razor-sharp separation between the realms of good and right, and thus the moral domain is specifically confined to the realm of right, we cannot have a critical debate on the ethical aspects of the conduct of the positional self. In other words, within the limits of law, the positional self is entitled to accomplish whatever strategic goals corporations and political organizations set for themselves. The positional self becomes the foremost agent in maximizing corporate profits and concentrating organizational power. Habermas's moral reconstruction can only supply us with a minimalistic solution to the moral predicaments of the positional self, because the moral character of the positional self is negatively construed in the sense of "not to break the law."

4

The Moral Predicament of the Positional Self
Niebuhrian Analysis

Introduction

In the previous two chapters, by focusing on Jürgen Habermas's critical theory and discourse ethics, we have not only analyzed the moral predicament that identifies the positional self as a colonizer of the lifeworld but have also reviewed a moral prospect that characterizes the positional self as a responsible self from the discourse theoretic (procedural) perspective. Standing against the backdrop of constitutional democracy, Habermas argues that we can reconstruct the moral identity of the positional self in the organizational and corporate world with regard to a democratic lawmaking process that incorporates the idealization of the moral, the ethical evaluations of goals, and the technical-pragmatic assessment of efficient means and strategies.

Although procedurally enacted legal norms and regulations should accord with moral insights in that they are justified by all those affected by them, Habermas claims that since laws may also express such elements as existing interest positions and pragmatically chosen ends, laws differ from morality. While the morally autonomous will remains in some sense virtual because it states only what could be rationally accepted by each, laws as a legal community's political will are much more complex because they ought to take into consideration the ethical and pragmatic aspects of positions and ends. As Habermas claims, "political issues are such that in the medium of law, the normative regulation of behavior is also open for the evaluation and pursuit of collective goals."[1]

Habermas's understanding of law is critical for our further discussion because the incorporation of the evaluation (ethical) and pursuit (pragmatic) of collective goals in the lawmaking process requires us to think critically as to how it would affect the positional self's role-playing in the organizational and institutional world. Indeed, as a representative for a certain collective ideal, a positional self ought to deal with the collective good or interests of particular organizations, institutions, or groups. This becomes an important reason why the concept of the positional self ought to be differentiated from that of nonpositional, ordinary selves. Since the concept of the positional self cannot be imagined without its intrinsic connection with the reality of good, a positional self and its conduct ought to be evaluated and analyzed from an ethical as well as a moral perspective.

Indeed, unlike a nonpositional, ordinary self, the positional self must take into consideration the ethical aspects of its own conduct as the representatives of the collective good and interests. This recognition is important in distinguishing the positional self not only from a nonpositional, ordinary self but also from Habermas's intersubjective moral self. Differing from an intersubjective model, the positional self is required to be ethically as well as morally justified in its acts. Thus, with the method of Habermas's moral reconstruction only, the ethical aspects of the positional self cannot be fully recognized and valued. We need to make sure that the justification of the positional act should cover both moral and ethical aspects.

The ethical aspect of the conduct of the positional self will be examined in this and the following chapter by critically analyzing Reinhold Niebuhr's insights on the ethical predicaments of the positional self (chapter 4) and the ethical reconstruction (chapter 5). In the last chapter (chapter 6), I will integrate Habermas's moral reconstruction and Niebuhr's ethical reconstruction through a "co-reconstructive" method with a view to developing a more comprehensive and holistic norm that would justify both moral (formal) and ethical (substantive) aspects of the conduct of the positional self. In doing so, we will discover that the co-reconstructive moral/ethical norm for the conduct of the positional

1. Habermas, *Between Facts and Norms*, 152.

self ultimately originates in the law of the "positional freedom" itself, which not only resides at the juncture of moral and ethical dimensions of the positional act but also mediates the political (legal) and existential spheres of the positional selfhood.

Regarding the shift of the methodological perspective from a moral to an ethical orientation, we need to remember that this shift is necessarily entailed because the positional self is supposed to represent the collective good or interests of corporations, organizations, and institutions. This shift also reminds us that an important fact of the positional self is that it is uniquely posited between the individual and the group in that it has both individual and organizational elements within itself as a position holder in the organizational world. Using Niebuhr's terms, the positional self will be described hereafter as a mediated self between "moral man" and "immoral society." This requires us to analyze the distinctive character of the positional self from a "socio-existential" perspective because the positional self has in itself both sociological as well as existential elements as an inseparable reality. The positional self is neither detached from the collectivity of groups nor separated from the individuality of members of society. Interestingly, just as we characterize the positional self as a mediated self between the lifeworld and the system in Habermas, we here define the positional self as a mediated self between the individuals and the group in Niebuhr, although in a quite different sense. While the former characterization is established from a moral perspective, the latter is from an ethical standpoint.

We need to remember that from now on the positional self as a position holder in organizations and institutions finds its own distinctive place between individuals and collective groups. This is the reason why we need to critically deal with the concept of the positional self from a socio-existential perspective. By a "socio-existential perspective," I mean a distinctive point of view that incorporates and integrates both social and individual aspects as well as institutional and existential spheres in evaluating and analyzing human conduct. The socio-existential perspective thematizes the positional self's distinctive situation uniquely structured between the social and the individual as well as between the institutional and the existential worlds. In the following, we will analyze specifically the ethical predicaments of the positional self that finds itself as a mediated self in between the individual and the group realms by drawing on Niebuhr's in-depth socio-existential analysis of a human being, particularly regarding his critical insight of human nature in both individual and collective forms.

Reinhold Niebuhr and the Positional Self

Reinhold Niebuhr neither used the term the "positional self" nor developed a similar concept as an independent idea in his writings. This, however, does not mean that such a concept has never been alluded to or suggested in his ethical or political writings. On the contrary, he shows us in various parts of his works that he has a deep and insightful understanding of the positional self and its ethical predicament. Certainly, differing from Habermas, who does not conceptually distinguish citizens according to their positional roles in the system, Niebuhr differentiates the concept of specific citizens who have higher ranks and power in the organizational system as an important theme in his political writings. For example, Niebuhr calls those who take a power position in society "the man of power" or "big men," in contrast to "little men" and "individuals." In *Reflections on the End of an Era*, Niebuhr remarks, "The recalcitrance and stubbornness of the man of power before the strictures and admonitions of the wise man are not simply due to personal defects or self deceptions. The real cause lies in the representative character of the oligarch. He expresses not only his own impulses but those of a social group, a class or a nation."[2]

Although he does not concretely theorize, Niebuhr has a substantive understanding of the positional self as one who has a power position in society and groups. Regarding the actions for those position holders, he has a clear idea that we, as observers, need to have a different moral criterion in appraising their social conduct. Niebuhr first epitomizes the ethical predicament that the positional self is facing as follows, "They could never extricate themselves completely from the sinfulness of power, even while they were wielding it ostensibly for the common good."[3] Niebuhr's writings show us that the moral criterion for the positional self is to be differentiated from nonpositional, ordinary people. For a better understanding of his implied concept of the positional self, we need to delve more deeply.

---

2. Niebuhr, *Reflections on the End of an Era*, 43.
3. Niebuhr, *Christianity and Power Politics*, 163.

In his 1926 article "How Philanthropic is Henry Ford?" Niebuhr raises the question whether Henry Ford is really as philanthropic as many people in the nation claimed. For Niebuhr, Ford is obviously distinguished from other ordinary people as a prominent positional self. Niebuhr first admits that he is the one who pays high wages, sells a cheap product, and yet accumulates vast riches. He even recognizes that Ford is acclaimed to have humanitarian characteristics because he donates money to humanitarian organizations and social-service agencies.

However, Niebuhr, criticizes Ford's public reputation by enumerating a list of contradictory points. Niebuhr posits that Ford has no concern for the well-being of his workers. "Not only is the Ford wage no longer a minimum subsistence wage, not to speak of a minimum comfort wage, but there is no conscience in the industry in the matter of unemployment or old-age insurance."[4] Niebuhr is even harsher in his critique against Ford regarding the latter's policy on social welfare, because he says that Ford's employment system is ruthless to old workers, with its systemic management of substituting young men for old.[5]

Judging that conscience is lacking in such a management system in which human material is ruthlessly used, Niebuhr's main point is that the careful study of Ford's managerial style does not prove the popular acclamation that he is the hero of average Americans for his seemingly humanitarian characteristics. Thus, Niebuhr remarks, "It is difficult to determine whether Mr. Ford is simply a shrewd exploiter of a gullible public in his humanitarian pretensions, or whether he suffers from self-deception."[6]

Niebuhr holds that the moral conundrum of Ford's case can be analyzed to have two originating sources: Ford himself and the American public itself. According to Niebuhr, as the "big man," Henry Ford should have been aware of long-term and in-depth social implications of his industrial policies. "He does not think profoundly on the social implica-

---

4. Niebuhr, *Love and Justice*, 100.

5. According to Niebuhr, while Ford employs five thousand boys from sixteen to twenty years of age to keep them out of mischief, he does this at a time when hardly any of his workers are working full time, and many are being discharged. Obviously, from Niebuhr's point of view, what Ford is doing is the exploitation of low-wage workers (ibid., 101).

6. Ibid.,102.

tions of his industrial policies."[7] By this, Niebuhr means that since Ford has taken an influential position in a great industrial company whose managerial policies and decisions can affect many people's lives directly and indirectly, he should be held accountable for the social outcomes brought about because of his positional actions.

For Niebuhr, the American public should be also held responsible for its naïve and uncritical attitude to the Ford case. He writes, "The tragedy of the situation lies in the fact that the American public is, on the whole, too credulous and uncritical to make any critical analysis of the moral pretensions of this great industry."[8] Regarding this phenomenon, Niebuhr diagnoses that this problem is universal rather than specifically American, because it is people's general tendency "to invest their heroes with moral qualities that they do not possess and to insist that the big man is also a good man."[9]

Here Niebuhr implies that positional selves in society are expected to have a certain moral character or moral identity. The case of Henry Ford is just one example of how Reinhold Niebuhr treats the socially powerful figures of industrial companies or political parties differently from the nonpositional ordinary people in the society.[10] Niebuhr

7. Ibid.
8. Ibid.
9. Ibid.

10. His poignant view on the immoral behaviors of the positional self is readily detected even in the works of his younger years. In a 1927 reflection later published in his 1929 *Leaves from the Notebook of a Tamed Cynic*, he talks about a business manager named "C" who allegedly recapitalized his business and added six million dollars in stock, but after "C" failed to invest in physical expansion, Niebuhr sarcastically writes, "What I wonder is whether the gentleman is deceiving himself and really imagines himself a Christian or whether he is really quite hard-boiled and harbors a secret contempt for the little men who buzz about his throne, singing their hallelujahs" (129). In his first book, *Does Civilization Need Religion?* Niebuhr critically points out the typical lack of moral imagination pervasive in many positional selves, which results in the their failure to maintain a distinction between utilitarian ethics and a religiously inspired moral life. He writes poignantly: "In modern industrial society those who are in position of power and privilege are most inclined to espouse an ethical ideal because it tends to stabilize social life and thus insures the perpetuations of privilege" (75). In his 1934 book *Reflections on the End of an Era*, Niebuhr identifies the positional self as the "modern oligarch" whose action is motivated subconsciously by the lust of power and the imperial impulse. He writes: "The lust of power and the imperial impulse may prompt this actions but they express themselves subconsciously rather than consciously. He is not fully conscious of life's brutalities. He may tenderly send his family to

dealt critically with the behaviors of many positional selves, including figures such as John D. Rockefeller, Franklin D. Roosevelt, Winston S. Churchill, Oliver Cromwell, Adolf Hitler, and Joseph Stalin. The cases of Hitler and Stalin, however, are extreme examples of how demonically positional selves can be dehumanized when they misuse the power they took over. Niebuhr's fundamental insight reflects the important point that the moral aspect of human action can be qualitatively differentiated among citizens according to their positional roles and characters. Niebuhr implicitly insinuates that the moral criterion for the positional self should be differentiated from the moral criterion for nonpositional, ordinary citizens of society because the widespread social, economic, and political impacts brought about by the positional acts tend to transcend the positional self's private and individual boundaries.

Niebuhr's general but critical insight regarding the concept of the positional self, however, needs to be further developed. Unfortunately, although Niebuhr insists that a "big man" should be differentiated from a "small man" with regard to the scope of the moral responsibility, Niebuhr stops short of developing the big man as a distinguished concept of a responsible moral self. Thus, I now radicalize Niebuhr's not so fully developed insight into a full-fledged theoretic conceptualization through a critical reading of his works. First of all, we will engage with his fundamental moral structure most notably known as the "dualism in moral thought," that is, the individual as a moral man versus the group as an immoral society. The purpose of this discussion is to reconstruct the Niebuhrian idea of the positional self through a critical and creative appropriation of Niebuhr's moral dualism. We will first investigate why Niebuhr fails to identify the moral issues of the positional self in organization as something qualitatively different from those of individuals in society. As a result of this investigation, we see more clearly that the positional self is an organizational self in whom both individual and group traits coexist. So the positional self will be described neither as a mere individual nor as a collectivity of the group, although both intrinsically constitute the moral identity of the positional self. As we will see shortly, the positional self is more concretely characterized as a responsible self posited in a constitutionally established group rather than a beleaguered ruler sandwiched between the individual and the group.

---

escape the winter's cold on the sands of Palm Beach while his workers starve to death amid the social confusion of an economic depression" (11).

While this chapter focuses on the moral predicament of the positional self based on Niebuhr's in-depth studies on the moral dynamics of individuals and groups, the following chapter explores the moral prospects through a critical study of his views on law, love, and justice.

We need to see why Niebuhr stops short of developing his moral concern into a full-fledged moral concept or theory trying to transcend the moral dualism of the individual and the group. First of all, for a structural reason, he could not develop his rough idea of the positional self into a full-fledged distinctive concept of a moral self because he cannot but identify it as a kind of individual based on his famous, but quite simplistic, schematic view that characterizes the basic social subject either "individual" or "group." From this perspective, the positional self cannot but be identified as a kind of individual rather than a group. No alternative conceptual tool or term would differently idealize the positional self neither as a mere individual nor as a group. Niebuhr has to reduce the distinctiveness of the positional self in order to fit it into his conceptual frame. In fact, the reduction of this distinctiveness is not just limited to the realm of the individual, because the group is also a largely truncated concept. When he talks about "group," Niebuhr typically lumps together races (racial groups), classes (economic groups), and nations (political groups) into a generic category that he calls "immoral society."

Niebuhr's tendency to bifurcate the social entity into two categories is not an accidental outcome. Niebuhr seems to develop such a view during his Detroit ministerial years through his personal and professional involvement in the labor movement and parish ministry. In a 1926 reflection, he writes, "If I viewed humanity only from some distant and high perspective I could not save myself from misanthropy. I think the reason is simply that people are not as decent in their larger relationship as in their more intimate contacts."[11] In his speech titled "Christianizing International Relations," delivered on September 18, 1928, at the seventh national convention of the Evangelical Brotherhood in Indianapolis, Indiana, Niebuhr reaffirms his view emphatically by saying, "But how about decency toward other groups—people in other racial, religious, and national groups? Here is the complication. Individuals find it difficult to deal justly with others within the group.

---

11. Niebuhr, *Leaves from the Notebook of a Tamed Cynic*, 94.

How much more difficult is it for the group as such to be decent in its international relations?"[12]

Niebuhr's professional experiences and personal reflections have led him to develop a theological antipathy toward liberalism that had been quite popular in the Western world since the eighteenth and nineteenth centuries. As he pointed out in the preface to a 1960 reprinting of his 1932 *Moral Man and Immoral Society*, he intended it to be a primary critique of the mistakes of "the Liberal Movement, both religious and secular."[13] Niebuhr perceives that liberalism is a great threat to humankind in that it infuses an illusive optimism in its followers, which later turn them into heartless cynics when they realize that the optimistic vision is only an illusion. The essence of liberalism lies in its belief that a universal moral law available to reason can gradually and progressively regulate and harmonize the special interests of individuals, groups, and governments into a grand, inclusive common good. Some of the leading proponents of this view, whom he identifies as "the children of light," were Adam Smith, Jeremy Bentham, and John Locke. Niebuhr also believes that Immanuel Kant is one of these culprits since his naïve confidence in the power of reason reflects the consistent feature of liberalism. Niebuhr regards the liberals as the "soft utopians" since they seem to imagine that "men of power will immediately check their ... pretensions in society, as soon as they have been apprised by the social scientists that their attitudes and actions are anti-social."[14] What Niebuhr was trying to do in his *Moral Man and Immoral Society* is to uncover the utopian illusion that lies at the heart of liberalism by revealing the recalcitrant and sinful aspects of the group, especially in the realm of power politics. Niebuhr's subsequent arguments supported by his elaboration of historical evidence are quite strong enough to crack down on the naïve belief of liberal views.

His political realism, however, is marked by his deep distrust of human reason: of its capacity to overcome the group egoism. It should be

---

12. Chrystal, *Young Reinhold Niebuhr*, 202. The thesis of *Moral Man and Immoral Society* can be also found in Neibuhr's first book, *Does Civilization Need Religion?* in which he epitomizes his view: "That is, groups as such find it even more difficult to maintain moral attitudes toward other groups than do the individuals within it toward individuals in other racial or political unities" (129).

13. Niebuhr, *Moral Man and Immoral Society* (1960 ed.), pref., ix.

14. Ibid., xviii.

noted here that Niebuhr does not regard highly the capacity of reason. Niebuhr holds that reason is not "the sole basis of moral virtue," even in interpersonal relationships. According to Niebuhr, individuals are born with "social impulses" that are more deeply rooted than the rationality. His strong distrust of human reason is captured by his own statement: "reason may extend and stabilize, but it does not create, the capacity to affirm other life than his own."[15] This, however, does not mean that reason does not play any role in making people moral. Indeed, he says that reason plays an important role in person-to-person or intimate group settings, such as in families or friendship. In individual relations, as Niebuhr writes, people are reasonable enough to take account of others' interest by submerging or even sacrificing certain of their interests to the good of others: "Reason enables him, within limits, to direct his energy so that it will flow in harmony, and not in conflict, with other life."[16] Niebuhr, however, believes that when it comes to group-to-group relations, "the limits of reason make it inevitable that pure moral action, particularly in the intricate, complex and collective relationships, should be an impossible goal."[17] In group relations, Niebuhr views, people will never be wholly reasonable because their common mind and purpose will always be more or less "inchoate and transitory."[18]

Niebuhr's distrust of reason becomes a decisive factor that characterizes his whole theological, ethical, and political viewpoint, which is largely known as Christian realism. His distrust of reason, particularly with regard to group relations, becomes a major theoretic perspective through which he deals with various national and international issues, leading him to develop a critical view not only against rationalistic liberalism but also against various versions of natural law theory, particularly against the Catholic view. Deeply grounded in the Christian tradition of original sin, Niebuhr's distrust of reason enabled him to launch a long list of attacks against all human endeavors to establish a "perfect society" by human efforts, whether though education (John Dewey) or proletarian revolution (Karl Marx). With regard to his dualism in morals (moral man and immoral society), however, Niebuhr's

---

15. Niebuhr, *Moral Man and Immoral Society*, 26.
16. Ibid.
17. Ibid., 34–35.
18. Ibid., 35.

strong distrust of reason sometimes renders him blinded and thus uncritical with regard to the legitimate distinction among various kinds of groups according to their constitutionality. For example, he lumps together an unconstitutional group such as "race" with a constitutional group such as "nation."

Although it may not be a serious mistake, the lack of a legitimate distinction among various groups sometimes means that Niebuhr is less critical about the possible political outcomes of different kinds of economic or political enterprises developed by liberal groups. For example, in 1932 and again in 1936, Niebuhr voted for the socialist Norman Thomas, pouring scorn on what he called "the futilities of Rooseveltian liberalism," with its aimless experiments and "whirligig reform."[19] However, throughout the 1940s and 1950s, Niebuhr changed his political view on Rooseveltian policies. In fact, Niebuhr voted for Franklin Roosevelt in 1940, by revoking his previous criticisms. The "unplanned improvisations of our early New Deal," which he once termed "whirligig reform," he then recognized as a "purposeful pragmatism" that would appear to be better than other alternatives.[20] Niebuhr later acknowledged the shortcomings of his view on liberalism by saying that his criticism against liberalism had been extravagant and exaggerated. Niebuhr writes:

> My second account of a gradual revision of my originally held opinions must deal, of course, with my rather violent, and sometimes extravagant, reaction to what I defined as the "utopianism," i.e., the illusory idealist and individualist character, of a Protestant and bourgeois culture before the world depression and two world wars. I must confess to some radical contradictions in my attitude.... And my reaction to bourgeois individualism prompted me to the error of using Marxist ideas to emphasize our new collective realities.[21]

We can also find Niebuhr's unsettled view on liberalism and the moral capacity of groups, particularly with regard to the formation of international politics. In 1932, Niebuhr clearly developed his skeptical

---

19. Schlesinger, "Reinhold Niebuhr's Role in Political Thought," 141–42, cited in Little, "Recovery of Liberalism," 172.

20. See Niebuhr, "Plutocracy and World Responsibilities," *Christianity and Society* 14 (Autumn 1949), cited in Little, "Recovery of Liberalism," 187.

21. Niebuhr, *Man's Nature and His Communities*, 21.

view of the possibility for international cooperation. He writes, "There is nevertheless little hope of arriving at a perceptible increase of international morality through the growth of intelligence and the perfection of means of communication. The development of international commerce, the increased economic interdependence among the nations, and the whole apparatus of a technological civilization increase the problems and issues between nations much more rapidly than the intelligence to solve them can be created."[22] During the 1940s and 1950s, however, he developed a somewhat different view on the possibility and necessity of international unity and politics. He was impressed by the achievements of democratic nations during the postwar era of the 1940s and 1950s.

As opposed to his earlier assessment of the mitigated reason in intergroup relations, Niebuhr eventually recognized that "effective democratic communities might actually elevate moral sensitivity and responsibility above what individuals can achieve in small, intimate groups, and thereby facilitate and enhance moral development rather than frustrate it."[23] Niebuhr's realistic approach toward international politics is well developed in the series of his columns and articles published in several journals, such as *Christianity and Crisis, Christian Century,* and *Foreign Affairs*. For example, in "World Community and World Government" (*Christianity and Crisis*, 1946), Niebuhr emphasizes that the world community should be established gradually along with the establishment of "mutual trust" and "forces of cohesion." In "Plans for World Reorganization" (*Christianity and Crisis*, 1942), Niebuhr cautiously lays out his Christian realist view of world reorganization by enumerating several conditions: "There must be tolerable equilibrium in it, and that equilibrium must be politically implemented; there must be an organizing center for it; and that center must be surrounded by checks to prevent its power from becoming vexatious; the organization must include many regional arrangements; and yet these regional arrangements must not run counter to the basic fact that the economic and political life of the nations is integrated in world, rather than regional, terms."[24] As David Little points out,[25] despite his well-known

---

22. Niebuhr, *Moral Man and Immoral Society*, 85.
23. Little, "The Recovery of Liberalism," 190.
24. Niebuhr, "Plans for World Reorganization," 6.
25. Little, "The Recovery of Liberalism," 190.

attack on the illusions of world government,[26] Niebuhr not only defended the usefulness of international constitutional guarantees but also tried to save the rights of smaller nations, defeated nations, and dependent peoples by actively supporting the United Nations.[27] Niebuhr's active support of the United Nations is noted in his 1952 pamphlet *The United Nations and the Free World*, in which he states:

> When the United Nations was launched at San Francisco in 1945 our readiness to commit ourselves to it represented a new chapter in the spiritual pilgrimage of our nation. The tragedies of World War II had convinced many peoples, and not merely us, that world community was waiting to become actual, that the days of unqualified sovereignty were over and that it was important to have such a constitutional instrument of world order.[28]

As we can see in the above, Niebuhr's early distrust of reason seems to be significantly seasoned and nuanced by his gradual adoption of the pragmatic stance, especially on the issues of national and international politics. This, however, does not mean that he deserted his earlier view of moral dualism, which still resonates in his later works.[29]

Although Niebuhr does not explicitly explain the reason why and how he came to have a nuanced view on human reason as opposed to his early distrust of reason,[30] we can conjecture the development of his later

---

26. In his well-known article "The Illusion of World Government," Niebuhr argues that given the situation in which the social forces operating to integrate the world community are limited, the hope to create a world government by the "fiat of the human will" is a sheer fallacy. He insists that the Lockean "social contract" conception should not be "workable."

27. Holleman, "Reinhold Niebuhr on the United Nations and Human Rights," 344.

28. This essay was first published as a pamphlet, *The Moral Implications of Loyalty to the United Nations*, by the Edward W. Hazen Foundation, New Haven, Conn.: July 1952. The essay was later reprinted in Ernest W. Lefever, ed., *The World Crisis and American Responsibility*, New York: Association Press, 1958, cited in Little, "Recovery of Liberalism," 191.

29. In his 1946 article "World Community and World Government," he still confirms his earlier insight. "It is very difficult to establish peaceful and just human communities, because the collective behavior of mankind is even more egoistic than individual behavior; our job is therefore to establish a tolerable community within the limits set by man's recalcitrance" (5).

30. Niebuhr now redefines *reason* more elaborately as follows: "Because reason is something more than a weapon of self-interest it can be an instrument of justice" (*Children of Light and the Children of Darkness*, 72).

view through the critical reading of his writings. The most important reason for this change lies in his mature thought on politics, an example of which we can find in the 1965 *Man's Nature and His Communities*. Niebuhr confesses that he made an "unpardonable pedagogical error" in *The Nature and Destiny of Man* (1943). He writes that he hopes to correct the earlier mistake: "My theological preoccupation prompted me to define the persistence and universality of man's self-regard as 'original sin.' This was historically and symbolically correct. But my pedagogical error consisted in seeking to challenge modern optimism with the theological doctrine which was anathema to modern culture."[31] By "politics" Niebuhr means the collective human effort to approximate the ethical ideal. In the approximating process, he discovers the place where reason can find its role. With regard to reason, however, Niebuhr stops short of developing it in the form of what we now call public reason, which has recently been developed by political philosophers, most notably John Rawls (*Political Liberalism, The Law of Peoples*) and Jürgen Habermas (*The Inclusion of the Other*). For Niebuhr, the reason is still a suspicious human capacity that can only lead people into utopian illusion or cynical realism unless it is properly checked by its own limitations.

Niebuhr's mature thought on politics implies an important point that he could differentiate the constitutionally established group from nonconstitutional groups. He now sees clearly that the careful differentiation of groups within the group can be more important than the categorical separation between individuals and groups in moral discourse. Facing a potential global calamity such as nuclear stalemate, the cold war, and the rampant poverty in the Third World, Niebuhr comes to realize that although limited, politics is a most viable option for the ailing humankind. In his *The Children of Light and the Children of Darkness*, Niebuhr argues that the relational character between the individual and the community is significantly affected by how the community is constituted as a political entity. Niebuhr's thesis is that for the common good of the world community, democracy is not only possible but also necessary among nations with a shared belief that "the task of building a world community is man's final necessity and possibility."[32] Thus it becomes clear why we need to deconstruct Niebuhr's dualism

---

31. Niebuhr, *Man's Nature and His Communities*, 23.

32. Niebuhr, *Children of Light and the Children of Darkness*, 187. Of course, he immediately delimits this possibility by adding a condition that the task of building a world community is his final impossibility.

in morals (moral man and immoral society), which somehow Niebuhr himself tries to exercise. In an increasingly diversified but progressively interconnected global society through the media of economic transactions and political reorganizations, we need to give due consideration to the critical roles of constitutional groups: to save themselves from themselves.

Now it becomes much clearer how we define the positional self in its socio-existential context between the individual and the group. Indeed, the positional self can be roughly characterized as an organizational self, which has both individual and group traits. However, as we have already seen, the positional self needs to be more carefully delineated as a constitutional self in that it finds its moral responsibility not only as an individual who has transcending capacity (freedom) but also as a position holder in constitutional groups established by law and policy (public reason). The inevitable conflict and the uneasy compromise between these two elements that characterize the moral sphere of the positional self (freedom and public reason) will be discussed when we explore the moral prospect of the positional self (chapter 6). For now, we will focus on the question: What is the moral predicament of the positional self?

In order to uncover the Niebuhrian moral predicament of the positional self, we begin with a critical analysis of Niebuhr's socio-existential condition of the positional self posited between the individual and the group. As we will see shortly, in several aspects, Niebuhr's socio-existential analysis of the moral predicament of the positional self is quite different from Habermas's historical-practical analysis. Most conspicuously, while Habermas's analysis focuses on the system's colonizing effect on the positional self (the positional self as a mediated self between the lifeworld and the system), Niebuhr's analysis is centered on the collective effects of group egoism on the positional self. Through Niebuhr's analysis, we see that the internal mediation of "individual" and "group" ethos in the positional self is also marked by a pathological trait just as in the case of Habermas's external analysis. Another significant difference will be that while Habermas's analysis can only provide us with a procedural and formalistic analysis of the moral predicament, Niebuhr's analysis allows us to have a much more substantive understanding of the moral predicament of the positional self. Most notably, the issue of money and power will be no longer be treated here "delinguistified media." Instead, money and power are now identified and analyzed as substantive "demoralizing sources" in the sense that they have inherent tendency to "concentrate" themselves to the extent of defying the moral ideal. The formal concept of power and money as delinguistified media thus must be differentiated from the substantive understanding of money and power that can turn into a demoralizing source for the sake of their own "concentration." When money and power become concentrated through organizations or corporations, they would not be regarded any longer as media because they would begin to claim themselves as ends or goals.

The concentration of power and money is indeed deeply related to the moral formation of the positional self because the concentration itself cannot be established without considering the role of positions. The enormous burden of managing the concentration of money and power is inevitably laid upon certain positions in the group. Thus, we will here focus on how the concentration of money and power could affect the moral imagination and responsibility of the positional self rather than on the money and power as media. The purpose of this analysis is then to uncover the moral circumstance of the positional self through a critical analysis of the inevitable imposition of power and money on the position holders of the group.

The Positional Self and the Concentration of Power and Money

Although we have briefly reviewed this above, it is important to be aware that Niebuhr's early political works, particularly *Moral Man and Immoral Society* (1932) and *Reflections on the End of an Era* (1934), were written in a period in which he disagrees more and more with the prevailing liberal views of his time (1925–1935).[33] Rooted in the eighteenth-century European Enlightenment and in new developmental forms in the nineteenth century, American liberalism represents a continuous and evolutionary development in human civilization as well as in human rationality and morality. In this period, according to Langdon Gilkey, "liberals tended to believe in the developing goodness and rationality of people, in the growing health of democratic and economic institutions,

---

33. Gilkey, *On Niebuhr*, 29.

and in the certainty of a better and better tomorrow."³⁴ The problem with this view lies in its relative and proportional downplay of historical realities such as perennial conflicts among peoples and nations as well as the persistence of selfishness, irrationality, brutality, and terrors. Niebuhr holds that by looking at the good side only, liberals wrongfully imagine that "the egoism of individuals is being progressively checked by the development of rationality or the growth of religiously inspired goodwill and that nothing but the continuance of this process is necessary to establish social harmony between all the human societies and collectives."³⁵

Against the stream of the nineteenth century's optimistic liberalism, Niebuhr argues that human efforts to develop rationality (social science) and religiously inspired goodwill (moral education) cannot reverse the fundamental tendency of human reason with its relation to the interest of groups. Niebuhr asserts, "What is lacking among all these moralists, whether religious or rational, is an understanding of the brutal character of the behavior of all human collectives, and the power of self-interest and collective egoism in all intergroup relations"³⁶ Thus, one of the important reasons that motivated Niebuhr to write *Moral Man and Immoral Society* is to warn the contemporary public as well as those liberal and religious moralists particularly about their optimistic view of the development of the human species along with their naïve belief in reason.³⁷

---

34. Ibid., 31.

35. Niebuhr, *Moral Man and Immoral Society*, xii. In contrast to many liberals, particularly John Dewey and George Stratton, in 1920s and 1930s Niebuhr first differentiates the role and scope of reason in its relevance to physical science and to social science. He holds that the development of reason in the field of physical science should not become the model in the field of social science. He particularly criticizes Dewey for his optimistic belief that just in the way modern people built up physical science, we need to take the road that leads to the assured building up of social science. See Niebuhr, *Moral Man and Immoral Society*, xiii.

36. Ibid., xx.

37. Niebuhr's view is often criticized because his rather pessimistic stance can be interpreted as defending the status quo. In his book *Wilderness Wanderings*, Stanley Hauerwas argues that the irony of Reinhold Niebuhr is that his Christian realism would only end up supporting the very liberalism he tried to undo. Hauerwas writes: "The irony of Reinhold Niebuhr is that it is precisely his antiliberal social criticism that turns out to provide a justification of liberal politics" (49). According to Hauerwas, by turning the human condition (particularly the ontology of the group) into the "truth," Niebuhr

Niebuhr tries to prove his own argument by uncovering the morally intractable aspect of power and money regarding their mode in intergroup relations. Niebuhr's point is that there is an inherently "concentrative" element in money and power that needs to be differed from their "mediatory" function in society. Niebuhr explains this with his penetrating insight on the qualitative difference between the individual's and the group's orientations toward the money and power. He points out that it is much more unlikely for a group to give up their quest for the concentration of power and money than for an individual to do so. Since this is an essential point in analyzing the moral predicament of the positional self, we need to take a closer look at his understanding of power and money. Since Niebuhr does not clearly differentiate between power and money with regard to their concentrative mode, and he also uses the term "power" indistinctively implying money, our analysis will focus on his understanding of power.[38]

First of all, by "power" Niebuhr means it not only a political power but it is also an economic and military power. Of course, individuals can have physical, psychological, monetary, or moral power with which they can realize their personal goals and interests. For example, emphasizing the possibility of personal moral power, Niebuhr says, "He may be personally the kindest and most considerate of man, in which case

---

allows such "truths" to succeed in "naturalizing a social setting of conflict that then becomes the rationale for structures of liberal social control and those who benefit from such arrangements" (57). Hauerwas's critique is not entirely right, because Niebuhr's theological liberalism (along with his Christian doctrine of sin) is always coupled with his political progressivism and activism (along with his realistic view of justice). His socialist ministerial legacy in Detroit in the 1920s and his political activism in 1928, 1930, and 1932 (his race for the state Senate as a nominee in the Socialist Party) are only a few examples for this. Niebuhr's main point in *Moral Man and Immoral Society* lies not in rebutting liberalism as such, but in presenting an alternative politically progressive realism that could better deal with the group-involved sociopolitical problems that could not be resolved by relying only on liberalist individual-oriented moral vision. See Niebuhr, *Moral Man and Immoral Society*, 21; and Fox, *Reinhold Niebuhr*, 121–24.

38. According to Gilkey, there are four major theses in *Moral Man and Immoral Society*: the ambiguity of power, the ambiguity of reason, the ambiguity of religion, and the immorality of groups. Among these themes, the first (the ambiguity of power) and the last (the immorality of groups) are particularly important for our discussion. Let us first analyze Niebuhr's understanding of power, because this leads us not only to substantively differentiate human beings into two categories, individuals and groups, but also to explain the distinctive moral and ethical predicament that the positional self encounters in between the two forms. See Gilkey, *On Niebuhr*, 33–41.

he will do what he can to soften the inevitable injustice of his rule by personal generosities."[39] By "power," however, Niebuhr generally means socioeconomic and sociopolitical power. He also perceives that a political society devoid of any concentration of power would not be possible, because political existence represents a contest of power.[40] Unlike Habermas, who configures power and money as delinguistified media opposed to the intersubjective use of language, Niebuhr primarily concerns himself with power's tendency to concentrate itself as a dominating drive. According to Niebuhr, groups are dominated by their own interests, which are stubborn and resourceful, and most problematically these interests cannot be checked, limited, or overthrown except by the opposition of another and stronger group. The interests of groups reveal themselves as their will, and this will is none other than the "will to power." Niebuhr explains this genealogically by saying that power was originally formed by individuals for their own survival, but this instinct of survival soon extends beyond it to become the will to power.[41]

In my view, Niebuhr provides us with an important insight regarding the concentration of power. Niebuhr perceives that the concentration of power has a certain meaning-creating element within it, which would allow the "average man" to transcend his individual limitations to become his own meaning. He writes, "The frustrations of the average man, who can never realize the power and the glory which his imagination sets as the ideal, makes him the more willing tool and victim of the imperial ambitions of his group. His frustrated individual ambitions gain a measure of satisfaction in the power and the aggrandizement of his nation."[42] Niebuhr argues that Tolstoian pacifists and other advocates of nonresistance cannot succeed simply because their views lack in realistic understanding of power and its concentrative drive. For this reason, he criticizes their view as an "illusion." Their problem lies in their ignorance or disbelief that "there are definite limits of moral goodwill and social intelligence beyond which even the most vital religion

---

39. Niebuhr, *Reflections on the End of an Era*, 43.
40. Ibid., 33.
41. Niebuhr, *Moral Man and Immoral Society*, 18.
42. Ibid.

and the most astute educational program will not carry a social group, whatever may be possible for individuals in an intimate society."[43]

Niebuhr correctly points out that the single most troubling impediment to the achievement of justice is the group's will to power, which is inevitably realized in the form of concentration of power. He writes:

> The fact is that the interests of the powerful and dominant groups, who profit from the present system of society, are the real hindrance to the establishment of a rational and just society ... Politics are given their general direction by the pressure of interest of the groups which control them; the expert is quite capable of giving any previously determined tendency both rational justification and efficient detailed application.[44]

According to Niebuhr, the concentration of power not only obstructs justice but also breeds further injustice as a form of inequality. "Our interest at the moment is to record that any kind of significant social power develops social inequality."[45] The group with dominant power, out of their desire to concentrate their power, always takes to itself most of society's privileges and would not voluntarily relinquish any significant portion of them unless somehow forced to do so. Niebuhr remarks that since society will probably never be sufficiently intelligent to bring all power under its control, the dream of "perpetual peace" and "brotherhood" for human society is one that will never be fully realized.[46]

Concerning the concept of power, perhaps the most ironic point will be its necessary presence despite its uncertainty and danger. First of all, power is necessary to bring unity and order to a society. Niebuhr is fully aware of the two possible idiosyncratic phenomena that can be constituted as a result of the misuse of power: anarchy and tyranny. While the perils of anarchy reside in the place where there is no central unifying power, the excess use of power may also bring tyranny to the society. Regarding this uncertainty of power in its lack of concentration and excessiveness, Gilkey asserts, "Because of the necessity and yet the ambiguity of power, society is continually, and inescapably, threatened with the dialectic of anarchy and tyranny and so continually plagued

43. Ibid., 20.
44. Ibid., 213–14.
45. Ibid., 7–8. In the same manner, Niebuhr also writes: "The basis of inequality is the disproportion of power in society" (ibid., 167).
46. Ibid. 21.

by injustice and potential conflict."⁴⁷ Niebuhr himself acknowledges the conundrum of political power by saying, "While no state can maintain its unity purely by coercion, neither can it preserve itself without coercion."⁴⁸

We now need to take a look at how the ambiguity of power is related to the concept of the positional self. Niebuhr's insight on the ambiguity of power enables us to see that the ambiguity of power, especially regarding its tendency to concentrate, can surely affect the moral and ethical identity of the positional self. The ambiguity of power becomes evident when power is connected to a positional self who has both individual and group traits at the same time. The positional self is certainly an individual who is capable of realizing his or her own moral conviction or identity, but it is simultaneously a representative and a manager of a group, whose interests it is supposed to advocate and promote. Thus the obvious moral predicament that the positional self faces as a manager of a group is that it cannot realize its personal moral conviction or vision through its positional role-playing. Personal moral integration certainly will be at odds with the group's tendency to concentrate its power and money. Although Niebuhr does not directly mention or deal with this issue, we can develop this idea by analyzing one of his main insights in *Moral Man and Immoral Society*.

According to Niebuhr, there is a certain discrepancy between the individual and the group in their moral capacity and imagination: while individuals can be moral, groups cannot. Thus, there should be a distinction between the moral conduct of individuals and the social behavior of groups. He also argues that individuals do not have adequate rational or religious resources to counter the collective pride of groups. Niebuhr states his thesis in the following way:

> The central thesis was, and is, that the Liberal Movement, both religious and secular seemed to be unconscious of the basic difference between the morality of individuals and the morality of collectives, whether races, classes, or nations. This difference ought not to make for a moral cynicism, that is, the belief that the collective must simply follow its own interests. But if the

---

47. Gilkey, *On Niebuhr*, 35.
48. Niebuhr, *Moral Man and Immoral Society*, 3.

difference is real, as I think it is, it refutes many still prevalent moralistic approaches to the political order.[49]

By the "morality of individuals," Niebuhr primarily means the individual's capacity to transcend one's own self-interests. According to Niebuhr, while an individual may sacrifice his or her own interests for the sake of others, groups such as classes, nations, and races, however, are incapable of doing so. For example, an executive in a commercial company may be reasonably moral and even godly as an individual, but when economic justice is at issue, he or she will act as a class representative to protect his or her group interests. One misconception, however, regarding Niebuhr's *Moral Man and Immoral Society* is that an individual person is naturally moral. Niebuhr has never proposed such an idea. Later, Niebuhr even suggests that the book should have been called *The Not So Moral Man in His Less Moral Communities*.[50] However, he continued to maintain that the distinction between individuals and groups in terms of their moral capacity as well as their moral imagination is an important one. Hence the possibilities of individual selflessness can in no case provide the plausibility of a corresponding group selflessness.[51]

Regarding this point, Gilkey finds three important reasons why groups find it almost impossible to overcome this collective selfishness (power's tendency to concentrate itself).[52] First, unlike for an individual, there is no single, unified, self-transcending consciousness in a group. Although it is true that the whole group is unified by a certain section of the community such as a class or a dominant minority, its consciousness is not identical with the consciousness of the whole. He says, "The interests that motivate the exercise of its power are by no means self-transcendent, selfless, or even the interests of the group as a whole; on the contrary, they represent the particular interests of a given

49. Ibid., ix.

50. Niebuhr, *Man's Nature and His Communities*, 22. Niebuhr actually introduces his friend's comment on his earlier work, *Moral Man and Immoral Society*, by writing, "A young friend of mine recently observed that, in the light of all the facts and my more consistent 'realism' in regard to both individual and collective behavior, a better title might have been *The Not So Moral Man in His Less Moral Communities*."

51. Gary Dorrien describes the thesis appropriately: "Morality was for individuals. If individuals occasionally overcame their inevitable egoism in acts of compassion or love, there was no evidence that human groups ever overcame the power of self interest and collective egotism that sustained their existence" (Dorrien, *Soul in Society*, 91–92).

52. Gilkey, *On Niebuhr*, 38–40.

class concerned with maximizing its own special power and privileges."[53] Second, called on by the group to be moral, individuals would become moral by supporting, enacting, defending, and even sacrificing himself or herself for the group policies and interests. Sometimes these include any group's frequent immorality toward other communities. True morality should be realized by challenging and even opposing communal immorality rather than furthering the group's interests.[54] Third, each group is universally hypocritical. In order to ease the consciences of individual members, the group claims to embody and pursue the highest values rather than admitting the relatively dubious interests and the particular self-interests. It is inevitable that "the group pretend not only that the values the community espouses are more universal than they truly are, but also that those values are the sole 'reasons' why it does whatever dubious things it does do."[55]

Now we have a more comprehensive view on the moral predicament that the positional self cannot but face and deal with in its situation. Being individual and thus potentially moral in its conviction and action, beleaguered by the group dynamics, particularly by its unchecked drive for the concentration of power, the positional self is inevitably shadowed by the group's blind passion for power and its concentration. In other words, the internal possibility of the positional self's moral transcendence becomes obscured by the external realities that characterize the positional roles: to serve for the concentration of power. Niebuhr describes this predicament as follows: "It is impossible completely to disassociate an evil social system from the personal moral responsibilities of the individuals who maintain it."[56]

This description clearly shows us that Niebuhr has developed a distinctive socio-existential understanding of the positional self and its moral predicament. Niebuhr's characterization of the moral predica-

---

53. Ibid., 38.

54. Niebuhr, *Moral Man and Immoral Society*, 248. Patriotism is an ambiguous virtue for this reason, because it combines the self-sacrifice of the individual with the self-interest of the group that the individual serves. Gilkey thus emphasizes, "To be 'morally' against the immorality of one's group is hence to become oneself immoral in the eyes of the wider community: a traitor to one's family, one's class, one's race, one's nation" (Gilkey, *On Niebuhr*, 39).

55. Ibid.

56. Niebuhr, *Moral Man and Immoral Society*, 249.

ment for the positional self is actually based on his fundamental belief that "individuals are never as immoral as the social situations in which they are involved and which they symbolize."[57] Why is it so? According to Niebuhr, as individuals, they are still free from the inevitable evils of the social system rooted in groups' blind interests in power and its concentration. Individual moral goodwill (ethics) thus must be differentiated from the imperative of groups (politics), and the former cannot substitute for the latter in reality: "Every effort to transfer a pure morality of disinterestedness to group relations has resulted in failure."[58]

Niebuhr's socio-existential analysis of the positional self, related to individual and group ethos, cannot be fully attained without looking at his ontological analysis of human nature represented by the concepts of freedom and original sin. Thus our discussion turns to these concepts in order to find the moral dualism of the individual and the group.

The Positional Self and Human Nature

The main question we need to answer in this section is, why can't the individual moral goodwill of the positional self realistically overcome the positional burden incumbent upon itself in the form of the concentration of power? In the above discussion, we have developed an idea (the moral conundrum of the positional self) by relying on Niebuhr's socio-ontological insight that although the positional self may be conceptually portrayed as one of the kinds of "moral man," it cannot realistically identify itself as a "moral man." Why is this so? What is the fundamental justification for the identification of the moral predicament of the positional self? We now try to answer this question by analyzing Niebuhr's anthropology: his ideas of freedom, original sin, and anxiety.

For Niebuhr, human beings are fundamentally paradoxical: on the one hand, they are part of nature; on the other hand, they can transcend the natural process.[59] It thus turns out to be a failure to reduce this para-

---

57. Ibid., 248.

58. Ibid., 268.

59. According to Gilkey's analysis, Niebuhr suggests four interrelated sets of paradoxes. They are as follows: first, humans are animals, a part of nature, and yet they are free and so both rational and responsible; second, humans are responsible, moral, and idealistic while they are continuously and universally immoral and often cruel, even evil; third humans seek and require meaning, and yet they despair; finally humans seem on the one hand bound in evil, while on the other hand they experience them-

doxical nature into a simplistic formula of human nature. Niebuhr, as a realist, tries to appreciate this paradoxical nature with an equal sympathy. He writes, "The obvious fact is that man is a child of nature, subject to its vicissitudes, compelled by its necessities, driven by its impulses, and confined within the brevity of the years which nature permits its varied organic form ... The other less obvious fact is that man is a spirit who stands outside of nature, life, himself, his reason and the world."[60]

Niebuhr points out how difficult it is to do justice to both features of the human being. According to Niebuhr, Western philosophies (rationalism) historically tend to forget humankind's relation to nature while describing and emphasizing its rational faculties and capacities for self-transcendence. Naturalistic philosophies, to the contrary, do not give due attention to its self-transcending unique capacity. He writes, "Naturalistic philosophies may (and in modern nationalism do) destroy individuality by emphasizing consanguinity and other natural forces of social uniformity as the only basis of meaning; spiritualistic philosophies may on the other hand prompt the transcendent ego (spirit) to flee from history with all its perils of particularity and its uncertain vicissitudes into a realm of meaning which negates history and individuality."[61] Since the human spirit is revealed in the form of freedom, it is important to understand that as part of nature, freedom is the capacity to stand outside given conditions.

This capacity, according to Niebuhr, plays an important role in human history, although it is often interpreted as an inevitable consequence of a previous event or action.[62] Niebuhr argues that the proofs of freedom are the endless variety and unpredictability of the historical dramas themselves. Freedom is the fundamental ground on which we can defeat historical determinism. However, this should not mean that history can be interpreted solely as the result of human freedom, because to some degree the inevitable consequence of a previous event

---

selves as both necessitated and responsible, as both guilty and free. Among these four kinds of paradoxes, the first is most important in that it is the fundamental paradox that ultimately entails the rest of the paradoxes. See Gilkey, *On Niebuhr*, 80–81.

60. Niebuhr, *Nature and Destiny of Man*, 1:3.

61. Ibid., 69–70.

62. Niebuhr, *Faith and Politics*, 80.

or action is an important aspect of history. For this reason, Niebuhr says that the good historian should be "half artist and half scientist."[63]

We need to look more closely at Niebuhr's view of freedom. The self-transcendence of spirit is in fact the possibility of intellect and of reason, and this possibility is the source of creativity, through which novelty is introduced into historical time. Freedom as self-transcendence both in space and time stipulates a human as a self-determining being: "Man is self-determining not only in the sense that he transcends natural process in such a way as to be able to choose between various alternatives presented to him by the process of nature; even more he transcends in the sense that he transcends himself in such a way that he must choose his total end."[64]

According to Robin W. Lovin, for Niebuhr, while freedom is "indefinite transcendence" of our circumstances and ourselves, freedom first starts from its concrete situation. Lovin thus contrasts Niebuhr's view of freedom with the concept of "freedom from nowhere." Lovin says, "Freedom is not the 'view from nowhere' that provides an objective picture of everything as it is. Freedom starts from somewhere, and views that starting point in relation to other possibilities."[65]

In Lovin's analysis, freedom is also a basic human good, like reason, in that "life without freedom is not something we would choose, no matter how comfortable the material circumstances might be."[66] But freedom is more than a good, because "it is also the capacity by which we know the good and identify the things that are good."[67] This capacity, however, is something that has limitations. Freedom is fundamentally a capacity of finite, limited persons whose capacities for change are also limited. For this reason, any exercises of freedom that attempt to deny or alter this reality become wrong. Since every human being has free-

---

63. Ibid. Niebuhr claims, "He [the good historian] is a scientist in that he may analyze causes and historical trends. He is an artist in that he must interpret the meaning of an historical structure according to a general system of meaning, which his imagination partly imposes upon them and partly elicits from them" (ibid.).

64. Niebuhr, *Nature and Destiny of Man*, 1:163.

65. Lovin, *Reinhold Niebuhr and Christian Realism*, 125. In the footnote, Lovin explains that he quotes the term "view from nowhere" from Thomas Nagel's work *The View from Nowhere*. Nagel originally employs the phrase to characterize the Enlightenment view of reason.

66. Ibid., 126.

67. Ibid.

dom and freedom has both a transcendental and a finite character, any attempt to deny or overemphasize one of those characters would also become inadequate.

According to Niebuhr, the true and in-depth study of human freedom can be better attained through biblical faith. Since rationalism, naturalism, and even Nietzschean romanticism fail to appreciate either the total stature of freedom in humanity or the complexity of the problem of human evil.[68] Biblical faith becomes an important view with which we can be more fully aware of the true and complex image of the human being.[69] Niebuhr is fully aware that freedom as an ability to stand outside and beyond the world can "tempt man to megalomania and persuade him to regard himself as the god around and about whom the universe centers."[70] Since the rational faculty itself is part of the finite world, the only principle to comprehend both man and his world is inevitably beyond his comprehension: "Man is thus in the position of being unable to comprehend himself in his full stature of freedom without a principle of comprehension which is beyond his comprehension."[71]

For Niebuhr, this in an important reason why so many mystic faiths have arisen in many parts of the world. Biblical religion, however, differs from other mystic religions in some important points. In particular, as a religion of revelation, biblical religion is "alone able to do justice to both the freedom and finiteness of man and to understand the character."[72] Perhaps the most critical characteristic that brings a difference between biblical religion and many mystic faiths would be the idea of sin (or original sin).

---

68. Niebuhr's critique of "romanticism" is more fully delineated in the third chapter of his *The Nature and Destiny of Man*, vol. 1. According to Niebuhr, while the classic romanticism subordinates the individuality of the person to the unique and self-justifying individuality of the social collective, Nietzschean romanticism later turns into a vehicle of demonic religion that has no law but one's own will to power as well as no God but one's own unlimited ambition. See Niebuhr, *Nature and Destiny of Man*, 1:81-92.

69. Niebuhr asserts that modern culture, in its controversies between rationalism and romanticism, has not been able to arrive at any satisfactory solution to the problem of the unity of nature and spirit. Niebuhr, *Nature and Destiny of Man*, 1:27.

70. Ibid., 124.

71. Ibid., 125.

72. Ibid., 127.

Niebuhr makes clear that the contradiction of finiteness and freedom is not a problem as such. It would be rather a human situation, but it becomes problematic when the problem of finiteness is subordinated to the problem of sin. Based on a biblical faith, he interprets sin in both religious and moral terms. He writes:

> Man is insecure and involved in natural contingency; he seeks to overcome his insecurity by a will-to-power which overreaches the limits of human creatureliness. Man is ignorant and involved in limitations of a finite mind; but he pretends that he is not limited. He assumes that he can gradually transcend finite limitations until his mind becomes identical with universal mind. All of his intellectual and cultural pursuits, therefore, become infected with the sin of pride. Man's pride and will-to-power disturb the harmony of creation. The Bible defines sin in both religious and moral terms. The religious dimension of sin is man's rebellion against God, his effort to usurp the place of God. The moral and social dimension of sin is injustice. The ego which falsely makes itself the center of existence in its pride and will-to-power inevitably subordinates other life to its will and thus does injustice to other life.[73]

Niebuhr emphasizes that the contradiction of finiteness and freedom itself is not the direct cause of sin. If the contradiction itself is the cause of sin, then the problem of human responsibility will be eclipsed by this contradiction between finiteness and freedom. Sin is definitely occasioned by this contradiction between finiteness and freedom, but it certainly does not cause sin: "Sin is not caused by the contradiction because, according to Biblical faith, there is no absolute necessity that man should be betrayed into sin by the ambiguity of his position, as standing in and yet above nature."[74]

According to Niebuhr, this contradiction rather should be understood with regard to anxiety. For him, anxiety is the psychological state that also has an ontological connotation. By "anxiety," Niebuhr means the "internal precondition of sin," standing in the paradoxical situation of freedom and finiteness.[75] Niebuhr's most ingenious insight on human anxiety is his uncovering of its dual aspects. For Niebuhr, as a necessary

---

73. Ibid., 178–79.
74. Ibid., 178.
75. Ibid., 182.

concomitant of freedom, anxiety is both the "source of creativity" and a "temptation to sin."[76] Niebuhr captures the idea that no one is able to choose one without being involved in the other by making a simple separation between the dual aspects. Niebuhr writes, "His creativity is therefore always corrupted by some effort to overcome contingency by raising precisely what is contingent to absolute and unlimited dimension ... It is always destructive."[77]

In Niebuhr's analysis, humans are paradoxical because they are free and bound, limited and limitless, and this is the source of their anxiety. He goes on further, saying, "It [anxiety] must not be identified with sin because there is always the ideal possibility that faith would purge anxiety of the tendency toward sinful self-assertion. The ideal possibility is that faith in the ultimate security of God's love would overcome all immediate insecurities of nature and history."[78] From the perspective of a biblical faith, thus, freedom from anxiety can only be possible in perfect trust in the divine security. The dynamic of anxiety and freedom as an internal precondition for sin cannot be resolved where there is no such perfect trust.

For Niebuhr, telling the difference between anxiety and sin is important because without this distinction, sin would be readily interpreted as a hereditary element in its character.[79] For this reason, Niebuhr works hard to excise any "literalistic" element from his explication of the doctrine.[80] From Niebuhr's perspective, an Augustinian literalistic understanding of original sin is problematic because the literalistic-hereditary interpretation of original sin is likely to reduce human responsibility for misbehavior. Niebuhr tries to emphasize human responsibility as well as freedom of the will in the act of sin. He writes, "Original sin, which is by definition an inherited corruption, or at least inevitable one, is nevertheless not to be regarded as belonging

---

76. Ibid., 185.

77. Ibid., 185–86. According to Niebuhr, creativity and temptation to sin are so inextricably bound together in the human being that it is not possible to separate them.

78. Ibid., 182–83.

79. By distinguishing anxiety from sin, Niebuhr carefully differentiates the inevitability of sin and the responsibility of sin. The theory of an inherited second nature could reduce this paradox to a simplistic theory that attributes human evil to the inertia of nature. See Niebuhr, *Nature and Destiny of Man*, 1:262.

80. Rees, "Anxiety of Inheritance," 75.

to his essential nature and therefore is not outside the realm of his responsibility. Sin is natural for man in the sense that it is universal but not in the sense that it is necessary."[81] Sin may be inevitable in human anxiety, but it is not necessary. The main point implied in this assertion is that while sin is inevitable, human will in its freedom still plays an important role in the act of sin. This is why Niebuhr claims that sin is not necessary. From Niebuhr's interpretation of original sin, no one can rationalize his or her own sinful action as a necessary outcome of his or her own nature. Even in the act of sin, a human is still free, and thus he or she is responsible for his or her action. The inevitability of sin does not remove the burden of responsibility from the sinner.

Although Niebuhr denies the Augustinian hereditary concept of original sin, he stands in the orthodox line that sin proceeds from a defect of the will. "Sin is to be regarded as neither a necessity of man's nature nor yet as a pure caprice of his will. It proceeds rather from a defect of the will."[82] According to Niebuhr, in its own anxiety, the defect of the will is realized in the form either of "pride" (inordinate self-love) or of "sensuality." While "man falls into pride, when he seeks to raise his contingent existence to unconditioned significance; he falls into sensuality when he seeks to escape from his unlimited possibilities of freedom."[83]

Niebuhr understands that biblical and Christian thought consistently maintains that "pride is more basic than sensuality and that the latter is, in some way, derived from the former."[84] From Augustine to our contemporaries, Western theologians continuously hold that pride and self-love are what compose original sin. For Niebuhr, pride as the primary original sin comes into being when humanity seeks to overcome insecurity by relying on his own power, by rejecting his limited creatureliness. Man commits the sin of pride by overestimating his freedom and intelligence when he seeks to gain security "by enhancing his power

---

81. Niebuhr, *Nature and Destiny of Man*, 1:242.

82. Ibid.

83. Ibid., 186.

84. Ibid. Feminist theologians and ethicists often criticize Niebuhr's emphasis on pride for failing to consider the socially marginalized, who do not even claim their own self as their own. See Dunfee, "Sin of Hiding"; Hess, "Gender, Sin, and Learning"; and Plaskow, *Sex, Sin, and Grace*.

individually and collectively."[85] The sin of pride occurs when people think more highly of themselves than they actually are. It is also the intentional usurpation of the prerogative of God. Niebuhr categorizes pride into three types: pride of power, pride of knowledge, and pride of virtue.[86] He is particularly interested in the third type in that it can rise to a form of spiritual pride as a worst kind.

Meanwhile, Niebuhr defines sensuality as "the inordinate love for all creaturely and mutable values which results from the primal love of self, rather than love of God."[87] Sensuality is indeed a pathological choice of free will, which man chooses in the form of self-love, but at the same time it is as an effort to escape self-love.[88] The fundamental reason for the sin of sensuality is the loss of the true center of one's life in God. In the absence of the true center, one reifies another or mutable objects as the meaningful center of one's life. But since it cannot provide the ultimate meaning to oneself, sensuality ultimately turns out to be a flight to nothingness.[89] For Niebuhr, while sin as pride realizes itself through the denial of finiteness, sin as sensuality comes into being through the escape from freedom.

The Positional Self and the Ethical Predicament: Positional Pride and Sensuality

In order to define the ethical predicament of the positional self, we need to go further to correlate Niebuhr's anthropological account with his

---

85. Niebuhr, *Children of Light and the Children of Darkness*, 20.

86. Niebuhr, *Nature and Destiny of Man*, 1:188.

87. Ibid., 232.

88. Ibid., 239. Sensuality, on the one hand, is a form of self-love in that one chooses to devote to particular impulses and desires as one's own good; however, on the other hand, it is also a form of escape from self-love in that one negates one's freedom to transcend the mutable and the external.

89. Lovin interprets Niebuhr's idea of sin as sensuality to be reminiscent of Karl Barth's understanding of sin as "sloth." Unlike the implied meaning of *sloth* in the sense of laziness and inertia, Barth's real meaning of sin as sloth is an active flight from God. Barth defines sin of sloth as follows: "At every point, as we shall see, this is the strange inactive action of the slothful man. It may be that this action often assumes the disguise of a hate which wants to be free of God, which would prefer that there were no God, that God were not the One He is—at least for him, the slothful man" (cited in Lovin, *Reinhold Niebuhr and Christian Realism*, 147). The original paragraph is from Karl Barth, *Church Dogmatics*, IV/2, 405.

socio-existential analysis of the positional self between individual and group ethos. According to Niebuhr, the most critical difference between group and individual dynamics is that while the lower morality of the individual can be regarded as the consequence of the inertia of "nature" against the higher demands of the individual's reason (spirit), the lower morality of the group cannot be regarded as the consequence of the inertia of the group's nature (of the group's will) against the higher demands of the group's reason.[90] Niebuhr accepts the possibility that a group can have reason or mind as an organ of "self-transcendence and self-criticism," as in the case of an individual. The "prophetic minority" is the most prominent example of the group's reason or mind. This instrument of the group's self-transcendence, however, in Niebuhr's own interpretation, is not only unstable but also ephemeral and shifting compared to the group's will, which is a counterpart of an individual's nature. Unlike an individual, a group finds it almost impossible to transcend itself relying on the voice of a prophetic minority. Thus it is inevitable that the higher demands of reason cannot help groups transcend themselves. The higher demands of reason become muted when forced to confront the nature-like "will of group." Niebuhr thus writes, "For this reason the immorality of nations is frequently regarded as in effect their unmorality, as the consequence of their existence in the realm of 'nature' rather than the realm of reason."[91]

Niebuhr holds that there is a legitimate reason why it is impossible for groups to transcend themselves, particularly when their survival is at stake. In this sense, he sympathizes with political scientists who treat government "not as a conscious contrivance, . . . but as an half-instinctive product of the effort of human beings to ward off from themselves certain evils to which they are exposed."[92] Niebuhr's ingenuity, however, lies in another point. He discovers that the nature-like will of the group does not remain in its inchoate level because it later takes on the "spiritual" character by providing a spiritual meaning to those who belong to the group. A group's inchoate "will to survive" is later transformed into its "will to power" by enabling the egotism of the

90. Niebuhr, *Nature and Destiny of Man*, 1:210.

91. Ibid.

92. Ibid. This is the only section that Niebuhr quotes from his earlier political work *Moral Man and Immoral Society* (88) in his *Nature and Destiny of Man*, reaffirming his earlier conviction that the group cannot transcend itself, unlike individuals.

group to become the characteristic of the spiritual life. The place for the spiritual self-transcendence of the prophetic minority is then filled up by a pseudo-spiritual characteristic. Niebuhr writes,

> The most conducive proof that the egotism of nations is a characteristic of the spiritual life, and not merely an expression of the natural impulse of survival, is the fact that its most typical expressions are the lust-for-power; pride (comprising considerations of prestige and "honor"); contempt toward the other (the reverse side of pride and its necessary concomitant in a world in which self-esteem is constantly challenged by the achievements of others); hypocrisy (the inevitable pretension of conforming to a higher norm than self-interest); and finally the claim of moral autonomy by which the self-deification of the social group is made explicit by its presentation of itself as the source and end of existence.[93]

Now we have a better view of the positional self, especially its moral predicament in comparison to other ordinary individual selves. Unlike individuals, whose anxiety lies between the capacity of transcending oneself (freedom of spirit) and the finiteness of nature, the positional self finds a third category that characterizes its anxiety in a quite different way from that of individuals. The third category that influences the positional self's anxiety is the pseudospiritual characteristic of the group (the group's will to power), which realizes itself through the concentration of power and money. As the representative of groups, the positional self will be forced to comprehend that the spirit of the will to power of groups is such a pressing and dominant force that it can even obliterate its personal capacity to transcend itself. If such analysis is right, then the positional self cannot but be deeply involved with two different spiritual identities: the spirit of one's own self-transcendence through an individual freedom and the spirit of the group's will to power. Beleaguered between these two spiritual aspects, the positional self finds itself being increasingly expected to realize the spirit of the group's will to power (i.e., the spiritual manifestation of group egoism) that comes into being through the concentration of power and money. In my view, this is exactly what characterizes the ethical predicament of the positional self in the most essential way.

93. Ibid., 211.

The ethical predicaments of the positional self can be further described by answering the following question: How do the dual pathologies of sin (pride and sensuality) take on their distinctive features with regard to the conduct of the positional self? To put it simply, the sin of pride is realized in the positional self in the form of exploitation and abuse of power, whereas the sin of sensuality is materialized in the form of blind subordination to the spirit of the group's will to power. In the former case, the positional self realizes its inordinate love of itself through its positional power either explicitly in the name of group pride or surreptitiously through substituting its will for the spirit of the group's will to power. In contrast, in the latter case, the positional self becomes selfless by succumbing to a group's will to concentrate its power. For the positional self, thus, the sin of sensuality would mean the blind adherence to the spiritual egoism of the group. Niebuhr's *Moral Man and Immoral Society* shows us in a most persuasive way how the sin of sensuality would be an inevitable reality to most position holders. Self is then held as a hostage by the position itself when the positional self gives way to the sin of sensuality. It is my contention, though, that just as the reality of sin does not obliterate the reality of responsibility among individuals, the position-mediated sins (e.g., self-aggrandizement and blind subordination to a group egoism) do not exonerate the moral responsibilities from the positional self. We can affirm this important point in Niebuhr's well-known analysis of "equality of sin and inequality of guilt."

Equality of Sin and Inequality of Guilt

We have examined thus far that although Niebuhr does not directly theorize about the concept of the positional self and its moral predicament as such, his socio-ontological insights and theological anthropology help us conceptualize substantive understanding of the positional self and its ethical predicaments. Regarding the ethical predicaments of the positional self, Niebuhr particularly emphasizes that the universality of sin or original sin should not be interpreted as a pretext to equivocate on the question of responsibility neither for ordinary individuals nor for position holders. Thus, Niebuhr's understanding of sin in the sense of the "equality of sin" among all people as well as all groups entails the following question: "If every group is equally characterized by sin, what is the basis for any sort of social action for justice?"[94] Fully aware of this problem, Niebuhr develops another paradoxical formula, which he calls "equality of sin and inequality of guilt." Here Niebuhr claims that although human beings are all on a certain equal horizon in that they are all marked by sin, the moral and ethical differences between individuals cannot be eclipsed or ignored by this condition at all. He first defines guilt as a consequence of sin: "Guilt is distinguished from sin in that it represents the objective and historical consequences of sin, for which the sinner must be held responsible.... Guilt is the objective consequences of sin, the actual corruption of the plan of creation and providence in the historical world."[95]

According to Gilkey's interpretation, while sin refers to the vertical relation to God, guilt refers to the horizontal, social, and moral consequences of sin to fellow humankind in its injustice: "In other words, sin refers to the vertical relation to God, which in all of us has become characterized by a break in that relation which Niebuhr has defined as pride, lack of trust, and 'centering the world around the self.' Guilt, on the other hand, refers to the consequences of this break, namely the injustice we inflict on others."[96] The methodological benefit we can receive from this paradoxical formula is that even though sinners are we, the crucial distinction of guilt still enables us to have options to choose the least guilt with a view to the concepts of justice and responsibility.

Niebuhr's paradox regarding sin and guilt is especially conducive to our task of defining and analyzing the idea of the positional self and also its moral predicament, because it clearly implies the idea that while all are equally sinners, some would be guiltier than others. First we need to identify who the guiltier ones might be. According to Niebuhr, the prophetic notes in Scripture specifically exemplify them as those who are guilty of moral wrongdoing; for example, "the rich and the powerful,

---

94. Gilkey, *On Niebuhr*, 112. According to Gilkey, Niebuhr's discussion of sin—the equality of sin and the inequality of guilt—is the most "intriguing" and most frequently "misunderstood" paradox. Gilkey continues, "it also illustrates the strong influence of modernity (liberalism) on his reinterpretation of the Biblical viewpoint and of Christian tradition" (111). As for Niebuhr, it is the tendency of orthodox Protestantism to efface all moral distinctions of history in light of a religious conviction of the undifferentiated sinfulness of all. See Niebuhr, *Nature and Destiny of Man*, 1:221.

95. Niebuhr, *Nature and Destiny of Man*, 1:222.

96. Gilkey, *On Niebuhr*, 113.

the mighty and the noble, the wise and the righteous."[97] Niebuhr quotes Amos 4:1, which condemns those who "oppress the poor, which crush the needy." Niebuhr also emphasizes that moral discrimination between the rich and the poor, between the powerful and the weak, and between the proud and the meek is also maintained in the New Testament.[98] In other words, the guiltier ones can be defined as those who hold great social, economic, and political power who tend to be "more guilty of pride against God and of injustice against the weak and those who lack power and prestige."[99] In describing those holding power as the guiltier ones, Niebuhr goes further by saying that even the "men of intellectual, spiritual and moral eminence" ought to fall under "men of power."[100] Niebuhr perceives that an anti-aristocratic analysis of the Bible does indeed agree with the historical facts in that those holding great power have been historically more guilty and unjust both to God and to fellow human beings. He writes, "Gentiles are not naturally more sinful than Jews. But Gentiles, holding the dominant power in their several nations, sin against Semitic minority groups more than the latter sin against them. White men sin against Negroes in Africa and America more than Negroes sin against white men."[101]

Although we ought to be cautious in identifying the positional self with the guiltier groups in Scripture, Niebuhr's paradoxical formulation enables us to see that the positional self could be readily identified with the guiltier ones because power is concentrated on the position that they hold. Niebuhr, however, emphasizes that there is no difference between wealthy capitalists and poor laborers in terms of their natural depravity. The inherent sinfulness of human beings is universal, and in that regard, people are equal regardless of their social, economic, and political privileges and ranks. But, as he argues, people's actual and artificial sins and thus their results (guilt) must be brought into our consideration. Niebuhr is absolutely sure that "those who hold great economic and political power are more guilty of pride against God and of injustice

---

97. Niebuhr, *Nature and Destiny of Man*, 223.

98. Ibid., 224. The best example is found in Mary's Magnificat. St. Paul's judgment stands in the same prophetic line. Most important, we can discover that Jesus maintains moral discrimination in his sermons written in Luke.

99. Ibid., 225.

100. Ibid., 227.

101. Ibid., 225–26.

against the weak than those who lack power and prestige."¹⁰² Niebuhr's analysis of the equality of sin and inequality of guilt obviously portrays the positional self as the guiltier one in society. Once again, however, we need to be aware of the fact that the weak, the dominated, and the exploited are, by the same token, not necessarily at all less sinful, or potentially less sinful.

In my view, the concept of the positional self cannot be fully understood without an understanding of its own paradoxical elements. First of all, a positional self, in comparison with a nonpositional self, is distinguished by its own positional transcendence, which comes along with the position itself in such a way that the sociopolitical or socioeconomic result of its acts goes beyond the perimeter of an individual freedom. A position provides a position holder with a distinctive possibility (positional freedom) to transcend its individual sphere of freedom.¹⁰³ But it also provides the position holders with the burden of the "concentrating tendency" of power. Being a position holder, a positional self is expected to wield the power through its positional freedom. This freedom, however, is accompanied by the spirit of a group's will to power. Although transcendent, but now being confined to and beleaguered by the spirit of the group's will to power, the positional self encounters a unique problem. Paradoxically, a positional self's unique transcending capacity (positional freedom) becomes its own shackle that binds its own freedom.

This ironic circumstance of the positional self, in my view, gives rise to both epistemological and ethical conundrums. From an epistemological perspective, on the one hand, the positional self is facing an issue whether it regards the paradox (the possibility of self-transcendence and the reality of hostage-ship) as a possibility of freedom or as a destiny of a position holder. From an ethical perspective, on the other

102. Ibid., 225.

103. "Positional freedom" is similar to Niebuhr's idea of "social and political freedoms." In Niebuhr's account, social and political freedoms are necessarily allowed to position holders ultimately for the sake of their social and political community. He writes, "The community must give the person a social freedom which corresponds to the essential freedom of his nature, and which enables him to express hopes and ambitions and to engage in interests and vitalities which are not immediately relevant to the collective purposes of the community, but which in the long run enrich the culture and leaven the lump of the community's collective will and purpose" (Niebuhr, *Faith and Politics*, 81).

hand, the positional self faces a conundrum of responsibility: What kind of responsibility (individual or group) should the positional self take up as an executive of the group? Should a positional self be held responsible for the sin of the group, that is, the systemic incarnation of the spirit of group egoism? Or should it be held responsible only for itself? Along with these questions, it now becomes important to answer the following question: How do we make it possible for the positional self to transcend the group egoism of the concentration of power (a major source of social injustice)?

Conclusion

As a result of the above discussion, we come to have a substantive view on the moral-ethical predicament that the positional self faces as a position holder. Indeed, economic and political systems cannot be established without social positions, in that positions are an indispensable structure of the establishment and development of the system. Positions, however, provide important opportunities for the members of society to realize their own individual freedom, talents, beliefs, virtues, dreams, and even higher callings. Particularly in today's highly and increasingly sophisticated society, any discussion about the moral virtue of "self-realization" would be certainly meaningless and pointless if we fail to take the social position into our consideration. Holding a position is indeed important to many people because it is intrinsically related to their own self-understanding of who they are in a systemic world. Thus the conundrum that the positional self finds in the social system is that in the course of realizing itself, the positional self is inevitably guilty either of pride by misconstruing itself as an exploiter, or of sensuality by relegating itself to a slave. Niebuhr writes, "The same man who can become his true self only by striving infinitely for self realization beyond himself [through position] is also inevitably involved in the sin of infinitely making his partial and narrow self the true end of existence."[104]

We need to understand that the moral predicament for the positional self appears in the dual forms that correspond to Niebuhr's dual identifications of sin: pride and sensuality. While, for the positional self, the sin of pride as an inordinate love of oneself is disclosed in the form

104. Niebuhr, *Christianity and Power Politics*, 2.

of exploiting others or other groups, the sin of sensuality as self-abnegation or self-abeyance is realized in the form of blind submission to the spiritual egoism of groups. For the positional self, sensuality would mean the loss of its true selfhood at the expense of a group interest, whereas pride would mean the aggrandizement of its fake selfhood for the sake of domination and control. In sum, using Niebuhr's famous axiom, we can finally identify two dimensions of the moral predicament of the positional self as follows: the *Scylla* of misconstruing oneself as an exploiter and the *Charybdis* of relegating oneself to a slave. In the following chapter, we will discuss Niebuhrian moral vision in situating the positional self as a moral self in organizational and corporate settings.

5

Niebuhr's Theological Reconstruction and the Positional Self

Introduction

IN THE PREVIOUS CHAPTER, WE REVIEWED THE ETHICAL PREDICAMENT of the positional self, the *Scylla* of corrupting oneself as an "exploiter" and the *Charybdis* of relegating oneself to a "slave," through Niebuhr's analysis of human nature and sin. We have also observed that power and money, especially their concentrating tendency, play an important role in disfiguring the ethical identity of the positional self. While the sin of pride evolves into an exploitative form, the sin of sensuality devolves into a slave figure in the positional self. In contrast to the previous chapter, however, we now turn our attention to a different sphere in Niebuhr through which we can uncover something positive about the moral prospectus of the positional self. In doing so, I portray Niebuhr as a theological reconstructionist by focusing on his reconstructive elements most conspicuously represented by his *justitia originalis*, *agape*, and justice. Of course, this does not mean that I challenge the popular image of Reinhold Niebuhr as a prominent Christian realist. Indeed, he was a Christian realist, but the point I flesh out here is that his Christian realism is significantly affected and molded by a theological reconstructionism. So what is "theological reconstructionism"? In short, with regard to ethics, theological reconstructionism is a critical-reflective method to ground a universal norm in ethics and morality through a reconstructive reading of Scripture and theological doctrines. In Niebuhr's case, mainly by focusing on theological anthropology and Christology, he found his theological reconstructionism in ethics through his critical-reflective reinterpretation of classical theological ideas such as original sin, original righteousness, and the crucified Christ in classical doctrines of Christian churches and Scripture.

Niebuhr's Theological Reconstructionism

With regard to Niebuhr's theological reconstructionism, first of all, we ought not to overlook the important point that there is not only a theological reason but also a historical background behind his reconstructionism. What historical situation, then, led young Niebuhr to become a theological reconstructionist? In my understanding, just as young Habermas was motivated to save Western civilization and culture from the despair of the "iron cage" in the aftermath of modernization and rationalization, young Niebuhr was motivated to save humanity and society from the illusory, cynical, and annihilative forces of idealism, naturalism, and romanticism that dominated his era. In a little-known essay titled "Tyrant Servants," the young Niebuhr of 1926 sincerely expresses his reconstructive vision.

> If the factory robs men of personal values it must be changed until it builds character and creates happiness. If the city imperils virtue it may have to be destroyed, providing it cannot be reformed. If the nation outrages the diviner qualities of human life and sacrifices eternal values for petty ends, it must be reformed until it becomes a true servant of human personality... Let us look through the eyes of Jesus with His cool discernment upon all our social customs and traditions, upon all our economic practices and industrial methods, upon our great communities of race and class and ask: Are these man's servants or his oppressors?[1]

In developing his theological reconstructionism, Niebuhr regards that modern non-Christian anthropologies are most problematic in that they have distorted the two elements in human nature: the self's natural limitations and the self's spiritual freedom. By "distortion," he means the sacrifice of one at the expense of the other. Niebuhr perceives that idealism (derived from Kant and Hegel) is problematic since it overemphasizes the rational freedom of a human being

---

1. This essay appeared in Ralph Milton Pierce, ed., *Preachers and Preaching in Detroit* (New York: Revell, 1926). This was Niebuhr's first article printed in a book. See Chrystal, *Young Reinhold Niebuhr*, 172–73.

to the extent of identifying human reason with the absolute. Idealism narrowly identifies human consciousness and spirit with reason and eventually identifies reason with some kind of absolute or divinity. Naturalism (as expressed in Francis Bacon and Montaigne), however, is also one-sided in that it reduces the human ego to a stream of consciousness in which personal identity is at a minimum.[2] As Niebuhr criticizes them, both idealism and naturalism ultimately annihilate spirit in such a way that, while naturalism does not comprehend the self-transcendent human spirit, idealism loses spirit as the pattern of rationality substitutes its place.

The most serious problem that Niebuhr finds in both idealism and naturalism is that spirit is largely ignored and annihilated through either deification or abasement. According to Niebuhr, romantic naturalism (as originated in Sigmund Freud and Karl Marx) is distinguished from idealism and naturalism in that it disapproves not only the claim of idealism that freedom and rationality are synonymous but also with the claim of naturalism that a human being is nothing but a mechanical nature. From Niebuhr's perspective, romanticism also errs in several aspects. Most important, it errs in its interpretation of human vitality when it attributes to the biological what obviously belongs to the creativity of the spirit.[3] While Freudianism errs in misinterpreting human complex spiritual phenomena in terms of biological sexual impulses, Marxism makes the same mistake by ascribing vitality to the desires of the social classes. As with the cases of idealism and naturalism, romanticism fails to penetrate to the paradox of the human spirit.[4] In sum, by critically analyzing the core deficiencies of idealism, naturalism, and romanticism, Niebuhr tries to meet and overcome the various spiritual, cultural, and political challenges of the modern world, such as liberalism, capitalism, Nazism, and modern nationalism. What Niebuhr discovers in his debate with idealism, naturalism, and romanticism is the loss of authentic and truthful understanding of individuality, and this is the fundamental problem for various kinds of the cultural, social, and political issues.[5]

2. Niebuhr, *Nature and Destiny of Man*, 1:75.
3. Ibid., 40.
4. Ibid., 53.
5. Niebuhr's analysis shows that in idealism the individual is only to be absorbed in the universalities of the impersonal mind, whereas in naturalism individuality is

Based on this criticism, Niebuhr maintains that we can find in Christianity a vantage point that offers a rightful balance of both freedom and natural vitality. This is how Niebuhr's theological reconstructionism begins with theological anthropology. Niebuhr recognizes that Christianity answers an anthropological question with its doctrines of a human being as made in the image of God and as creature. These two aspects constitute the core individuality of a human being as universal elements. Because of this mixture, human beings are fundamentally paradoxical. The image of God is the aspect of human nature that enables people to transcend the world of finitude, allowing them to see the world from the perspective of eternity. Through the capacity of transcendence, a human being can transcend both natural finitude and oneself. So the image of God is deeply related to the freedom side of human individuality. The creature side is also an essential element that constitutes human nature, which is not only transcending but also determined and limited. Niebuhr explains this uneasy combination of the spiritual side of the image of God and the creature side by drawing on the psychological concept of anxiety. The concept becomes important in developing his theological reconstructionism because anxiety is deeply related not only to the doctrine of original sin but also to the idea of freedom. We should notice here that Niebuhr's psychological analysis of anxiety is deeply influenced by Søren Kierkegaard.

Kierkegaard first lays out the psychological structure of the human self as a dialectical kind that Niebuhr adopts. In a similar pattern, although using different terms, Kierkegaard describes the existential-psychological structure of the human self as follows: "The self is composed of infinity and finiteness. But the synthesis is a relationship, and it is a relationship which, though it is derived, relates itself to itself, which means freedom. The self is freedom. But freedom is the dialectical element in the terms of possibility and necessity."[6] In conjunction with this existential-psychological structure of the human self, Kierkegaard

---

quickly lost since nature knows nothing of self-transcendence. In romantic naturalism, too, a person's individuality is quickly subordinated to the unique and self-justifying individuality of the social collective, with the exception of Nietzschean romanticism. Niebuhr, however, finds nothing hopeful in Nietzschean romanticism, in that Nietzsche "knows no law but his own will-to-power and has no God but his own unlimited ambition" (Niebuhr, *Nature and Destiny of Man*, 1:92).

6. Kierkegaard, *Sickness unto Death*, 162.

also renews the doctrine of original sin by giving it a psychological explanation. Niebuhr adopts this account too. Since we have reviewed the psychological explication of original sin in the previous chapter, we now focus on the creative elements of Niebuhr's explanation of human anxiety, especially with regard to the creative aspect of human anxiety. By exploring the reconstructive moral meaning of the creative aspect of anxiety, we further develop what Niebuhr's theological reconstructionism has to do with the positional self.

As Niebuhr describes it, human anxiety originates in a condition that encompasses both limits and higher possibilities in a human being. Indeed, no one knows the limits of one's own possibilities as well as one knows one's own limitations. Niebuhr points out that in anxiety, human beings readily commit sin through their own freedom, ignoring the possibility to transcend their own limitations. Niebuhr, however, is clear that anxiety is a precondition of sin, not its direct cause. It is no less important as well that anxiety is at the same time the precondition of human creativity. In the phenomenon of anxiety, Niebuhr perceives both "destructive" and "constructive" elements. Niebuhr emphasizes continuously that anxiety is not sin in itself. He writes, "It [anxiety] must be distinguished from sin partly because it is its precondition and not its actuality, and partly because it is the basis of all human creativity as well as the precondition of sin."[7] Niebuhr goes on by saying, "Man is anxious not only because his life is limited and dependent and yet not so limited that he does not know of his limitations."[8]

According to Niebuhr, it is ultimately up to our choice and thus our responsibility whether we choose to commit sin or choose creativity in meeting the challenges of our life. If Niebuhr's analysis and argument are justified, then we can certainly discuss the creative moral possibility of the positional self going beyond the established moral limitations of the positional self: the positional self either as an exploiter or as a slave. In my view, compared to that of ordinary individual citizens, the most formidable limitation for the creative behavior of the positional self is the nature of the group, which always tries to promote its group egoism through the concentration of power and money. In this respect, we can say that the positional self has different kinds or levels of anxiety.

---

7. Niebuhr, *Nature and Destiny of Man*, 1:183.
8. Ibid.

This, however, should not be translated in such a way that there is no transcending possibility in the actions and choices of the positional self. With regard to the anxiety of the positional self, we need to consider two aspects. First, unlike the existential anxiety of ordinary individuals that is composed of the image of God and nature, the anxiety of the positional self is constituted by two elements: the image of God and the image of the group. Second, by "group," we mean it only as the constitutional kind, which is organized and established by the shared will of the people. I have already defined the character of the group in the previous chapter, where I deconstruct Niebuhr's rather vague concept of the group.

Let me explain what these two conditions would mean. First, as we have seen, in the case of existential anxiety, individuals commit sin through their own freedom, ignoring the possibility to transcend their own limitations: the limitations set by nature. In the case of the anxiety of the positional self, the only difference from existential anxiety lies in the kind of limitations. For the positional self, the limitations are not the limitations set by nature, but instead, they are the limitations set by the image of the group. Between two moral dynamics (the image of God and the image of the group), the positional self is likely to commit sin by ignoring the possibility to transcend the limitations set by the group. Second, as we have also seen, in the case of existential anxiety, it is not necessary for individuals to ignore the possibility to transcend their limitations. Likewise, in the case of the anxiety of the positional self, it is not necessary for the positional self to ignore its transcending possibility, because the group is constituted in such a way as to guarantee its position holders the right to express and utilize their freedom within the limits of the law. We see here an interesting dialectical tension or paradox between the positional self and the group. On the one hand, the group expects the positional self to stick to the interests of its own group image; on the other hand, the group permits the positional self to express its creative freedom. Just as in the case of ordinary individuals' existential anxiety, the anxiety of the positional self becomes the source of creativity as well as the temptation to sin.[9]

Until now we have reviewed the anthropological aspect of Niebuhr's theological reconstructionism, and as a result of this study,

---

9. Ibid., 185.

we come to understand that for Niebuhr, the dimension of freedom is the most significant element in human nature. Indeed, it is the essence of a human being in the image of God. In this sense, Niebuhr's theological reconstructionism is deeply related to the restoration of the original image of God, and Niebuhr envisions it by reconstructing the doctrine of original righteousness: *justitia originalis*. Before we discuss his theological reconstruction of *justitia originalis* and its reconstructive meaning for restoring the original image of God in human beings, we need to pay attention to his Christology because he identifies Christ as the "perfect norm of human nature."[10]

For Niebuhr, reconstructing Christology is as important as reconstructing theological anthropology in developing his theological reconstructionism, and, of course, there is a historical background behind this. In his 1939 article "Ten Years That Shook My World," Niebuhr explains how he came to have a theological interest in Christology.[11] We can conjecture from this article that he was considering liberal Christianity of the nineteenth century and its continuous influence in the United States when he felt the need for a reconfigured Christology. He acknowledged some contributions that liberal Christianity made to "true Christianity," particularly with regard to its contributions in bridging religion and civilization, faith and intelligence, and mythology and science. Niebuhr was critical, however, of liberal Christianity especially its "pathetic" effort to justify itself before the "modern mind." He states clearly: "But liberal Christianity quite obviously accepted the prejudices as well as the achievements of modern culture. It was pathetically eager to justify itself before the 'modern mind' and failed to realize that this modern mind was involved in a very ancient human sin."[12]

Niebuhr's discontent with liberal Christianity, however, was focused on its mistaken Christology. He criticizes liberal Christianity by claiming that for the sake of persuading the modern mind, liberals sacrificed most of the essential Christian positions, including Christology. He deplores the phenomenon that Christ was transmuted into the good man Jesus, who could challenge all to become as good as he was.[13]

10. Niebuhr, "The Problem of the Love Ethics in Politics," in David and Good, *Reinhold Niebuhr on Politics*, 131.

11. This article was published in the *Christian Century*.

12. Ibid., 544.

13. Ibid.

It would not be too much to say that Niebuhr's theological reconstructionism was his heartfelt response to the radical destruction of classical Christology by liberalism in theology. Niebuhr believed that although it sounds "absurd," the doctrine of the God-man Christ contains the whole essence of the Christian faith. How, then, does he characterize the essence of the Christian faith? For Niebuhr, the essence of Christian faith lies in its belief: "belief that God transcends history and makes himself known in history; that history measured by Christ is tragic and ends tragically for it crucified Christ; that only God is able to resolve the conflict between what man is and what he ought to be."[14]

With regard to Niebuhr's theological reconstructionism, we especially need to attend to his statement that Christ is the true nature of the self and the perfect norm of human nature. He acknowledges that Christ appears in many guises to the believer, such as in the form of the judge and the redeemer. Niebuhr emphasizes, however, that Christ is also "the law, the logos, the essential structure of life, which I must seek to obey, even though I fall short in my obedience. He is what I am essentially, and therefore what I ought to be."[15] In other words, for Niebuhr, at the core of Christian theology and human morality lies Christ. In his sermonic essay entitled "As Deceivers, Yet True," Niebuhr epitomizes his Christology as follows: "In Christian thought Christ is both the perfect man, 'the second Adam' who had restored the perfection of what man was and ought to be; and the Son of God, who transcends all possibilities of human life.... The only adequate norm of human conduct is love of God and man, through which all men are perfectly related to each other, because they are all related in terms of perfect obedience and love to the center and source of their existence."[16] It is important to understand that Niebuhr makes great effort to uncover the ethical meaning of Christology through his theological reconstructionism. Niebuhr's theological reconstructionism, thus, culminates in ethics rather than in doctrinal theology as such. Niebuhr is very explicit about this because he is adamant about his belief that Christ is the perfect norm of human nature, and the perfect norm is expressed in the form of sacrificial love. Niebuhr writes, "The Christian faith affirms, further, that the same

---

14. Ibid.
15. Ibid., 545.
16. Niebuhr, *Beyond Tragedy*, 16.

Christ who discloses the sovereignty of God over history is also the perfect norm of human nature. This perfection is not so much a sum total of various virtues or an absence of transgression of various laws; it is the perfection of sacrificial love."[17] By showing that sacrificial love is the perfect norm of human nature, Niebuhr also renders all moral standards devised by humankind short of perfect and infinite love.

Now with regard to Niebuhr's theological reconstructionism that culminates in his ethics of sacrificial love, some might argue against him by saying that since his reconstructionism is specifically a Christian kind, it is absurd for him to argue that all moral standards turn out to be deficient before the Christian perfect norm of sacrificial love. This is a legitimate concern, and I believe that Niebuhr was fully aware of this aspect. How would he, then, respond to this problem? It is my contention that Niebuhr tries to resolve this difficulty through the concept of *justitia originalis*. In other words, what Niebuhr was trying to do is to universalize the perfect norm of sacrificial love, revealed in Christ, by converting it into the perfect norm of human nature through the concept of *justitia originalis*. Christ is hidden in *justitia originalis*; *justitia originalis* is realized in Christ. Thus the sacrificial love revealed in Christ is the perfect fulfillment of the universal moral norm that is already universally contained in human nature.

From an ethical point of view, it is Niebuhr's genius to connect Christology with *justitia originalis*. In this respect, Niebuhr incorporates the Pauline characterization of Christ as the "second Adam." When Niebuhr affirms that Christ is the "second Adam," this means that Christ "clarifies and redefines" the law of their being, which is the law of love.[18] In other words, Niebuhr regards it possible to universalize the Christian moral norm of sacrificial love without specifically referring to the name of Christ. For Niebuhr, Christ can be both a universal norm and its specific realization. For believers, Christ is a specific realization of *justitia originalis*; yet for nonbelievers, Christ is a universal norm of human nature. In this sense, Niebuhr may be regarded as truly a public theologian. In the following pages, we will deal more extensively with Niebuhr's reconstructed vision of *justitia originalis* and its ethical im-

17. Niebuhr, "Problem of the Love Ethics in Politics," 131. The quotation can be found also in Niebuhr, *Nature and Destiny of Man*, 2:68.

18. See Niebuhr's 1940 article "Christian Faith and Natural Law." This important article can be found in Niebuhr, *Love and Justice*, 53.

plication for the establishment of the moral norm for the positional self. For this, first of all, we begin by examining Niebuhr's critical appropriation of the Catholic natural law tradition, which separates the realm of natural law from that of the supernatural grace. What Niebuhr tries to do through his critical appropriation of Catholic natural law is to reconstruct *justitia originalis* as a universal moral law by dialectically bridging the realms of nature and supernatural grace.

Natural Law and *Justitia Originalis*

In the above discussion, we have examined the general background of Niebuhr's theological reconstructionism, and from here we focus on the ethical aspect of his theological reconstructionism through which we will explore the possibility of establishing the positional self as a moral self. The ethical aspect of Niebuhr's theological reconstructionism is best elucidated by his reconstructive study on *justitia originalis* (original righteousness). In a nutshell, Niebuhr's ethical reconstructionism is distilled through his theological response to this apparent conundrum: How do we integrate the seeming discrepancy between the pure ethical norm and fallen nature in reconstructing our moral identity? Broadly speaking, Niebuhr tries to solve this conundrum through his dialectical method, and he begins by critically appropriating the Catholic version in answering the conundrum. From Niebuhr's perspective, Catholic rationalism tries to resolve the question by clearly separating nature and *justitia originalis*. According to Niebuhr, however, since Catholic rationalism makes too complete a distinction between natural law and *justitia originalis*, it subsequently differentiates too completely between a relative and an absolute natural law.[19] Whereas by "relative natural law," Niebuhr means the general concept of natural law, by "absolute natural law," he means original righteousness (*justitia originalis*), which is lost in the fall but later substituted by theological virtues. Against this clear-cut model of Catholic rationalism, Niebuhr posits as follows.

> The real situation is that "original justice" in the sense of a mythical "perfection before the Fall" is never completely lost. It is not a reality in man but always a potentiality. It is always what he ought to be. It is the only goodness completely compatible with his own and his fellow man's freedom—that is, with their

19. Niebuhr, *Nature and Destiny of Man*, 1:297.

> ultimate transcendence over all circumstances of nature. Man is neither as completely bereft of "original justice" nor as completely in possession of "natural justice" as the Catholic theory assumes.[20]

In Niebuhr's analysis, if Catholic rationalism is right, then there can be ultimately no connection between the law of justice and the law of love. Niebuhr does not deny a distinction between the two, but he perceives that a complete distinction makes it impossible "to define the limits of the force of sin or of the ideal possibilities which transcend sin."[21] We first need to define what this means by dealing with Niebuhr's view of natural law and his account of theological virtues and *justitia originalis*. For this, we need to begin with his theological understanding of the fall and its subsequent relevance to natural law.

According to Niebuhr, the idea of the fall has long been a difficult problem to Christian churches throughout their history, and the most significant reason for this lies in the church's attempt to view the matter as a historical and chronological event. From Niebuhr's point of view, although Western Christian churches have roughly developed two perspectives in dealing with this issue: Catholic and Protestant views, they all tumble into confusion in understanding the relation of the human being's essential nature to his or her sinful condition. For Niebuhr, this confusion is actually the consequence of the chronological and thus the literalistic understanding of the fall. Niebuhr states:

> In Protestant thought it aggravated the tendency toward extravagant statements of man's depravity and confused the effort to moderate such statements by the admission that some little power of justice remained to man.... In Catholic thought, chronological literalism encouraged the definition of the state of original righteousness [*justitia originalis*] as a special supernatural gift, a DONUM SUPERNATURALE which was added to the PURA NATURALLA, that is to the essential humanity which Adam had as man.[22]

As a result of this understanding of the fall, the consequence of sin ("the corruption of man's true essence, but not its destruction") becomes

---

20. Niebuhr, "Christian Faith and Natural Law," in *Love and Justice*, 50.
21. Ibid.
22. Niebuhr, *Nature and Destiny of Man*, 1:268-69.

obscured in both Catholic and Protestant thought: "In Catholicism the Fall means the loss of something which is not essential to man and does not therefore represent a corruption of his essence. In radical Protestantism the very image of God in man is believed to be destroyed."[23] In Niebuhr's account, then, the chronological version of the perfection before the Fall is problematic because it fails to provide us with an undistorted and unbiased view of the relation between "man's essential nature" and "his sinful state." Instead of a chronological and literalistic approach, through his own symbolic approach, Niebuhr now tries to show an alternative view that although sin is a corruption of the human being's true essence, it is not destruction. In fact, "the human sin cannot destroy the essential character of man to such a degree that it would cease being implied in, and furnishing a contrast to, what he had become."[24] By "a contrast," he means the law of love, which is also the "requirement of freedom." We will shortly deal with this more extensively.

In light of his symbolic interpretation of the fall, Niebuhr particularly finds it problematic for Catholicism to signify through its natural law an aspect of the eternal or divine law manifested in human reason. Niebuhr points out that at the center of the natural law tradition lies an important belief that human reason is in basic harmony with, and thus can mirror, the universal law of nature. Niebuhr recognizes correctly that because of natural law, the Catholic Church has established a meeting ground with non-Catholics or non-Christians, compared to the Protestant church, which generally separates the world into two kingdoms: the heavenly kingdom and the earthly kingdom. Niebuhr, however, claims that natural law can turn out to be a rigid legalism that

23. Ibid., 269. Niebuhr is aware that there is some ambivalence in Protestant thought regarding the total depravity of the human being. He notices that the most extreme statement of the doctrine of total depravity can be found in the Lutheran Formulary of Concord, which reads: "They are also likewise repudiated and rejected who teach that our nature has indeed been greatly weakened but nevertheless has not altogether lost all goodness relating to divine and spiritual things." Indeed, differing from this extravagant statement of the depravity of the human being, as Niebuhr observes, there have been other views in Protestantism, which hold that "some little power of justice remained to man." Thus, the remnant of original perfection, which was conceded to the first human being was later falsely identified with the capacity for "civil justice." According to Niebuhr, the best example of this can be found in Augsburg Confession, Article 18. See Niebuhr, *Nature and Destiny of Man*, 1:268.

24. Ibid., 267.

can ironically create a tension between Catholics and non-Catholics.[25] Niebuhr's critical response to classical, medieval, or modern natural law theories is twofold. First, natural law theories are biased in their understanding of history; second, love is regarded as an addendum to natural law. Niebuhr epitomizes his criticism as follows:

> The one point is that these concepts [natural law theories] do not allow for the historical character of human experience. They are rooted in a classical rationalism which did not understand history. They therefore do not understand the uniqueness of historical occasion or the historical biases which creep into the definitions of natural law. This criticism is not met by calling attention to the distinction between the jus natura, the jus gentium, and the jus civilis. Of course, every natural law theory allows for the application of general principles to particular situations. But the question is whether its general principles are not too inflexible on the one hand, their definition too historically conditioned on the other hand.... The other point of my criticism of natural law concepts is the tendency to make the law of love an addendum to the natural law, so that the one defines the determinate possibilities and the other the indeterminate possibilities of good. My point is that it is not possible to draw a neat line between determinate and indeterminate possibilities. Justice is an application of the law of love. The rules are not absolute but relative. They are applications of the law of love and do not have independence apart from it.[26]

Niebuhr's critique of natural law needs to be understood in light of his distinctive understanding of history. Referring to the first criticism, Niebuhr holds that history shows us an important aspect that such concept as "essential" social structure does not exist. Niebuhr states emphatically that there are "always historically contingent elements in the situation which natural law theories tend falsely to incorporate into the general norm, and there are new emergents in the human situation which natural law theories tend to discount because their conception of an immutable human nature can not make room for them."[27] Niebuhr

25. See Niebuhr, "A Protestant Looks at Catholics" in *Catholicism in America*, 30–31.

26. Kegley and Bretall, *Reinhold Niebuhr*, 435.

27. Niebuhr, *Faith and History*, 180–81. For example, in his article "Christian Faith and Natural Law," Niebuhr argues that bourgeois idealists of the eighteenth century developed their version of natural law theories justifying the bourgeois classes in a

thus focuses his criticism on both the relativities of history and the indeterminate character of the self in its freedom. He writes, "The whole concept of natural law rests upon a Stoic-Aristotelian rationalism which assumes fixed historical structures and norms which do not in fact exist. Furthermore, it assumes a human participation in a universal reason in which there is no ideological taint."[28]

In Niebuhr's account, Catholic tradition on natural law is problematic in identifying the immutability of human nature with the rational capacity of the human being. As is well known, Catholic rationalism holds that human reason is not only unimpaired by the fall but also participates in the eternal law whose knowledge it possess to some degree.[29] What is lost, according to Thomistic doctrine, is a capacity for faith, hope, and love, but not rational capacity or natural justice. For this reason, Niebuhr maintains that there is an essential relation between Catholic theory of natural law and human reason. Niebuhr argues that Catholic theory of natural law is derived from human reason through both intuitive and inductive (analytical) ways.

> Sometimes it would seem that the natural law consists of moral judgments which reason knows *intuitively*, or as *"self-evident" deductions* from the primary proposition that "good" is to be done and promoted and evil is to be avoided. Usually the "self-evidence" of more detailed requirements of the natural law consists in their derivation in a "necessary," that is logical, manner from the primary proposition that good is to be done and evil avoided ... reason, according to the theory, sometimes seems to arrive at the truths of the moral law *inductively* and *analytically*, rather than deductively. It seeks to discern the permanent structure of human existence ... In this sense the law is "natural" not so much because it embodies the self-evident truths of practical reason as because reason discerns analytically the permanent structure of human nature.[30]

According to Daniel F. Rice, as Niebuhr holds, we can find a certain irony in the second way in which Catholic natural law theory derives

---

way similar to that of the older natural law in the Middle Ages that justified the feudal aristocrats justifying their ideals. See Niebuhr, *Love and Justice*, 48-49.

28. Niebuhr, *Christian Realism and Political Problems*, 172.
29. Niebuhr, *Man's Nature and His Communities*, 49.
30. Niebuhr, *Faith and History*, 180 (italics original).

specific laws from reason. Insofar as reason arrives at a certain structure of nature, including human nature based on its analytic way, Catholic theory exhibits "the very methods of the Enlightenment's theory of natural law which it ostensibly abhors."[31]

Niebuhr is critical of the Catholic understanding of reason. Differing from Catholicism, Niebuhr argues that the most important feature of reason lies in its equivocal characteristic since it can serve both the self as transcending itself and the anxious self in action. Niebuhr captures succinctly the equivocality of human reason in his following remarks: "[Reason] can be alternately the instrument by which the self-as-subject condemns the partial and prejudiced actions of the sinful self, and the vehicle of the sinful self by which it seeks to give the sanctity of a false universality to its particular needs and partial insights."[32] From Niebuhr's perspective, classical Catholicism has too much undue confidence in human reason believing in the ability of an unspoiled reason. Relying on this concept of unspoiled reason, Catholicism ultimately arrives at definitive standards of natural justice by having recourse to the concept of unspoiled reason: "The confidence of medieval Catholicism in the ability of an unspoiled reason to arrive at definitive standards of natural justice thus became the very vehicle of the sinful pretensions of the age."[33] Niebuhr criticizes Catholicism by saying that Catholic confidence in unspoiled reason only reveals its unexamined embodiment of the contemporary social consciousness. Niebuhr writes, "The social ethics of Thomas Aquinas embody the peculiarities and the contingent factors of a feudal agrarian economy into a system of fixed socio-ethical principles."[34] From Niebuhr's point of view, since it is not possible "to exempt 'reason' or any other human faculty from the disease of sin," there can be no uncorrupted natural law.[35] Catholic undue confidence in human reason fails to show the full scale

---

31. Rice, "Spirit of the Law in the Thought of Reinhold Niebuhr," 259.

32. Niebuhr, *Nature and Destiny of Man*, 1:284–85.

33. Ibid., 281.

34. Ibid. According to Niebuhr, "the same indictment holds for Enlightenment theories of natural law, in which natural rights or inalienable rights proved to be as influenced by bourgeois interests as the old system was by feudal interests" (Niebuhr, *Man's Nature and His Communities*, 50).

35. Niebuhr, *Nature and Destiny of Man*, 1:277.

of human reason because, as Niebuhr holds, reason can serve both the self as transcending itself and the anxious self in action.

There is, Niebuhr tells us, a historical factor behind Catholicism's confusion regarding its theory of natural law and its misplaced confidence in the ability of an unspoiled reason. The main culprit for this confusion is the early influence of Stoicism, particularly its concepts of man and nature. Niebuhr argues, "Stoicism confuses the relationship between reason and nature through its inability to understand the character of the self in its freedom. Classical rationalism generally erred in identifying 'reason' and 'freedom,' thereby assuming that whatever freedom man has over nature is contained within 'rational' boundaries."[36] It is thus Niebuhr's critique against the classical rationalists that they "do not understand that man's rational capacity involves a further ability to stand outside himself, a capacity for self-transcendence, the ability to make himself his own object, a quality of spirit which is usually not fully comprehended or connoted in 'ratio' or 'nous' or any of the concepts which philosophers usually use to describe the uniqueness of man."[37] It is important to understand that although man transcends his own reason with his freedom, since the sin of man is effective in man's reason, there is therefore no uncorrupted natural law drawn from reason. While human freedom renders the fixed structures of human nature assumed by natural law theories contradicted to itself, human sinfulness makes the supposedly absolute standards of human reason the sinful pretensions of the age. This is why natural law cannot be understood as something like an uncorrupted universal law of all generations and ages.

According to Niebuhr, the critique of the Catholic natural law tradition must incorporate its view on *justitia originalis*: the self's "original righteousness" or "original perfection." As we have seen above, Catholic thought claims that human beings lost their original righteousness in the fall, but not their essential humanity. Niebuhr is critical of this view because he perceives that *justitia originalis* is not totally separated from natural law, as Catholic thought portrays. According to Niebuhr, Catholic thought is right in its layout that the self is distinguished between "man-as-creature" and "man-as-spirit," but it is erroneous to

---

36. Rice, "Spirit of the Law in the Thought of Reinhold Niebuhr," 263.
37. Niebuhr, *Nature and Destiny of Man*, 1:4.

separate them in such a radical way that results in the total separation of natural law and the virtues of faith, hope, and love that correspond to the self in the freedom of its spirit. In critiquing Catholic natural law, Niebuhr actually denies its two main claims: the doctrine of human capacity for natural justice and the interpretation of love as a *donum superadditum* (a superadded gift).[38]

Niebuhr's critique leads him to develop his own understanding of *justitia originalis* in the sense of the law of love as the "requirement of human freedom." From his Christian realist perspective, Niebuhr not only rejects the doctrine of rational capacity for natural justice but also tries to transform the "theological virtues" of Catholic tradition from their position as "supernatural additions" to something as fundamental aspects of the self. In order to bring about that change, Niebuhr finds it is necessary "to eliminate the unwarranted distinction between a completely lost original justice and an uncorrupted natural justice,"[39] which occupies the essence of natural law theory in Catholic tradition. According to Niebuhr's analysis, what is called *justitia originalis* in Catholic thought is in fact the love that is the requirement of human freedom. For Niebuhr, thus, *justitia originalis* should not be understood as either the theological virtues of Catholic thought or the human standard of natural justice constructed by human reason. He writes, "These ultimate requirements of the Christian ethic are therefore not counsels of perfection or theological virtues of the sort which merely completes an otherwise incomplete natural goodness or virtue. Nor can they be subtracted from man without making his freedom a source of sinful infection."[40]

Ultimately, with his new understanding of *justitia originalis*, Niebuhr tries to overcome the Catholic dualism between natural law and theological virtues. He writes:

> We have suggested that what is usually known as "natural law" in both Christian and Stoic thought is roughly synonymous with the requirements of man as creature and that the virtues, defined in Catholic thought as "theological virtues," that is the

---

38. Niebuhr epitomizes a Thomistic view on natural law: "The Fall robbed man of a donum superadditum but left him with a pura naturalia, which includes a capacity for natural justice" (Niebuhr, "Christian Faith and Natural Law," in *Love and Justice*, 47).

39. Niebuhr, *Nature and Destiny of Man*, 1:276.

40. Ibid., 1:272.

> virtues faith, hope and love, are the requirements of his freedom and represent the justitia originalis. This righteousness, we have suggested, is not completely lost in the Fall but remains with sinful man as the knowledge of what he ought to be, as the law of his freedom.[41]

Niebuhr makes it clear that since *justitia originalis* remains in us as the knowledge of what we ought to do, it becomes possible to connect social justice to the vision of love. According to Rice, by postulating that love is the requirement of the self-as-freedom, and justice is the requirement of the self-as-creature, Niebuhr conveys that "love as the basis of the self in its freedom is the ultimate ground of all justice in historical life."[42] This, however, should not mean that love becomes the historical possibility. We need to be aware that love as the basis of the self in its freedom is not a realizable perfection. Paradoxical as it may sound, "Love, for Niebuhr, is experienced as a 'lack,' and therefore as an 'ought,' in the highest levels of self-transcendence."[43]

Niebuhr's discovery of love as the requirement or law of freedom, which "sets every standard of justice under higher possibilities," gives us an important insight with regard to our common quest for the moral prospectus of the positional self as a moral self. Broadly speaking, compared to the philosophical reconstructionism of Habermas, Niebuhr's theological reconstructionism enables us to see that the moral injunction "keep the law" is only a basic requirement in reconstructing the positional self as a moral self because to keep the law is in fact only a minimal moral imperative for the positional self. It is certainly better for a positional self to abide by the law in playing his or her role as a position holder than to violate the law of society, but he or she should be aware that there is a "higher-ought" aspect in exercising his or her freedom as a position holder. Indeed, no one can perfectly realize the law of one's freedom, but one needs to think seriously that a positional self is required to transcend the standard of justice symbolized minimally

---

41. Ibid., 1:280.

42. Rice, "Spirit of the Law in the Thought of Reinhold Niebuhr," 268.

43. Ibid. Niebuhr makes it clear that we have to view *justitia originalis* not as a historically realizable reality because it remains in us as a law "in moments of the self's morally reflective self-transcendence." Niebuhr's claim is reminiscent of Kant's categorical imperative, which is known to us apodictically as the fundamental moral law of the self in its freedom.

in the form of "keep the law." Thanks to Niebuhr's theological reconstructionism and its ethical implication, we come to see more clearly that the moral norm for the positional self ought not to be exhausted by the minimalistic injunction to keep the law. Of course, the positional self should abide by the law of society, but it must remember that love as *justitia originalis* is the law of its freedom that requires it to transcend the mere bottom line set by the political institution. Thus we can say that there are two kinds of *ought* for the positional self: the "lower *ought*" and the "higher *ought*," and the law of freedom requires that the positional self should conform to the higher *ought*'s transcending the lower ought. However, since the higher *ought* can never be fully realized in the fallen world, we need to take into consideration that there is always a limitation in terms of the positional self-fulfilling the higher *ought*.

Agape and the Positional Self

In the above discussion, we have uncovered a different layer or level of the moral norm for the positional self through a critical analysis of Niebuhr's theological reconstructionism. This development, however, should be further enhanced because we have not yet analyzed the substance of *justitia originalis*, especially in relation to the positional self in its organizational and corporate context. Thus, we turn to the following issues: What moral significance or relevance does the law of love have in the organizational or corporate world? What are the possibilities and limitations of the law of love with regard to positional acts? Could love be the law or requirement of positional freedom? In order to answer these questions, we hereafter engage in an in-depth analysis of Niebuhr's understanding of *justitia originalis* and justice.

We first need to understand why Niebuhr identifies love as law. What makes love as law? Can love ever be a law? What does it mean that love is law? According to Niebuhr, love is the only "structure" for the life of the self in its essential nature (freedom), but the sin of self-love makes it not as a mere possibility but as the form of law. This law, as Niebuhr clearly asserts, is the claim of his or her essential nature upon him or her as obligation. "This sense of obligation is, in fact, the claim which the essential nature of man makes upon him in his present sinful state. The virtue that corresponds to the true nature of man therefore appears to sinful man in the form of law."[44] It is crucial to recognize that Niebuhr understands love as an independent requirement of human freedom. This, of course, does not deny an important theological point that love is derivative of faith. As we have seen above, however, "The Christian faith affirms, further, that the same Christ who discloses the sovereignty of God over history is also the perfect norm of human nature."[45]

According to Niebuhr, human community itself is good evidence of why and how love is an independent requirement of human freedom. In order to establish community, there should be something deeper than the mere "gregarious impulse" of the human being, and this something, for Niebuhr, is an aspect of love: "Love is a requirement of freedom because the community to which man is impelled by his social nature is not possible to him merely upon the basis of his gregarious impulse. In his freedom and uniqueness each man stands outside of, and transcends, the cohesions of nature and uniformities of mind which bind life to life."[46] By saying this, Niebuhr claims that the law of love is not an alien or supernatural norm, but rather it "is given by the very constitution of selfhood."[47] According to Niebuhr, human conscience and memory not only conveys the unforgotten sphere of this law but also betrays the glimpse of its negative aspect: "No man, however deeply involved in sin, is able to regard the misery of sin as normal. Some memory of a previous condition of blessedness seems to linger in his soul; some echo of the law that he has violated seems to respond in his conscience. Every effort to give the habits of sin the appearance of normality betrays something of the frenzy of an uneasy conscience."[48] Indeed, it is Niebuhr's main point that *justitia originalis* continuously remains in us as the law and requirement of freedom.

Regarding the complex and paradoxical relation between love and law, Daniel F. Rice notes two aspects of this relationship in Niebuhr's theological system: a subjective and an objective side.[49] While law in its objective or material sense is characterized by duty and obligation, law

---

44. Niebuhr, *Nature and Destiny of Man*, 1:272.
45. Ibid., 2:68, cited in David and Good, *Reinhold Niebuhr on Politics*, 131.
46. Niebuhr, *Nature and Destiny of Man*, 1:271.
47. Niebuhr, *Self and the Dramas of History*, 232.
48. Niebuhr, *Nature and Destiny of Man*, 1:265.
49. Rice, "Spirit of the Law in the Thought of Reinhold Niebuhr," 273.

in its subjective sense is realized as some form of coercion or restraint originated in either the "mores and customs of a community" or in the "compulsion of conscience" as opposed to other impulses in the personality.[50] On both sides, however, the dialectical character can be found. The subjective side of "thou shalt" requires that love is to be commanded as if it is law, whereas the objective aspect represents the detailed duties and obligations in the form of law.[51] In Niebuhr's account, while love is not a simple achievement of the historical human being, it is still commanded to us as a law. Niebuhr captures the dialectical relation between love and law by saying that love both completes and contradicts law. For Niebuhr, love is also the fulfillment and the negation of law because, paradoxical as it may sound, love in its universality points not only to its transcendence over law but also to the summary of all law.[52]

Niebuhr thus defines love as the "higher law," which "even sinful man has, not as a possession but in his sense of something lacking."[53] Niebuhr also holds that love must be further explicated in a way that contains three terms with a view to the self's tripartite relation: to God, to oneself, and to others. He writes,

> The specific content of this higher law ... has been tentatively defined, and this definition must now be further explicated. It contains three terms: (a) The perfect relation of the soul to God in which obedience is transcended by love, trust and confidence ("Thou shalt love the Lord thy God"); (b) the perfect internal harmony of the soul with itself in all of its desires and impulses: "With all thy heart and all thy soul and all thy mind"; and (c) the perfect harmony of life with life: "Thou shalt love thy neighbor as thyself."[54]

Among these three terms, the last explication is particularly important to us because love as the perfect harmony of life with life reveals the essential elements of universal love for all human beings: "the sum total of

---

50. Niebuhr, *Christian Realism and Political Problems*, 148.

51. The best example for this can be found in the scripture, which says "Thou shalt love the Lord they God with all thy heart, and with all thy soul, and with all thy mind. This is the first and greatest commandment. And the second is like unto it, Thou shalt love they neighbor as thy self" (Matthew 22:37–39).

52. Rice, "Spirit of the Law in the Thought of Reinhold Niebuhr," 274.

53. Niebuhr, *Nature and Destiny of Man*, 1:288.

54. Ibid., 289.

all our obligation to our fellow men without specific detail."⁵⁵ According to Niebuhr, to the extent that the universal kind of love "expresses our obligations beyond the boundaries of the natural communities of family, tribe, and nation, the love of 'mankind' must be by law . . . our concern for those beyond our circle, our obligation to the peoples of the world and the community of mankind . . . [and this love] comes to us very much with the push of the 'ought' against the force of our more parochial habits of grace."⁵⁶ In Niebuhr's analysis, Jesus's life and his message reveal the positive essence of what this love is through the form of *agape*, and agape becomes the most crucial ideal to describe the law of love. Niebuhr is clear that "Agape" differs from either "the classical Philia or Eros, that is . . . mutual love or the love which calculates its relations to other from the standpoint of its need of others."⁵⁷ *Agape* is characterized in the New Testament as the heedless, sacrificial, and forgiving love of Christ, which is most distinctively revealed on the cross. The ethic of Jesus, thus, represents an "impossible possibility" in that human self-realization is possible only through loving self-sacrifice. This, however, paradoxically shows us that at the center of *agape* lies the concept of grace.

The sacrificial love of *agape*, the essence of *justitia originalis*, is in stark contrast to the concept of sin: the inordinate love of oneself. Since our world is no longer the original society of Adam and Eve before the fall, Niebuhr acknowledges that *agape* "cannot be formulated as an obligation, nor can it be achieved under the whip of the sense of obligation."⁵⁸ In this sense, *agape* is the negation of love as mere law. In Niebuhr's account, *agape* is not a law because it is not an obligation that can be enforced. Niebuhr's dialectical understanding of love develops out of this situation. On the one hand, *agape* is stipulated as the law of freedom; on the other hand, *agape* is not to be recognized as a law. Niebuhr explains that the simple commandment "Thou shalt love" is indeed the paradox: "the paradox of stating a possibility as an obligation when the obligatory feature destroys it is a possibility."⁵⁹ If Niebuhr is right, then

55. Niebuhr, *Interpretation of Christian Ethics*, 155.
56. Ibid., 152.
57. Niebuhr, *Faith and History*, 176.
58. Niebuhr, *Christian Realism and Political Problems*, 159.
59. Niebuhr, "Problem of the Love Ethic in Politics," in David and Good, *Reinhold Niebuhr on Politics*, 134.

we cannot but be moral, not because we are moral, but because we are paradoxical; morality lies in the paradox of the human situation. For Niebuhr, in this sense, both legalism and relativism in morality are mistaken. Ethics for humankind ought to be dialectical: dialectical not in a sense of mere contradiction, but in a sense of impossible possibility. This possibility, however, comes along with suffering because we are still living in a fallen world. Thus, according to Niebuhr, history after Christ is conceived as an "interim between the disclosure of its true meaning and the fulfillment of that meaning, between the revelation of divine sovereignty and the full establishment of that sovereignty, a continued element of inner contradiction in history is accepted as its perennial characteristic."[60]

Niebuhr's dialectical ethics is best exemplified in his in-depth discourse on the dialectical relation between the self-sacrificial love of *agape* and the mutual love of *philia*. He epitomizes the dialectical relationship between *agape* and *philia* as follows:

> Mutual love (*philia*) is also a form of love, for the life of the other is enhanced. Yet, on the other hand, such expressions of love fall short of love in its ultimate form. For they are mixed with a careful calculation of interest and advantages in which the self always claims an equal share. The final form of love is bereft of such calculation and meets the needs of the other without calculating comparative rights. Sacrificial love is therefore a form of love which transcends the limits of love.[61]

According to Niebuhr, just as there is a dialectical relation between love and law, so is there between heedless love and mutual love. Niebuhr seems to be concerned with the problem that mutual love can inevitably degenerate into mere loveless calculation. Niebuhr also seems to believe that with mutual love only, society cannot be established and maintained, because "mutual love has the root of selfishness in it that it lends itself so readily to a justification of egoism if it does not stand under the scrutiny of the higher ideal of disinterest or sacrificial love."[62] Thus according to Niebuhr there is an inherent conundrum in regard to political society, because *agape* must be presupposed even though it is not

60. Ibid., 135.
61. Niebuhr, *Christian Realism and Political Problems*, 160.
62. Niebuhr, "Letters to the Editor," 364.

a realizable possibility of historical life. Niebuhr tries to overcome this conundrum with his concept of "approximation" as a dialectical reality between *agape* and mutual love. According to Niebuhr, the idea of the fall has long been a difficult problem to Christian churches throughout their history, and the most significant reason for this lies in the church's attempt to view the matter as a historical and chronological event. In other words, in order for mutual love to stand without falling into mere calculative egoism, mutual love is necessarily sustained by the dialectic in its relationship with *agape* even though the latter is not a historically realizable possibility.

Niebuhr explains this with the metaphor of the "end of history." Indeed *agape* is not "in history" as a possibility, or "outside history" as an unrelated principle; however, the ethics of the impossible possibility remains as the approximation that can approach the final goal indefinitely within history. The reference to the final goal beyond history is thus regarded as an eschatological love of the kingdom of God, and with this, the relative nature of the approximation comes to have more than relative significance in each historical situation. We, however, should be aware that Niebuhr's vision of approximation only remains as approximation, no matter how much it may approach the final goal. Ultimately what Niebuhr does is to bring moral tension in between *agape* and *philia* with his idea of approximation. This tension is not only worthwhile but also necessary to prevent ethical relativism and egoism. Niebuhr's understanding of this relation has invited considerable critique from both Christian theologians and philosophers.

In his major study *Agape: An Ethical Analysis* (1972), Gene Outka raises questions against Niebuhr's conception of love as "self-sacrifice." Outka believes that if *agape* is regarded as self-sacrifice as its quintessence, then it entails several "serious difficulties." The first of its problems is the "blank check" issue. Outka writes, "The feature of self-sacrifice in itself would appear to provide no way of distinguishing between attention to another's needs and submission to his exploitation and no warrant for resisting the latter."[63] He warns us that if *agape* as self-sacrifice is not checked or amended by some additional principle, such as justice, it can be misused or abused as a blind rule. Outka also points out that Niebuhr's conception of love is insufficient in according the distinc-

---

63. Outka, *Agape*, 275.

tion "between the treatment of someone else in relation to myself and the treatment of someone else in relation to still another (or others) than myself."[64] This problem is not something unfamiliar to Niebuhr either. As Outka rightly alludes, Niebuhr is aware of this difficulty readily related to "collective action" rather than to the "individual."[65] I will come back to this issue of collective action shortly since it is deeply related to the moral conundrums of the positional self. First though, there is, according to Outka, another problem: the unintelligibility of *agape* as self-sacrifice with regard to its application to the several parties in a given transaction. In explaining this unintelligibility, Outka states, "What decisively identifies self-sacrifice for Niebuhr is not so much its promotion of other-regarding attitudes and actions but simply the process of non-accommodation to self-interest."[66] For this reason, Outka argues that a considerable modification is in order to define the concept of *agape*.

Instead of *agape* as self-sacrifice, Outka now redefines *agape* as "equal regard."[67] However, he acknowledges that Niebuhr's *agape* should not be simply discarded, because it can still be appropriated as an "instrumental warrant," by which Outka means that although self-sacrifice may not be the purest and most perfect manifestation of *agape*, it must be appropriated as "one possible exemplification and by-product of devotion to others for their own sake."[68] For this reason, Outka develops a new understanding of *agape*: *agape* as equal regard. By "equal regard," Outka means commitment to the well-being of the other "inde-

---

64. Ibid., 276.

65. Niebuhr says, "For as soon as the life and interest of others than the agent are involved in an action or policy, the sacrifice of those interests ceases to be 'self-sacrifice.' It may actually become an unjust betrayal of their interests. Failure to understand this simple fact and this paradoxical relation between individual and collective action has resulted in the unholy alliance between Christian perfectionism and cowardly counsels of political expediency in dealing with tyrants in our own day" (Niebuhr, *The Nature and Destiny of Man*, 2:88, cited in Outka, *Agape*, 276).

66. Outka, *Agape*, 276–77.

67. Agape as "equal regard" is now widely accepted as one of the major interpretations of neighbor love in the academic Christian arena. See Browning, "Altruism and Christian Love," and *Religious Thought and the Modern Psychologies*, 150-59; Janssens, "Norms and Priorities in a Love Ethics"; Tracy, *Analogical Imagination*, 435; Porter, "De Ordine Caritatis"; and Pope, "'Equal Regard' versus 'Special Relations'? Reaffirming the Inclusiveness of Agape."

68. Outka, *Agape*, 278–79.

pendently" and "unalterably" and a viewing of the other as irreducibly valuable.[69] Outka observes that the independent and unalterable other regard entails two implications: "(1) he is valued as, or in that he is, a person qua human existent and not because he is such-and-such a kind of person distinguishing him from others; and (2) a basic equality obtains whereby one neighbor's well-being is as valuable as another's."[70] To regard, thus, means to consider the interests of someone, to have active concern for what she or he wants or needs, to commit oneself to meeting the needs of her or his "psycho-physical existence."[71]

As Outka acknowledges, *agape* as equal regard is something that Kierkegaard conveys through his conceptual contrast between neighbor love with other forms such as friendship and erotic love. Forecasting Outka's equal regard, Kierkegaard asserts that love toward one's neighbor is "eternal equality" in loving. Kierkegaard writes, "Love to one's neighbor is therefore eternal equality in loving, but this eternal equality is the opposite of exclusive love or preference . . . Equality is just this, not to make distinctions, and eternal equality is absolutely not to make the slightest distinction."[72] In this sense, Kierkegaard is adamant in denouncing comparison, particularly those comparisons between his love and that of someone else. "If you will preserve love, you must preserve it in the infinitude of debt. Watch out, therefore, for comparison! . . . Watch out for comparison!"[73] For Kierkegaard, the moment of comparison is a selfish moment, and through comparison love becomes defiled as a form of economy. "In comparison everything is lost; love is made finite and the debt something to repay just like any other debt, instead of love's debt having its own characteristic of infinitude."[74]

Outka's equal regard, however, is questioned by scholars regarding the relation of equal regard and partiality. Julia E. Judish, for example, asks the question: "How are the claims of friendship and kinship to be

---

69. Ibid., 10.

70. Ibid., 12. Outka's equal regard stipulates that each one's well-being is as valuable as another's, no more, no less. In this sense, he writes, "At the most basic level there ought to be no exclusiveness, no partiality, no elitism" (Ibid.).

71. Ibid., 264.

72. Kierkegaard, *Works of Love*, 70.

73. Ibid., 180.

74. Ibid., 178, cited in Outka, *Agape*, 15.

fitted into the framework of equal regard that defines agape?"[75] This question originates in Outka's clear position on the worthiness of the other. Outka maintains that the neighbor must be regarded as a human being prior to a particular human being. In other words, when it comes to equal love, what matters is not "suchness" of a person, but a person's "thatness."[76] Since equal regard should "remain as the center of gravity," the "thatness" of each individual, including oneself, has equal worth. Careful reading of Outka, however, enables us to see that he is well aware of this issue: the uneasy relation between "thatness" and "suchness," "equal regard" and "partiality," "sameness and differences," and so on. Referring to this issue, Outka points out the need to differentiate between "equal consideration" and "identical treatment." He says that "agape requires the former, but not always the latter."[77]

Between equal consideration and identical treatment, there is a caveat in which a place for partiality (special relations) resides without contradicting the principle of impartiality. Stephen J. Pope explains this by developing the concept of a "weak version of impartiality" composed of the moral requirements of "role reversibility" and "interpersonal consistency." According to Pope, Outka forms an alliance between a "weak" form of impartiality and *agape* in such a way that although we must recognize the worth of all people equally, not all people are expected to be treated equally. Pope writes, "When Outka adds the caveat that one is 'at least not required' to give more weight to others, he makes room for generosity, kindness, and altruism that transcends duty."[78] Pope's point is epitomized by Outka's later work, in which he writes, "Full inclusion can always mean genuine inclusion, but not always equal inclusion."[79] Indeed, "one should love others neither more nor less than oneself" and thus each one's good is "equally worthy of consideration," but Outka adds the important qualification that every person's good is not "on an equal footing."[80] Thus Pope concludes that "the full scope of agape en-

75. Judish, "Balancing Special Obligations with the Ideal of Agape," 21. See Sommers, "Filial Morality."

76. Outka, *Agape*, 23.

77. Ibid., 20.

78. Pope, "'Equal Regard' versus 'Special Relations'? Reaffirming the Inclusiveness of Agape," 367.

79. Outka, "Universal Love and Impartiality," 3.

80. Ibid., 78, cited in Pope, "'Equal Regard' versus 'Special Relations'? Reaffirming the Inclusiveness of Agape," 367.

compasses *both* 'special relations' and universal love, *both* deep mutual affection and unilateral respect."[81]

In several aspects, Outka's *agape* as equal regard seems to be more relevant in terms of reconstructing a moral norm for the positional self than is Niebuhr's self-sacrifice. Most conspicuously, as we have reviewed above, Outka's equal regard can more aptly resolve dilemmas that require one to resist exploitation or oppression on behalf of an innocent third party in "other-other" interactions. Outka's equal regard is also helpful in justifying actions that would benefit both oneself and others without disqualifying them from the realm of *agape*. Further, Outka's equal regard is more inspiring to guide a positional self as a moral self, in that it concerns those who are affected by the agent's actions, which is an essential aspect in position-mediated relations. Outka writes, "The 'other' to be regarded in this generic sense therefore appears to mean anyone and everyone affected by the agent's actions."[82]

Outka's delineation of other-other interactions, however, needs to be further analyzed, because the agent's relation to other-other interactions is not that simple. Outka's other, first of all, is conceived negatively as opposed to the agent. Thus, Outka's other is a negative other. By "negative other," I mean the concept of an other that is relatively conceived in the sense of a "non-agent." There is no concrete name, no concrete character, no concrete face, and no concrete position of its own that pertains to this other. In my view, it is no accident that when Outka describes the other, he uses the term "generic sense" to define it. When the other is conceptualized in the generic sense, then the concept of sacrifice is no longer viable, because self-sacrifice is always concrete and particular. Now we need to go back to a problem we have discussed: the integration of equal regard and special relations. Interestingly, when Stephen J. Pope develops an idea of the weak version of impartiality, with which Outka agrees, those who are allowed to have a concrete name, character, and position are the other in the region of special relations such as family, relatives, and friends; the other in the region of equal regard is, however, conceptualized in the generic sense. The conceptual division between the weak version and the strong version is problematic, not

---

81. Pope, "'Equal Regard' versus 'Special Relations'? Reaffirming the Inclusiveness of Agape," 379.

82. Outka, *Agape*, 12–13.

because the division does not make sense, but because it makes sense only at the expense of rendering a certain other generic and negative.

When the other is generically conceived, then the other's needs and interests easily become the matters of mathematics and economics. We can see this phenomenon in Outka's critique of Niebuhr's self-sacrifice. Outka introduces a passage from the earliest halachic midrash, the *Sifra*, which says the following: "If two men are traveling on a journey and one has a pitcher of water, if both drink they will both die, but if only one drinks, he will reach civilization."[83] Outka uses this case to show that exhorting everyone to act self-sacrificially is "self-defeating" and "contradictory." In my view, however, the real problem lies not in whether self-sacrifice is self-defeating but in whether we really know who these two men are. In other words, self-sacrifice appears to be self-defeating in this case not because the self sacrifice itself is deficient but because these two men are "generically and negatively" conceived. I am not arguing here that equal regard is problematic as the principle of *agape*. Rather, what I am questioning here is how it is possible to maintain equal regard without rendering a certain other generic or negative other.

Compared to Outka's generic other, Niebuhr's other is particular, especially when he attempts to apply self-sacrifice to the intersubjective relation. Niebuhr's other is not conceived "negatively" or "generically" in the mere sense of "non-agent." Niebuhr's other is, rather, characteristically specified, such as immigrants, union workers, racial minorities, and oppressed nations beyond individuated others who have their specific names, characters, faces, and positions. With regard to the concept of the positional self, Niebuhr's basic view of the other is helpful because reconstructing the positional self as a moral self necessarily requires the positional self to recognize the other not as the negative other in the sense of the nonpositional self, but as a concrete and particular other whose specific interests are to be carefully considered. Speaking concretely, others for the positional self can be enumerated as suppliers, stockholders, employees, consumers, constituencies, manufacturers, customers, and local communities. In a global capitalistic society, others can oftentimes be coffee growers in Ethiopia, street children in Honduras, or sweatshop workers in South Asian or Latin American

---

83. Ibid., 277.

countries. These particular others may be invisible to many of us, but their "particularity" ought not to be "departicularized" as negative and generic others. One way to enliven their particularity is to view their needs from a universal and holistic perspective, and this is particularly important to the positional self.

I agree that Outka's "equal regard" is helpful, particularly in overcoming some ethical conundrums that self-sacrifice finds it hard to resolve, but I would like to go further by presenting the concept of "universal regard," which modifies the idea of equal regard through rediscovering and reencountering the negative and generic others whose names and faces are veiled or buried by organizations and corporations. Universal regard is particularly relevant to the positional self because others for the positional self are essentially mediated by organizational or corporate systems, rather than by the immediate or interpersonal self-other or other-other relations. Unlike interpersonal relations, relations of the positional self are oftentimes characterized as "organizational self–organizational other" or "organizational other–organizational other" relations, which typically capture the organizational other as generic others. In order to unveil or rediscover the other, we ought to view "the interests of the other as vividly as those of the self,"[84] and we need to see these interests of others not from a negative or a generic perspective, but from a universal and holistic perspective by situating the positional self and others in the large context of economic organization or political structure. Referring partially to this aspect, Niebuhr writes, "Furthermore the realization of any such system of harmony would require more than individual action. It would require the organization of vast economic and political structures in defiance of, and transcendence over, the contingencies of geography, the fortuitous differences of natural resources, etc."[85]

Therefore, in the following I will use the term *universal regard* to distinguish the ultimate moral norm for the positional self from other definitions such as equal regard or self-sacrifice. Universal regard is established in such a way to integrate both equal regard and self-sacrifice. Self-sacrifice is an integral aspect of universal regard on the condition that all others are no longer negative or generic others, but

---

84. David and Good, *Reinhold Niebuhr on Politics*, 136. See also Niebuhr, *Faith and History*, 197–98, and Niebuhr, *Nature and Destiny of Man*, 1:296.

85. Niebuhr, *Nature and Destiny of Man*, 1:296.

rather that they are concrete and specific others whose names and faces are known by the positional self. Universal regard, thus, is *agape* love as the requirement of positional freedom, which is especially relevant to the positional self. However, the ideal of universal regard may only be approximated by the positional self. It is impossible for the positional self to see all others affected by its actions as others in themselves rather than as negative or generic others because the moral imagination tends to be limited and diminished in organizational relations compared to interpersonal or intersubjective relations, as Niebuhr's *Moral Man and Immoral Society* poignantly points out.

Justice and the Positional Self

Niebuhr's concept of justice is particularly important in reconstructing the ethical norm for the positional self. First, his concept of justice is deeply related to the idea of tension as an achievable historical reality that must be directed to the goal of eschatological love that is yet beyond history. For Niebuhr, humans are paradoxical beings from a moral perspective: on the one hand, they have the possibility of transcending natural limitations (because a human being has freedom as his or her faculty); but, on the other hand, they are limited by their nature (because human beings have fallen by their sinfulness). Thus in order to discuss human morality, we need to consider these paradoxical elements. Niebuhr has developed his idea of justice based on this fundamental understanding by defining justice as "the relative embodiment of Agape in the structures of society."[86] Broadly speaking, for Niebuhr, justice is the practical answer to the question of "whether the original righteousness, the perfection before the Fall, which sinful man retains as law, can finally become a realized fact of history."[87]

In the above discussion, we have discovered that freedom is not only given to human beings universally; it is also structured in such a way that love is its law. We have also seen that although freedom is corrupted by sin, it is still possible to presuppose the law of love as the requirement of freedom. According to Niebuhr, *agape* love is indeed impossible to realize directly as historical reality but must be presupposed as a goal that provides direction to historical life. Without this,

---

86. Rice, "Spirit of the Law in the Thought of Reinhold Niebuhr," 279.
87. Niebuhr, *Nature and Destiny of Man*, 1:298.

in Niebuhr's analysis, the construction of human society is not conceivable, because mutual love (without being initiated by heedless love) will relapse into egotistical calculation and mere relativism. Meaningful society requires love as the goal of its law and the criterion of justice. In characterizing the positional self as a moral self, thus, Niebuhr's dialectical understanding of love and justice is critical for the establishment of the moral norm for the positional self.

What, then, does Niebuhr's dialectical understanding of love and justice have to do with the establishment of the moral norm for the positional self? According to Niebuhr, first of all, the positional self is an agent who is supposed to realize social harmony through exercising its moral faculties in economic and political organizations. It is important to see that the positional self has freedom as one of its triune moral faculties. Since the freedom of the positional self is intrinsically related to managerial or operational power, based on Niebuhr's ethical reconstructionism, we can develop the idea that the positional self is required to realize the system of harmony by approximating the norm of love in the organizations of economic and political structures. The main point is that the ethical norm of love can and should be applicable to the concept of the positional freedom that lies in the positional self. Using Niebuhr's theological term, the vision of the "kingdom of God" is not just an individual goal. It can also call for social, economic, and political transformation to enhance social harmony in society. This harmony is similar to what Niebuhr calls the "approximation" of love by law and justice. This, however, must not be identified as a direct and immediate vision, lest it turn out to be a kind of Christian utopianism. According to Niebuhr, "The Christian utopians think they can dispense with all structures and rules of justice simply by fulfilling the law of love. They do not realize that the law of love stands on the edge of history and not in history, that it represents an ultimate and not an immediate possibility."[88]

In the following, by focusing further on the dialectical relationship between love and justice, we will look more closely at how the positional self approximates the ethical norm of love in the organizational world. As we will see, unlike that of ordinary, private individuals, the positional self's moral actions are maintained through justice, which

---

88. Ibid.

would eventually require it to consider the good of others as much as its own. Niebuhr differentiates the possible moral actions of ordinary private individuals from those of the positional self: "It is possible, though not always advisable, for individuals to suffer injustice rather than let the dispute come to an ultimate issue. But *statesmen*, responsible for values beyond their own lives, do not have this option. They must seek for justice by an accommodation of interests and they must protect precious values by force if necessary."[89] The moral meaning of positional freedom is reconstructed primarily through justice, which is dialectically conditioned by the law of love: universal regard. Justice is a key for the positional self because it is impossible for the positional self to know all others affected by its actions as concrete and specific others. Although the law of love requires the positional self to treat all others as oneself, the system of organization makes it inevitable that certain others will be converted into negative or generic others.

Niebuhr's distinctive understanding of justice is first marked by its indeterminate character. He understands justice not as something that has its own criterion by its own principle or norm, but as something that can be understood only in its relation to ideal love. Hence without taking into consideration the higher vision of love, the concept of justice cannot be adequately explicated. According to Niebuhr, justice is most definitely understood in its relation to love. As he claims, "Love is both the fulfillment and the negation of all achievements of justice in history."[90] Niebuhr rewrites his claim "in reverse" as follows: "The achievements of justice in history may rise in indeterminate degrees to find their fulfillment in a more perfect love and brotherhood; but each new level of fulfillment also contains elements which stand in contradiction to perfect love."[91] Justice then can always be variant kinds of imperfect love. Imperfect love as it may be, justice is still the fulfillment of love.

---

89. David and Good, *Reinhold Niebuhr on Politics*, 143. See also Niebuhr, "Speak Truth to Power," 14.

90. Niebuhr, *Nature and Destiny of Man*, 2:246. We need to notice that in the previous section, Niebuhr says that love is both the fulfillment and the negation of all law. The relation between law and justice is best epitomized by Niebuhr as follows: "Broadly speaking, the end of the law is justice." See Niebuhr, *Christian Realism and Political Problems*, 171.

91. Niebuhr, *Nature and Destiny of Man*, 2:246.

Thus we see that Niebuhr's idea of justice is not only indeterminate but also complex. Part of this complexity comes from the presupposition that justice requires. For Niebuhr, justice paradoxically presupposes the sinfulness of the human being and the sinful element in society, which is the "tendency of various members of a community to take advantage of each other, or to be more concerned with their own weal than with that of others."[92] From Niebuhr's perspective, justice is supposed to be understood not only in its dialectical relation to ideal love but also in its paradoxical relation to human sin. Failing to bring a balance between these relationships, for Niebuhr, could result in inadequacy at best or danger at worst.[93]

Niebuhr tries to resolve the complexity of justice by distinguishing two dimensions: "the laws and principles of justice" and "the structures of justice." He writes, "The difference between the first and second dimension obviously lies in the fact that laws and principles of justice are abstractly conceived, while structures and organizations [of justice] embody the vitalities of history."[94] Since the establishment of the ethical norm for the positional self is for the most part related to the two principles of justice rather than to the structures of justice, we will examine the moral meaning of these principles of justice in light of their relevance to the moral behaviors of the positional self. First of all, the abstractly conceived principles of justice are exemplified by Niebuhr as "equality" and "liberty." For Niebuhr, equality and liberty are regulative principles, to which he adds "practical universality." They are regulative in that while equality requires persons to be treated as equal, liberty demands freedom to be allowed as much as possible within the limits of social cohesion. They are also "practically universal" in that the lack of universal reason in history leaves them to be guaranteed not by their logical system of justice but by the historical communities and

---

92. Ibid., 252.

93. For Niebuhr, sentimentalists and rationalists are good examples of this. While sentimentalists seek to substitute love for justice by ignoring the severity of human sinfulness, rationalists overestimate their rational capacity to realize justice without its dialectical relation to the ideal love.

94. Niebuhr, *Nature and Destiny of Man*, 2:247. By "the structures of justice," Niebuhr mainly means the arrangement of power, which has two social aspects: the central organizing power and the equilibrium of power. Niebuhr asserts that these two aspects are not only essential but also perennial to community organization.

individuals.[95] Indeed, "Regulative principles form a complex normative system in which they are in a dialectical relationship of affirmation and negation both to the law of love and to other regulative principles."[96]

For Niebuhr, equality is not an absolute law; rather, it is a relative norm. It is important to notice that when he talks about equality, he does not mean that everyone's need, power, and capacity should be the same. What he is saying is that people's different levels of need, power, and capacity are treated in light of the principle of equality for the purpose of a more just society. For this, the law of equality accepts the necessity "to calculate" the advantage among the group relations in which the concern for self-interests is imbedded. "Relative justice involves the calculation of competing interests, the specification of rights and duties, and the balancing of life forces."[97]

Niebuhr's Christian realism recognizes the fact that the claims about justice are historical and contextual.[98] This means that the quest for equality is limited by historical context and social consciousness as well as by what the social order requires. This, however, does not disrupt the principle that persons are to be treated as equals. According to Niebuhr, as a pinnacle of the ideal of justice, equality always implicitly points toward love as the final form of justice, because "equal justice is the approximation of brotherhood under the conditions of sin."[99] Niebuhr puts this limitedness of the principle of equality as follows: "The validity of the principle of equality on the one hand and the impossibility of realizing it fully on the other, illustrates the relation of the absolute norms of justice to the relativities of history."[100] Thus, for the positional self, the principle of equality becomes dialectically connected with universal regard as its approximation and negation.

---

95. Here the word "practical" must not be confused with "realizable" because the word "practical" only supports the next word "universality." "Practical universality" should be more legitimately connected with "transcendent." According to Niebuhr, Stoic, medieval, and modern theories of natural law rightfully understand both equality and liberty as transcendent principles of justice, whereas both the bourgeois as well as Marxists "falsely regard them as realizable rather than as transcendent principles." See Niebuhr, *The Nature and Destiny of Man*, 2:254.

96. Lovin, *Reinhold Niebuhr and Christian Realism*, 219.

97. Ibid., 207.

98. Ibid., 212.

99. Niebuhr, *Nature and Destiny of Man*, 1:254.

100. Ibid., 255.

Liberty is another regulative principle of justice. Although Niebuhr recognizes that equality has a certain priority to liberty, "a higher justice always means a more equal justice," equality is still one of the two regulative principles of justice.[101] For Niebuhr, liberty is primarily understood in relation to the political system. In other words, liberty is not about unchecked freedom or ambiguous potentialities of self-transcendence. Liberty is always situated in the political community. For the regular and orderly function of society, liberty is to be checked. Niebuhr explains this condition as follows: "Nevertheless, the tendency of the community to claim the individual's devotion too absolutely, and to disregard his hopes, fears, and ambitions which are in conflict with, or irrelevant to, the communal end, makes it necessary to challenge the community in the name of liberty."[102]

For Niebuhr, although liberty requires a critical attitude toward all governments to prevent them from relapsing into a totalitarian system, the more important political aspect of liberty requires people to participate in politics. In other words, liberty realizes itself through political participation. Thus, giving people a full share of their entitlements, although important, is not the entirety of justice. The principle of liberty requires them "to participate in the deliberations that determine what those entitlements are, and they must resist in the name of this more complete liberty any version of liberty that offers freedom without participation, or any version of equality that offers entitlements without deliberation."[103] There is, thus, a dialectic between participation and autonomy within liberty. This dialectic must be contrasted with the dialectic that can be found between liberty and equality.

According to Niebuhr, the balance between equality and liberty is always a major point for the problem of justice. In terms of quality, they are in a dialectical relation in that, on the one hand, they are in contradictory relations and, on the other hand, both are indispensable for the realization of justice. The dialectical relation can be exemplified as follows: If we have absolute liberty, then some of us will use the liberty

101. Ibid. 254.

102. The quotation originally appeared in "Liberty and Equality," which was published in the *Yale Review* 47 (September 1957). This article was later reprinted in his books, such as in *Pious and Secular America* and *Faith and Politics*. Here the quotation comes from *Pious and Secular America*, 66.

103. Lovin, *Reinhold Niebuhr and Christian Realism*, 230.

to establish inequality; and if we argue for absolute equality, then we sacrifice liberty, because people cannot use their liberty to do what they want. Absolutizing one of the regulative principles will bring about the loss of the other principle; and at the same time, ignoring either one of the principles will ultimately hinder justice from being fully established. In order for a political society not to degenerate into either anarchy or tyranny, both principles of justice must be realized in a balanced way.

How then are the principles of equality and liberty related to the positional self? In order to answer this question, we first need to see that, for Niebuhr, love reveals itself through "the general spirit of justice." According to Niebuhr, the general spirit of justice "expresses itself in the structures, laws, social arrangements, and economic forms by which men seek to regulate the life of the community and to which men seek to regulate the life of the community and to establish a maximum of harmony and justice."[104] As this key sentence indicates, justice is the primary and practical criterion that ought to shape the behaviors of the positional self. Indeed it is crucial to see that as the principles of justice are embodied and made historically concrete, although imperfectly, in the structures and systems, the organizations and mechanisms, of society, the positional self is also morally established and contextualized in and by organizational systems and institutional mechanisms.[105] By conforming to the spirit of justice, thus, the positional self approximates the law of love. More specifically, reflecting the spirit of equality defined as "an equal treatment of all others" and with liberty identified as "giving people a full share of their entitlements," the positional self is expected to realize these principles through its actions. Through this actualization, the positional self approximates the law of love: the universal regard.

Conclusion

Niebuhr's concept of justice (its principles) provides us with an important perspective in answering the question, how can we help the positional self constitute itself as a moral self? To summarize, the principles of justice specify that the positional self should responsibly exercise its

104. Niebuhr, "Love and Law in Protestantism and Catholicism," 107. See also Niebuhr's *Christian Realism and Political Problems*, 167.

105. David and Good, *Reinhold Niebuhr on Politics*, 179. See also Niebuhr, *Nature and Destiny of Man*, 2:256–57.

power not for the sake of the concentration of its power, but for the sake of the "practically universal" principles of justice: equality and liberty. What we have to recognize is that the dual principles of justice are regulative. Thus, from the moral perspective, it is imperative for a positional self to perform its positional role in a way to meet the principles of justice. The principles of equality and liberty will be better served when a positional self tries to realize brotherhood through its positional action, rather than just to meet the order of the legal system. It is important to notice that both abstract principles and structures of justice are not exhausted by law. Thus, regarding the above question, Niebuhr's main answering point would be that "keep the law" itself is neither complete nor comprehensive enough as the moral criterion for the conduct of the positional self.

We can generally say that in contrast to Habermas's philosophical reconstructionism, Niebuhr's theological reconstructionism promotes a maximal understanding of justice. The maximal understanding of justice requires the positional self to view and asses its positional actions not only against the backdrop of relative justice but also against the backdrop of absolute justice. The positional self is requested and expected to find itself in the dialectical relationship between love and justice. Understanding this dialectic between love and justice is crucial for providing moral guidance to the positional self, because justice aims at the harmony of life with life. This dialectic enables the positional self to recognize that in order to justify their actions on moral grounds, their positional actions are supposed to be instruments of love, on the one hand, and approximations of the law of love, on the other hand.

For Niebuhr, absolute justice is identical to love, although it cannot be realized in human history, in that the circumstance of justice makes it impossible. This is why we need to rely on relative justice. Represented by legal norms, relative justice turns on degrees of good and evil, taking into consideration the two structural aspects of the organization of power and the balance of power. Calculation of needs and interests must be incorporated in reconstructing the positional act. Lovin exhibits this in his analysis of *agape*. He says, "The requirements of agape exceed the possibilities of discursive formulations and can be grasped only in myth and symbol, but agape is approximated in history by certain clarity and honesty about my needs, which in turn allows me to see the needs of my neighbors on their own terms, rather than in terms of what I want and need from them."¹⁰⁶ According to Lovin, since "to love another is to wish that person's good, . . . a search for justice that is related to love must include an understanding of human good."¹⁰⁷

Lovin's analysis of Niebuhr's vision on justice in its dialectical relation to love is especially important to the moral prospect for the positional self. Since love is both the fulfillment and the negation of all achievements of justice,¹⁰⁸ "keep the law" cannot itself become the final standard for the moral behavior of the positional self. Insofar as the principles and rules of justice are instruments of mutuality and brotherhood, according to Niebuhr, they extend the self's obligation toward the other. This other-regarding element must be incorporated into the moral standard of the positional self even though it cannot be fully realized because of the historical and human condition tainted by sin. According to Rice, although "they [principles and rules of justice] necessarily reflect the vested interests of those in a position of power and prestige who articulate them, and thus embody the 'taint' of self-interest . . . they are more than this to the extent that the self can rise to the point of considering interests other than its own, thereby exhibiting some genuine sense of social obligation."¹⁰⁹

Since the law requires the positional self to follow the principles and rules of justice, and the positional self recognizes that love is the end term of any system of justice, it is required that the positional self approximate love in its institutional or organizational activities. The commitment to this approximation thus ultimately characterizes the moral identity of the positional self. In sum, going beyond the mere criterion of keeping the law, the positional self is required to approximate the law of love through adhering to the principles of justice. In Niebuhr's terms, although human beings' nature is corrupted by sin, the moral destiny of human beings still ought to be found in *justitia originalis*. This should also be applicable to the positional self, although it would be much complex and difficult. This is what a theological reconstruction stands for. Despite the inevitability of sin (the *Scylla* of misconstruing oneself as an exploiter and the *Charybdis* of relegating oneself to a slave), the

---

106. Lovin, *Reinhold Niebuhr and Christian Realism*, 200.
107. Ibid.
108. Niebuhr, *Nature and Destiny of Man*, 2:246.
109. Rice, "Spirit of the Law in the Thought of Reinhold Niebuhr," 288.

moral significance of the positional self ultimately can be found in the dialectical tension between love and justice, which gives rise to the law of love beyond the law.

6

The Co-Reconstruction of the Positional Imperative

Introduction

IN THE PREVIOUS CHAPTERS WE EXAMINED THE DISTINCTIVE MORAL predicaments of the positional self through in-depth analyses of Habermas's critical study of the evolution of society and Niebuhr's ontological critique of the human nature. Habermas's and Niebuhr's in-depth analyses are indispensable in identifying the distinctive moral predicaments of the positional self. Habermas allows us to see how the positional self's moral predicament is historically constituted as a result of the rationalization process that culminates in the uncoupling of the lifeworld and the system. Niebuhr's account, by contrast, helps us understand how the moral predicament of the positional self is construed as an existential problem that originates in the human nature.

With regard to the moral prospect of the positional self, we investigated how Habermas's philosophical reconstructionism and Niebuhr's theological reconstructionism can respectively formulate different sets of the moral norm for the positional self. While Habermas's moral project offers us a formal, procedural, and minimalist solution (to keep the law), Niebuhr's ethical stance provides us with a concrete, substantive, and maximal criterion—to do what perfect justice demands—in establishing the positional self as a responsible moral self in organizations and corporations. The purpose of this chapter is to integrate Habermas's philosophical reconstructionism and Niebuhr's theological reconstructionism through a method of the co-reconstructionism with the purpose of developing a holistic moral norm for the positional self, which I call the "positional imperative." In doing so, I will focus on two aspects: Why co-reconstructionism? And how is it possible?

As already described in the introduction, co-reconstructionism is a methodological endeavor to integrate two types of the reconstructionism: the philosophical reconstructionism of Habermas's discourse ethics and the theological reconstructionism of Reinhold Niebuhr's Christian realism. As we will see in this chapter, the method of the co-reconstructionism is deeply connected to the notion of position. It is critical to understand that a position not only mediates the positional self and the world of organizations and corporations regulated by laws, policies, and constitutions, but it also mediates the dual moral faculties of the positional self: freedom and communicative reason. By abiding by democratically constituted laws, regulations, and policies, the positional self appropriates the communicative reason on the one hand; by managing, directing, and supervising organizations and corporations, the positional self exerts its freedom on the other hand. Unlike other types of a moral self, the positional self comes to realize its moral identity by integrating these dual moral faculties due to its positionality.[1] The purpose of the co-reconstructionism is therefore to develop a moral norm for the positional self, which integrates these dual moral faculties holding the positional self responsible for its actions.

From Niebuhr to Habermas: Niebuhr's Conundrum and Habermas's Solution

The careful reading of Niebuhr enables us to realize a conundrum in his moral system, especially with regard to the concept of the positional self. In his *Moral Man and Immoral Society*, Niebuhr claims that the individual cannot justify the sacrifice of the interests of the group to which he or she belongs: "An individual may sacrifice his own interests, either without hope of reward or in the hope of an ultimate compensation. But how is an individual, who is responsible for the interests of his group, to justify the sacrifice of interests other than his own?"[2] In *The*

---

1. By "positionality," I mean the nature of organizational position, which *categorically* signifies the fundamental moral characteristics of the positional self as a responsible being. I use this term in order to differentiate the moral distinctiveness of the positional self from the other types of the moral self solely conditioned by individuality or intersubjectivity.

2. Niebuhr, *Moral Man and Immoral Society*, 269.

Nature and Destiny of Man, however, he argues that the ultimate moral law requires us to sacrifice our interests to approximate the law of love because "love is a requirement of freedom."[3]

If love is a requirement of freedom as Niebuhr argues, then we have to ask the following question: What does it mean for a positional self to realize its freedom as a position holder in organizations and corporations? Since it is obvious that a positional self has freedom, then we can suppose that the law of love also must be the moral requirement of a positional self. If this is right, then contradiction seems to be inevitable, because no one should justify the sacrifice of group interests while the sacrifice of group interests is a moral requirement for the positional self.

Niebuhr approaches this problem from a different vantage point insofar as we could defend his position by saying that the law of love can only be realizable in cases of individual-to-individual relations but not in group-to-group relations. Still, if this is right, then Niebuhr needs to redefine his concept of freedom and also the idea of *justitia originalis*. When he says that love is a requirement of freedom, Niebuhr does not differentiate the freedom of a non–position holder from that of a positional self: a freedom that must realize itself through an organizational or institutional position. The problem is that Niebuhr never argues that there is a qualitative difference between the freedom of non–position holders and that of positional selves when he claims that group-to-group morality ought to be qualitatively distinguished from individual-to-individual ethics. How should we, then, solve Niebuhr's moral conundrum?

First of all, we need to be precise about what is at stake in Niebuhr's rejection of applying the law of love to group-to-group relations. When Niebuhr says that the individual cannot justify the sacrifice of group interests, the subject matter is not whether an individual person can sacrifice interests other than his or her own, but rather whether one could justify the decision to sacrifice the interests of one's group. Thus what is more important in this case is not the possibility of sacrifice but the justification of sacrifice. A complete analysis of this problem of justification, however, must incorporate another aspect already presupposed in the positing of the question itself. The subject matter

---

3. Niebuhr, *Nature and Destiny of Man*, 1:271.

itself (whether one could justify the decision to sacrifice the interests of its group) cannot be fully posited without presupposing a political structure as its backdrop. Is it possible to consider the sacrifice of group interests without presupposing a certain political structure?

In other words, in order for a person to sacrifice his or her group interests, he or she must be necessarily situated in a certain political position that qualifies the decision to make the sacrifice. This qualification of the individual's decision cannot be imagined without presupposing a certain political dimension. Hence assuming that this reasoning is right, the subject matter of justifying a sacrifice of the group interests should ultimately incorporate a political dimension going beyond the horizon of individual morality. It is my contention that Niebuhr does not take into equal consideration both moral and political dimensions when he raises the question, how is an individual who is responsible for the interests of a group to justify the sacrifice of interests other than his own? Niebuhr here confounds two different spheres of analysis, that is, the moral and the political.

In my view, by relegating the subject matter to the moral sphere alone, ignoring the so-called political justification, Niebuhr commits a reductionist fallacy, namely, reducing the political-moral subject matter to an exclusively moral dimension (which Niebuhr defines in terms of individual-to-individual relations only). Indeed, Niebuhr formulates an important and essential question when he asks whether it is justifiable for an individual to sacrifice interests other than his or her group interests, but he mistakenly tries to answer the question from a too narrow and restrictive vantage point—from a moral perspective only. This becomes the reason why we ought to incorporate a political dimension into our discussion to assess the moral character of the positional self.

Now regarding the issue of political justification, we first have to answer the critical question of whether Reinhold Niebuhr's political philosophy could ever provide any justificatory criterion for the conduct of the positional self. Does Niebuhr's understanding of politics have to do with the political justification of the moral conduct of the positional self?[4] If it does, what is the source of its justification; if not, why is it so?

---

4. By "moral conduct of the positional self," I mean the decision to sacrifice the group interests for the sake of others.

In order to answer these questions, we have to explore the relation between Niebuhr's Christian interpretation of human nature and his realistic understanding of politics because Niebuhr always argues that politics should be grounded in the rightful understanding of human nature—in terms of both capabilities and fallibilities. For Niebuhr, political methods must be judged by two criteria: "first, do they do justice to the moral resources and possibilities in human nature and provide for the exploitation of every latent moral capacity in man? Second, do they take account of the limitations of human nature, particularly those which manifest themselves in man's collective behavior?"[5] In fact, Niebuhr not only tries to ground political realism in a Christian understanding of human nature but he also analyzes and judges the various forms of politics in regard to its often hidden but presupposed idea of human nature. Indeed, although Niebuhr acknowledges various understanding of human nature, he believes that a Christian view of human nature is more adequate than other possible kinds, such as optimistic or cynical views, for the development of a democratic society.[6]

For Niebuhr, democracy is the most adequate political system because it not only values the transcendent aspect of human nature, but it also recognizes and constrains its penchant for evil. Niebuhr understands that both bourgeois democracy and the collectivism of Marxism fail to become the most adequate political system, because they put inordinate emphasis on the transcendent aspect of human nature. Niebuhr calls bourgeois democrats the "soft utopians" and Marxist collectivists the "hard utopians." According to Niebuhr, even though their ideals and methods differ, both groups ultimately belong to the same circle, which he terms "the children of light." Niebuhr defines the children of light as "those who believe that self-interest should be brought under the discipline of higher law, universal law, or universal good."[7] Niebuhr describes "the children of darkness," or the children of

---

5. David and Good, *Reinhold Niebuhr on Politics*, 70.

6. Niebuhr, *Children of Light and the Children of Darkness*, xv. According to Niebuhr, while optimistic theorists of democracy (Locke and Rousseau) and utilitarian philosophers (Bentham) failed to measure the full dimensions and the dynamic quality of human vitalities, the undemocratic constitutionalists (Hobbes and Luther) saw the destructive but not the creative possibilities of individual vitality and ambition legitimizing the strong government. See ibid., 47.

7. Ibid., 9.

this world, by contrast, as "the moral cynics, who know no law beyond their will and interest."[8] Niebuhr's point is that although the children of this world are wiser with respect to the actual situation of existence since they recognize the power of self-interest, they are flawed in that they give the actual situation moral justification by ignoring the transcendental capacity of human freedom.

Although, for Niebuhr, the children of light are foolish in comparison with the children of darkness, because they underestimate the power of self-interest among the children of this world, he affirms that "our democratic civilization has been built, not by children of darkness but by foolish children of light."[9] Niebuhr is sympathetic with the children of light because of their virtue, but he warns that a politics based solely in their perspective can be seriously mistaken and even dangerous, because this perspective does not adequately account for the power of self-will. Niebuhr believes that by helping the children of light to become armed with the wisdom of the children of darkness, we can constitute a more valid and justifiable democracy. The following dictum reveals Niebuhr's point most succinctly: "Man's capacity for justice makes democracy possible; but man's inclination to injustice makes democracy necessary."[10] Again we come to see clearly that the most adequate form of politics is democracy, and its adequacy lies in a Christian understanding of human nature, which comprehends the transcendent aspect of human freedom as well as the selfishness of human vitalities. As a result of the above discussion, we come to understand that the ultimate justification of democracy as the most adequate political system lies in a religious basis: the Christian idea of human nature.

According to Niebuhr, although the Christian idea of human nature conceptually provides us with the most adequate criterion by which we may determine the validity of a political system, he argues that its validity must also be confirmed by historical facts and events. This is the point where Niebuhr's pragmatic approach to social ethics is most evidently displayed. He is an essentialist in that he believes that there is a definite understanding of human nature, but he is also a politi-

---

8. Ibid.
9. Ibid., 10.
10. Ibid., xiii.

cal pragmatist since he still argues that we are on our way to building a more just and legitimate political system in history.[11]

Niebuhr's political justification is deeply grounded in his substantive understanding of human nature. For that reason, his political justification is largely disconnected from the political process as such. It is almost impossible to disentangle his idea of politics from his Christian understanding of human nature. The two elements are inextricably intertwined, and Niebuhr's reductionist tendency is related to this aspect. Niebuhr does not successfully provide a political justification with regard to the positional self's possible decision to sacrifice the interests of its group to achieve a higher moral end. The political justification is subsumed in the moral justification.

It is my contention that Niebuhr's reductionist tendency makes it necessary for us to engage in a practical dialogue with Habermas because his political concept of "deliberative democracy" is designed to provide a "political justification" for the political problems purely from a political standpoint. To some, calling Niebuhr's way of formulating political justification reductionistic may sound too simplistic, given the complexity of his view of human nature. The point I am arguing here, however, is not that Niebuhr is a reductionist. Instead, what I am contending is that the political justification needs to follow a certain procedural paradigm not subsumed by a substantive view of human nature. For this reason, we need to take a look at Habermas's concept of deliberative democracy.

In his article "Three Normative Models of Democracy," Jürgen Habermas delineates the idea of deliberative democracy, critically amalgamating elements of liberal and republican conceptions of democracy by viewing deliberative democracy from the vantage point of discourse theory. Habermas's main point is that the ideal political system of modern Western society can be most validly attained through deliberative democracy. According to Habermas, the liberal view differentiates the state from society. While "the state is conceived as an apparatus of public

---

11. Niebuhr's essentialist and pragmatic approach is well depicted by the following sentences. "The democratic idea is thus more valid than the libertarian and individualistic version of it ... Since the bourgeois version has been discredited by the events of contemporary history and since, in any event, bourgeois civilization is in the process of disintegration, it becomes important to distinguish and save what is permanently valid from what is ephemeral in the democratic order" (ibid., 5).

administration,... society is conceived as a system of market-structured interactions of private persons and their labors."[12] The liberal understanding of politics stipulates that politics is about the citizens' political will formation, and it can be best established through "bundling together and bringing to bear private social interests against a state apparatus that specializes in the administrative employment of political power for collective goals."[13] Thus, in the liberal view, political efforts to occupy positions that would grant access to administrative power become a critical part of politics. Habermas describes the political process as follows: "The political process of opinion- and will-formation in the public sphere and in parliament is shaped by the competition of a strategically acting collective ... Success is measured by the citizens' approval of persons and programs, as quantified by votes."[14] The liberal view, according to Habermas, understands that the democratic process and the form of political compromises between competing interests cannot be separated. The fundamental criterion for justice is therefore deeply related to the rules of compromise formation, which are ultimately justified in terms of liberal notions of basic rights.

According to the republican view, in contrast to the liberal view, politics cannot be conceived in separation from a view of society based on the Hegelian notion of *Sittlichkeit* (ethical life). According to this view, judgments of the rightness of morality and political institutions cannot be separated from the substantive value commitments of a society, or a substantial ethical lifeworld. The republican view holds that society, deemed to be the carrier of substantial ethical life, occupies a central position in the legitimation of state power. Solidarity, gained through the political opinion and will formation in the public sphere and in parliament, becomes an important source of social integration in addition to an administrative apparatus and the market. According to the republican view, democracy is none other than the political self-organization of society. Habermas argues that both positions neglect the structural complexity of democracy. For example, both positions ignore a structural difference between communicative power realized in the form of discursively generated majority decisions and the administra-

12. Habermas, *Inclusion of the Other*, 239.
13. Ibid.
14. Ibid.

tive power possessed by the governmental apparatus. While the liberal view tends to reduce the essential element of politics to instrumental control of the governmental apparatus, the republican view tends to reduce politics, as democratic will formation, to the form of an ethical discourse of self-understanding. Ultimately political deliberation can rely for its content on a culturally established background consensus of the citizens.[15] Thus according to the republican view, the citizens' political opinion and will formation forms the medium through which society constitutes itself as a political whole.[16]

According to Habermas, an alternative type of democracy, that is, deliberative democracy, can be established by taking elements from both positions (liberal and republican) and integrating them through a concept of an ideal procedure based on discourse theory. Habermas initially draws on the idealization of liberalism and republicanism from Frank Michelman, but Habermas claims that the two types of politics can interweave and complement each other in a rational manner. He says, "Dialogical and instrumental politics can interpenetrate in the medium of deliberation if the corresponding forms of communication are sufficiently institutionalized."[17] Habermas understands that discourse theory makes it possible to realize deliberative democracy in that it brings an important concept into play: the procedures and communicative presuppositions of democratic opinion and will formation function as the most critical channel for the discursive rationalization of the decisions of a government and an administration bound by law and statue.[18]

Indeed, as Habermas argues, discursive rationalization enables deliberative politics possible not only through the institutionalization of the higher-level intersubjectivity of communication processes in parliamentary bodies but also through the informal networks of the public sphere. By connecting parliamentary politics and the general public lifeworld through the medium of communication and discourse, deliberative democracy makes available the integration of both functions into a single, unified view of political justification: on the one hand, the

15. Ibid., 246.
16. Ibid., 247.
17. Ibid., 245.
18. Ibid., 249–50.

function of legitimating the exercise of political power (the liberal view), and, on the other hand, the function of constituting society as a political community (the republican view). Habermas, however, acknowledges that although deliberative democracy has a stronger normative connotation than the liberal model, in that the deliberative model provides a legitimation process oriented to understanding, it is weaker than the republican model, because the republican view sees such legitimation as already constituted.[19]

Habermas's delineation of three types of democratic system makes it clear why his discourse-based deliberative democracy becomes the best model of the political system that can provide the required political justification to the organizational actions of the positional self. Although the republican model of political democracy is much stronger than the liberal model in affording such political justification, since its political justification relies heavily on the substantive contents of a particular culture and tradition, the political justification for positional actions is better grounded in Habermas's concept of deliberative democracy. In an increasingly pluralized contemporary society, the procedures of democratic opinion and will formation of public and parliamentary discourses become the crucial procedure in grounding in political justification the various organizational actions of position holders.

Since politically justified opinions and wills of the public are realized in the forms of law and statue, the demand for political justification of positional acts should be met and matched by the laws constituted through deliberative democracy. In this sense, Niebuhr is connected to Habermas in centering the moral and political justification of positional actions. However, this is only one side of the co-reconstructive integration between Niebuhr and Habermas. Until now, we have shown that Habermas's deliberative democracy and procedural law can resolve the moral conundrum, with which Niebuhr could not effectively deal due to his reductionist tendency in justifying the moral and political conduct of the positional self. For Niebuhr, societies are always immoral, and the positional self can never establish itself as a "moral man" in those contexts. We now have to consider whether Habermas's solution is sufficiently complete and comprehensive to resolve the tension that arises around the concept of the positional self. Do we need something more

19. Ibid., 248.

than the clear guideline of "keep the law" reconstructed by Habermas's deliberative democracy?

From Habermas to Niebuhr: Habermas's Conundrum and Niebuhr's Solution

If Habermas's solution by itself is complete and comprehensive enough, then all moral issues revolving around the positional self will be resolved by the simple and clear command to keep the law. Then does the adherence to the law provide us with the panacea to all the moral issues that a positional self encounters? What about the moral issues that develop in the areas of foreign policy or the global economy? These areas are important components of our contemporary political and economic life, in which a great number of positional selves discover their own positional roles and meanings by affecting many others' lives on a global scale.

It is true that the foreign policies of dominant countries as well as the business activities of multinational companies are increasingly affecting many peoples' lives with an impact that crosses national borders. Of particular relevance to our discussion is that the influential scope of these political and economic activities now increasingly transcends the municipal, national, and regional boundaries, typically regulated by civic and common laws. Environmental issues are just one example of this. Indeed the foreign policies of the United States, the European Union, Russia, China, and other powerful countries can have lasting political effects on other nations. We also know that the managerial decisions of upper-level executives in the multinational companies oftentimes decisively affect the interests of many stakeholders (e.g., suppliers, employees, customers, and consumers) in foreign countries as well as in domestic markets.

Perhaps the most significant point that should matter to us in this discussion is that more and more business activities in these areas are predominantly characterized by unilateral relationships between two parties: the affecting agencies and the affected subjects. The lawful actions of the affecting agencies oftentimes appear to be immoral from the perspective of the affected subjects. The radical unilateralism between affecting agencies and affected subjects in the political and economic world urges us to rethink Habermas's discourse principle[20] that provides the moral justification for the constitution of law. Since, as William Rehg argues, the legal-political structure institutionalizes the broader and more abstract discourse principle, and the discourse principle emphasizes the rational approval of the affected subjects in regard to subjective matters, we see here a greater discrepancy between the institutionalization of the discourse principle itself and the socioeconomic and political reality of lawful society. And this discrepancy makes it inevitable that keeping the law cannot in itself be the sufficient moral criterion against which we may morally judge the actions of the positional self. It is evident that the moral command to keep the law cannot be the comprehensive moral guidance for the positional self.

The inevitable discrepancy between the institutionalization of the law through the discourse principle and the socioeconomic and political reality of our world ultimately makes it necessary for the positional self to engage, with anticipation, in the moral-practical discourse with all those affected by its positional actions. This means that the positional self sometimes should go beyond the legal standard in order to fully establish itself as a moral self. Of course this anticipation is motivated solely by moral consideration of the universalizability principle, which Habermas calls "(U)."[21] According to Habermas, the universalizability principle "suggests the perspective of real-life argumentation, in which *all affected* are admitted as participants."[22] Thus, according to the universalizability principle, those affected by foreign policies adopted by neighboring countries and those affected by the managerial decisions of multinational companies are entitled to join the uncoerced argumentation about whether they would approve proposed administrative

20. Habermas defines the discourse principle ("D") as follows: "Only those norms can claim to be valid that meet (or could meet) with the approval of all affected in their capacity as participants in a practical discourse" (Habermas, *Moral Consciousness and Communicative Action*, 66).

21. According to Habermas, the universalizability principle ("U") is defined as follows: "*All* affected can accept the consequences and the side effects its *general* observance can be anticipated to have for the satisfaction of *everyone's* interests (and these consequences are preferred to those of known alternative possibilities for regulation)" (ibid., 65).

22. Ibid., 66, emphasis added.

and executive policies and decisions. The nature of this consideration, however, must be further elaborated because Habermas clearly asserts that the principle of universalization must be carefully distinguished from the following:

- Substantive principles or basic norms, which can only be the *subject matter* of moral argumentation
- The normative content of the presuppositions of argumentation, which can be expressed in terms of rules...
- The principle of discourse ethics (D), which stipulates the basic idea of a moral theory but does not form part of a logic of argumentation.[23]

Habermas's stipulation of the universalizability principle makes it clear that we must not confuse it with such concepts as substantive principles or normative content of the presuppositions of argumentation. In other words, we cannot argue in such a way that universal approval from all the affected parties is the only way that a positional self can become a moral self. This approach is mistaken because it misrepresents Habermas's universalizability principle as a substantive moral norm. As a bridging principle, the universalizability principle (U) is a rule of argumentation for moral-practical discourse.[24] If contested norms are verified by the principle of universalization, then they are supposed to be "generally observed" in such a way that general observance of them is "equally in interest of all" rather than equally good for everyone as such. Thus, the moral consideration of the universalizability principle must begin with the question of whether general observance of the law would be equally in the interest of all affected by it rather than whether the principle of universalization would substitute for the law as a universal moral norm.

In a situation where general observance of the law turns out not to be equally in the interest of all affected by it, which we have discussed above with regard to foreign policies and multinational companies,

---

23. Ibid., 93. Sections 3.1 and 3.3 describe the rules of discourse in an ideal speech situation. While 3.1 stipulates, "Every subject with the competence to speak and act is allowed to take part in a discourse," 3.3 states, "No speaker may be prevented, by internal or external coercion, from exercising his rights" (ibid., 89).

24. Ibid., 66.

the positional self should reconsider the legitimacy of the current laws and regulations. From the discursive moral perspective, if a certain law and public policy turn out to be invalid as a contested norm by the criterion of the universalizability principle, then it becomes evident that the current laws or public policy need to be substituted by a different set of laws or policies that meet the criterion of the principle of universalization. Given the situation that no alternative laws or policies are available, it would be ultimately up to individual positional selves how they would respond when they come to recognize that observance of the current laws or policies is not equally in the interest of all. It is my contention that in such a case Habermas's reconstructive moral understanding requires positional selves to engage in the "positional reflection" through which they are to search for the higher moral norm that would better meet the criterion of the universalizability principle. As we will see shortly, the co-reconstructive integration between two moral faculties (freedom and communicative reason) takes place in the positional reflection.

What then is the positional reflection? How is it possible? In order to answer these questions, we need first to recognize that in a normal situation, all actions of the positional self are necessarily accompanied by a discursive presupposition that its actions are legitimate, and thus justified by the standard of the law. When a positional self initiates an action with a reasonable belief that its actions are legitimate, it actually performs its action with a virtual argumentation that its actions are legitimate to all, particularly to those who are affected by them, because its actions are believed to be valid by the legal standard. Virtual argumentation is necessary because the positional self is posited in organizations and corporations, and these institutions are legally bound in their establishment, planting, and management. Thus, lest the positional self be out of its context, and thus supposedly illegal, it must consider its actions with regard to legal norms and regulations. Now we have to remind ourselves that according to Habermas's discourse ethics, legal norms and regulations are established by the discourse principle, along with other considerations such as ethical and pragmatic dimensions. Since the principle of discourse ethics already presupposes that we can justify our choice of a norm on the proviso of justifying the principle of universalization,[25] when the positional self performs its actions, the actions are accompanied by its virtual argumentation against all who are affected by them, and its actions are supposedly legitimate by the standard of the law.

The fact that positional action comes with the virtual argumentation that it is justified by all affected by the positional action necessarily entails positional reflection, particularly when those affected by positional action challenge the validity of the legal norms themselves. Positional reflection differs from a practical discourse in that while "practical discourses depend on content brought to them from outside,"[26] positional reflection depends on the virtual discourse situation in which the positional self is engaged in a debate with those affected by its positional acts. This reflection must be undertaken for the following reason: As we have seen in the above discussion, positional action is accompanied by a virtual argumentation that claims its legitimacy by the standard of the law. From the perspective of discourse ethics, law is to be established through practical discourse, which is a "procedure for testing the validity of norms that are being proposed and hypothetically considered for adoption,"[27] and this procedure is referred to as the principle of discourse ethics. Since discourse ethics depends on the universalizability principle to make possible discourse ethics, all argumentation referring to the principle of discourse ethics necessarily reflects the spirit of the principle of universalization.

According to Habermas, the universalizability principle is not only conceived as a rule of argumentation as the only moral principle but is also regarded as part of the logic of practical discourse.[28] The logic of practical discourse is what I term the "sprit" of the universalizability principle. The essence of this logic, or the spirit of the principle of universalization, can be best described as "the idea of impartiality." Habermas writes, "In doing so, it will become clear that the idea of impartiality is rooted *in* the structures of argumentation themselves and does not need to be *brought in* from the outside as a supplementary

25. Ibid., 66.
26. Ibid., 103.
27. Ibid.
28. Ibid., 93.

normative content."[29] After all, the logic or the spirit of the universalizability principle is the ultimate motivating source that makes the positional self engage in positional reflection when the legal or moral norms are contested, with which the positional self manages and organizes the system as a manager or an executive. The positional reflection is thus virtual, because of the virtual argumentation against those affected by its actions. Its significance, however, does not lie in the virtual argumentation as such but rather in its projection toward the practical discourse that deals with the contested norms in public space.

It is my contention that the moral-practical anticipation of the positional self to abide by the ideal of the principle of universalization, the logic of practical discourse, in its positional reflection ultimately leads us to go beyond Habermas's rigorous claiming of procedural justice. And it also renders both Niebuhr's idea of justice (the approximation of love) and political vision (the realization of love through politics) an inevitable moral requirement for the positional self. Then what makes it inevitable? To answer this question, we first need to take a look at the political reality that differentiates between positional reflection and practical discourse. Unlike positional reflection, practical discourse is bounded by the political reality of the society, such as the availability of the public sphere, the maturity of public reason, and the efficiency of parliament. To put it simply, the idea of positional reflection and the procedure of practical discourse can be greatly differentiated. Thus we need to admit that although positional reflection is a virtual discourse between the affecting agents and the affected subjects, it is still far different from intersubjectively, fully established practical discourse. Indeed in many cases, the sociopolitical reality of society may sometimes hinder those affected subjects from participating in practical discourse. For example, this reality may include the lack of political membership, the deficiency of extra time, and the fear of political retaliation or stigmatization on the part of those affected. All of these factors can contribute to the differentiation of practical discourse from positional reflection.

Political realities that lie between positional reflection and practical discourse make us realize that the moral ideas of the positional reflection may not be directly affirmed or accepted in the practical discourse. Political barriers inevitably make it difficult for the moral

---

29. Ibid., 75–76 (emphasis original).

ideas of positional reflection to be realized in practical discourse. Various interest groups and political factions and economic situations inevitably may make the moral views of positional reflection unrealistic, groundless, and unsubstantiated. After all, without a substantive moral imperative that clearly stipulates that the positional self should be impartial in regard to all affected, the moral ideas of positional reflection will be ultimately trumped by the legal measures of the practical discourse. This is why the universalizability principle ironically calls for the substantive understanding of justice that commands the positional self to go beyond the minimalistic injunction of the legal-practical discourse to keep the law. Since the criterion of impartiality cannot be possible without actively listening to the voices of the unjustly affected, and this active listening is indeed a form of love, the trial to go beyond the mere command of practical discourse makes love an essential aspect of discursive justice. This is how Niebuhr's justice, an approximation of love, is inevitably anticipated in establishing the positional self as a moral self.

What we have to see in this co-reconstructive process of establishing the positional self as a moral self is that Habermas's universalizability principle calls for a substantive concept of justice that approximates the law of love as a discursive anticipation. The anticipation of the law of love for the moral reconstruction of the positional self also makes us reconsider the purpose and meaning of politics, because the positional self is posited in the organizations and institutions formally regulated by laws and public policies. From a negative point of view, unless the political system is flexible enough to allow the positional self to attend to discursive anticipation, the substantive moral vision of the positional self will have no meaning at all. From a positive point of view, however, to the extent that the positional self is committed to a discursive moral anticipation through its positional actions, the public and the stakeholders are duly affected. Thus we need to see a reciprocal relationship between the moral understanding of the positional self and the political discourse of the public. Just as the deliberative enactment of legal norms of the political community influences the positional self, so the moral imagination, belief, and commitment of the positional self can affect the public consciousness and the political atmosphere.

Perhaps we can see more clearly how the moral understanding of the positional self can affect the public and politics by referring to

Reinhold Niebuhr. We first need to remember that for Niebuhr, theological anthropology is strongly related to the idea of politics. By incorporating human "freedom" into "politics," Niebuhr tries to ground politics in human freedom. Robin W. Lovin clarifies this by saying, "Politics begins with the capacity for indefinite transcendence of present circumstances."[30] Niebuhr's aspiration for a "realistic" liberalism is essentially directed toward a politics that can "affirm human freedom without neglecting the realities of power and self-interest in the formation of communities."[31] Niebuhr's Christian realism does not "assume" that politics can be reduced merely to anarchy or tyranny. Nor does it perceive that the purpose of politics is to bring an uneasy balance between anarchy and tyranny, which is something like Rawlsian "stability." Niebuhr's understanding of politics does not mean a mere tribunal adjustment among the various demands of self-interests. In the realm of politics, Niebuhr tries to see a more affirmative and positive purpose and meaning: the realization of love.

For Niebuhr, love is primarily understood as an indeterminate possibility and obligation in life. Niebuhr writes, "Life in history must be recognized as filled with indeterminate possibilities of love. There is no individual or interior spiritual situation, no cultural or scientific task, and no *social* or *political* problem in which men do not face new possibilities of the good and the obligation to realize them."[32] Niebuhr acknowledges, however, that the sinfulness of human beings makes it impossible for perfect love to be realized among group relations. For this reason, Niebuhr argues that perfect justice as an equal consideration of interests between the self and others is the practical goal that can be realizable in political and economic arenas. Although Niebuhr differentiates between "perfect love" and "perfect justice" by delimiting the realm for perfect love to individual relations, he still claims that "the love which is the final criterion is obviously a principle of criticism upon all *political* and *economic* realities, since it reveals the sinful element of self-seeking and of coercive restraint in all forms of human community."[33]

30. Lovin, *Reinhold Niebuhr and Christian Realism*, 188.

31. Ibid., 168.

32. David and Good, *Reinhold Niebuhr on Politics*, 154 (emphasis added). The same passage is found in Niebuhr, *Nature and Destiny of Man*, 1:207.

33. David and Good, *Reinhold Niebuhr on Politics*, 157 (emphasis added).

Niebuhr's understanding of perfect love and perfect justice has an interesting correlation with Habermas's ideas of the universalizability principle and the discourse principle. Just as the universalizability principle itself cannot become the substantive norm for the positional self, perfect love as such is a practically impossible norm for many positional selves posited in organizations and corporations. Conversely, just as the universalizability principle, as a bridging principle and also as the rule of argumentation, makes the discourse principle practical and normative, so the idea of perfect love, as the supreme moral ideal, renders perfect justice morally possible and anticipatory for the positional self.

Thus in reconstructing the positional self as a moral self, Niebuhr's perfect justice is crucial. What we can learn from Niebuhr is that as much as a positional self is politically conditioned, it is morally open ended in regard to the law of love. For Niebuhr, the open-endedness of the moral sphere of a positional action is best revealed in a struggle between the claims of the self and the larger claim of love, and it is ultimately a spiritual issue because of an aspect of certain transcendence in the mode of the struggle itself. With penetrating insight, Niebuhr states that the open-endedness of the moral prospect for the positional self is paradoxically affirmed in the form of a burden rather than an asset: "Here is the responsible self in the collective life of mankind. Insofar as nations, even more than individuals, never adequately meet the wider claim, the responsible self is also the guilty self."[34] According to Niebuhr, this makes it clear that "human life is under obligation not only to perfect every moral attitude in the direction of perfect love, but to extend it in the direction of universal love."[35] For Niebuhr, the purpose and the meaning of politics is ultimately to be found in regard to this direction.

In sum, in the above discussion we have seen that actions of the positional self reflect not only a political connotation but also a moral significance. In my view, while the analysis of Niebuhr's conundrum (i.e., how is an individual who is responsible for the interests of his or her group to justify the sacrifice of interests other than his or her own?) makes Habermas's deliberative democracy necessary, Habermas's universalizability principle makes Niebuhr's perfect justice (an ap-

---

34. Ibid., 160. The same passage is found in Niebuhr, *Faith and History,* 97.
35. David and Good, *Reinhold Niebuhr on Politics,* 154.

proximation of "universal regard") anticipatory as a moral norm for the positional self.

The Positional Self and the Co-reconstruction of the Positional Imperative

Thus far we have reviewed how the co-reconstructive integration between Niebuhr's and Habermas's perspectives is possible. One might still wonder, however, why we need co-reconstructionism. Is not the theoretical status of co-reconstructive integration finally Niebuhrian because moral reduction is not systematically required by his position? One may wonder also whether co-reconstructive integration is not finally Habermasian since the account of justice appropriated from Niebuhr appears to be nothing other than the universalizability principle.

It is my contention that if we try to establish the moral norm for the conduct of the positional self solely based either on Niebuhr's theological reconstructionism or on Habermas's philosophical reconstructionism, we fail to provide holistic moral guidance to the positional self. Neither Niebuhr nor Habermas recognizes the significance of positionality in reconstructing the moral norm for the positional self. The moral significance of positionality lies in the fact that the individual aspect and the intersubjective dimension compose the positionality of the positional self. The "individual aspect" here means the personal characteristics of the positional self, such as freedom, virtue, personality, a belief system, and so on. The "intersubjective dimension," by contrast, is exemplified in the form of law established through the exercise of communicative reason determining the formal aspects of the positionality. Unlike the individual aspect, the intersubjective dimension should be considered in conjunction with the system's "anchoring" in the lifeworld, because the anchoring allows the intersubjective moral reconstruction of the system through the discursive establishment of the law. If society's law is enacted through the democratic procedure among its people and thus enables the full scope of their communicative reason, the positional self realizes its intersubjective dimension by adhering to the law of society. Since the individual aspect includes freedom, and the intersubjective dimension incorporates communicative reason, co-reconstructive integration of Niebuhr's theological and

Habermas's philosophical reconstruction becomes possible, centering on the concept of positionality. For Niebuhr, love (perfect justice) is a requirement of freedom; for Habermas, the universalizable principle is embedded in the communicative reason as a rule of argumentation. This is why the actions of the positional self should meet both moral justification and legal justification.

Since the individual aspect and the intersubjective dimension form the positionality of the positional self, the moral norm for the positional self should be established through the co-reconstructive integration of Niebuhr's substantive and Habermas's discursive reconstruction. Centering on positionality, thus, the co-reconstruction of the moral norm for the positional self ultimately comes down to the integration of two moral faculties (freedom and communicative reason) and their principled norms. The possibility and necessity of co-reconstructionism is therefore a matter of integrating these dual moral faculties and their norms. If we miss this point, then we are likely to fall into either moral reductionism or legal reductionism.

Ultimately, the aspect of positionality is what makes the positional self a distinctive type of a moral self. In arguing that Niebuhr and Habermas cannot but fall, respectively, into moral and the legal reductionism, this means that positionality is reduced to a matter of individuality in Niebuhr, whereas it is subsumed by intersubjectivity in Habermas. This is why I argue that co-reconstructive integration should not be reduced either to Niebuhrian or Habermasian reconstructionism. By failing to recognize positionality as a fundamental moral characteristic that distinguishes the moral identity of the positional self from other types, the Niebuhrian and Habermasian reconstructive project cannot successfully overcome the moral and the legal reductionism in providing moral guidance to the positional self. Niebuhr's moral reductionism and Habermas's legal reductionism are in some sense an inevitable consequence of their own methodological approaches, because they both find the fundamental moral origins of the self in individuality and intersubjectivity rather than in positionality.

Paradoxically though, it is important to realize that the method of co-reconstructionism is deeply dependent on Niebuhr's and Habermas's reconstructive studies. In fact, without Niebuhr's theological and Habermas's philosophical reconstructionism, co-reconstructionism itself may not be well established. One should be reminded, however, that co-reconstructionism is not a mere combination of two different versions of reconstructionism. Even though it is true that the method of co-reconstructionism draws on both theological and philosophical insights from Niebuhr and Habermas, co-reconstructionism is developed here not for the sake of the mere amalgamation of two reconstructionisms but rather for the sake of formulating a distinctive moral norm for the positional self. In other words, what makes co-reconstructionism a possible and necessary project is the discovery of positionality that becomes the distinctive moral origin of the positional self. Let me describe further how co-reconstructionism stands.

Positionality in the "self-other" relation needs to be distinguished from the intersubjectivity in the "self-other" relation, because while intersubjectivity is characterized by such qualities as communicative and interpersonal immediacy, positionality is not. We should note that the parameters of the positional relation exceed the typical interpersonal proximity mediated by linguistic deliberation. Since the positional relation is keyed to or centered on the position of managing power and money, the position-mediated "self-other" relation is largely characterized by impersonal, legal, or formal relations. However, this does not mean that the ethical aspect is eclipsed, nullified, or bracketed in this relationality. On the contrary, the ethical aspect of the positional relation happens through the co-reconstructive integration of two moral faculties: communicative reason and freedom. These two moral faculties are paired off into "positional-practical reason" in positionality. While the moral faculty of communicative reason renders the positional self liable to democratically constituted regulations and laws, the moral faculty of freedom requires the positional self to transcend minimalistic legal norms when these norms fail to do justice to all affected by his or her positional act. Indeed, the moral faculty of "communicative reason" is an essential element for the moral reconstruction of the positional self, given that the conduct of the positional self is bound by the laws, regulations, and policies established by the deliberative process of public discourse, which is basically facilitated by communicative reason. In a different venue, the moral faculty of freedom also becomes an indispensable element for the moral reconstruction of the positional self as well since the positional self is required to make organizational decisions as a responsible executive, administrator, supervisor, or representative. As a position holder and a moral self, the positional self is then required to integrate these moral faculties in taking on the responsibility of his or her position. As we will see shortly, the integration of two moral faculties is enabled not as a mechanical synthesis, but as a pragmatic approximation toward the moral ideal of love and justice.

Why then is the integration of two moral faculties possible? Their integration is possible as an indispensable aspect of the ontopolitical nature of the positionality. "Ontopolitical" means the incorporation of the ontological-existential sphere of an individual and the legal-political ethos of an organizational position. The ontopolitical nature of the positionality is thus deeply "phylogenetic" at its core, as distinguished from the solely "ontogenetic" aspects of individuality and intersubjectivity. This means that the positionality is to be conceived from the beginning in the organizational context of political and economic system regulated by democratically established rules and laws. The positionality is deeply interconnected with the evolvement of a group or political ethos as well as the growth of an individual moral responsibility. The ontopolitical fusion of the collective and individual spheres are continually revised, renewed, and reconstituted at various levels in a corporate and organizational system necessitating the integration of two moral faculties. In many cases, though, the integration of two moral faculties is concretized in the form of the positional self's personal commitment to the organization's mission statement and code of conduct. This is how the integrated practical reason of two moral faculties is largely reduced to the minimalistic moral guideline of "keep the law."

The dysfunctional integration of two moral faculties is the single most important moral problem for the positional self, and its moral reconstruction is impossible without the positional self's conscientious rediscovering of the "other" in the "self-other" relation. Who is, then, this other for the positional self? The other for the positional self includes not only the positional self's co-workers, supervisors, and supervisees in the corporations and organizations, but also the invisible but indispensable stakeholders in all corporate and organizational relations. From this perspective, the boundary of the other for the positional self may be indefinitely expanded to include, for instance, such stakeholders as coffee growers in Ethiopia or Columbia when it comes to multinational coffee companies. The minimalistic reductionism of "keep the law" cannot become a sufficient moral criterion for the positional self because the positional self would not "do full justice" to his or her *invisible* others on the basis of the reductive law only. Due to the moral faculty of freedom, the positional self is morally prompted and motivated to transcend the limitation of moral minimalism to do justice to all affected by his or her actions. Of course, this procedure is not always simple and clear-cut. We may not expect that the integration of the two moral faculties would operate as if it were a mechanical device. Although not opposing in essence, the two moral faculties (i.e., "freedom and communicative reason") would not be easily integrated due to organizational demand to concentrate on its interests. For this reason, the two moral faculties are rather integrated according to a pragmatic paradigm of continuous proximity to a moral ideal.

The co-reconstructive integration of dual moral faculties is methodologically delineated as follows: First, the co-reconstruction should take into consideration that the human nature (individual egoism) of the positional self in organizational settings necessitates legal justification for the positional act. Second, legal justification for the positional act is, however, shadowed by the political nature of the organization (group egoism). Third, the spirit of the universalizability principle embedded in legal justification calls for the moral justification of the positional act. Fourth, the call for moral justification for the positional act anticipates the realization of the substantive norm of perfect justice, and this requires the positional self to transcend the political nature of the organization (group egoism). One should here take note of an important aspect: when the positional self is anticipated to transcend the political nature of the organization (group egoism), this moral anticipation is put forward onto the positional self owing to its position. The positional self ought to acknowledge the moral anticipation in light of its positionality.

So what does it mean practically for the positional self to recognize moral anticipation? Does this mean that the positional self, in the end, should become a "moral man" in the Niebuhrian sense? If this is the case, then co-reconstructionism is ultimately nothing other than moral reductionism. On the contrary, if we claim that moral anticipation is impractical, and thus that we should be concerned about only the law with regard to the positional act, then co-reconstructionism is relegated to legal reductionism. How can we make sense of co-reconstructionism without falling into moral reductionism or legal reductionism?

In order to answer this question, we should realize an important point that Habermas's communicative reason is closely aligned with the basic philosophical stance of American pragmatism: communal investigation of truth. A philosophical connection between Habermas's discourse ethics and American pragmatism will be dealt with shortly. Suffice it to say here that it is no wonder that pragmatism has significantly influenced the fields of politics and law constituted through the deliberative process of public discourse. The significance of this point is that the co-reconstructive integration of dual moral faculties and their norms is considered as a pragmatic process toward a moral truth. From now on, I will focus on the methodological significance of the pragmatic aspect of integrating two reconstructive norms (the "minimal norm" of Habermas and the "maximal norm" of Niebuhr) through the pragmatist insight of "processivism." The co-reconstructive integration of the moral faculties between communicative reason and freedom becomes possible as a positional-practical reason in its pragmatic open-ended process.

One should note here, however, that co-reconstruction is distinguished from pragmatism as such. Although the co-reconstructive integration appropriates pragmatist insights, such appropriation only plays a limited role in completing the co-reconstructive project. One also should note that both Habermas and Niebuhr adopt pragmatist insights in developing their philosophical and theological reconstructionism, to which we turn shortly. In the following, we focus on how the pragmatic aspect plays an integrating role in the co-reconstructive establishment of the moral norm for the positional self.

The Positional Imperative as the Moral Norm for the Positional Self

My argument in the above discussion that Habermas's principle of universalization renders Niebuhr's idea of perfect justice an inevitable moral anticipation is based on an assumption that any supererogatory actions of the positional self—considerate actions to care for those affected by the acts of the positional self beyond the legal stipulation—are indeed equivalent to an approximation of love. Co-reconstructionism argues that perfect justice (universal regard) itself substantiates the moral ideal for discursive anticipation. Indeed the in-depth analysis of Habermas's universalizability principle with regard to the moral reconstruction of the positional self reveals a discursive anticipation that can only be met with a universal regard of all those affected by the positional action beyond the legal perimeter. Thus, based on this discursive anticipation, we can develop the idea that the moral reconstruction of the positional self requires us to go beyond the minimal moral provision to keep the law, and the actual concern for all affected subjects is what Niebuhr's perfect justice signifies. In this sense, we can argue that universal regard for all affected subjects in some way or another ought to be incorporated into a reconstructive moral norm for the positional self.

Pragmatist insight plays an important role in our co-reconstructionism because its emphasis on the processivism aiming toward the truth helps integrate the minimal moral provision of "keep the law" and the maximal moral prospect of the universal regard of all affected subjects. In other words, thanks to the pragmatist insight, co-reconstructionism becomes possible by bridging a gap between necessitation and anticipation. The ultimate justification for this integration lies in the important point that Niebuhr's maximal norm substantiates what is discursively anticipated. Thus, through the co-reconstructive appropriation of a pragmatist insight, we can attain a co-reconstructive synthesis between "discursive anticipation" (Habermas) and "approximation of the ideal" (Niebuhr). As a result of the co-reconstructive integration between two reconstructed norms for the conduct of the positional self, we discover a more integrative view of the moral provision for the positional self. In the following, we examine how American pragmatism contributes to the final co-reconstruction of the positional imperative.

Habermas's indebtedness to American pragmatism is evident in his works such as *Knowledge and Human Interests* (1968), *The Theory of Communicative Action* (1981), and *Postmetaphysical Thinking* (1988).[36] Particularly his early work *Knowledge and Human Interests* shows us clearly how he came to develop his own method of critical theory through his in-depth analysis of Charles S. Peirce. Habermas recapitulates Peirce's idea of truth as follows:

---

36. According to Dmitri N. Shalin, American pragmatism provides Habermas with prescriptive answers "by mobilizing the public, revitalizing public discourse, and getting personally involved in politics" (Shalin, "Critical Theory and the Pragmatist Challenge," 245).

> Under the impression of actual cognitive progress in the natural sciences, Peirce had defined truth in the following manner: First, so that universal propositions, above all, could be true; second, so that no certainty is possible about the definitive validity of every individual opinion before the completion of the process of inquiry; and third, so that to the degree that the sciences advance, there is, nonetheless, an objective accumulation of opinions whose validity does not have to be revised again before the completion of the process of inquiry as a whole.[37]

For Peirce, "'Truth' means that opinion which investigators are bound to come to in the long run, and the object of their convergent opinion would be the meaning of 'reality.'"[38] What Habermas finds appealing in Peirce is his exalted view of a community of rational investigators devoted to "critical inquiry and ceaselessly advancing toward the truth through uncoerced discourse, rational argumentations, and consensus building."[39] Emphasizing the importance of the community of rational investigators (philosophers), Peirce himself wrote in an 1868 article, "Finally, as what anything really is, is what it may finally come to be known to be in the ideal state of complete information, so that reality depends on the ultimate decision of the community."[40]

George Herbert Mead later developed Peirce's community of rational investigators into the concept of the interactive process of reaching understanding, which goes beyond the old "paradigm of the philosophy of consciousness."[41] The significance of pragmatists' influence on Habermas lies in their helping him to discover an alternative paradigm of reason, which Habermas calls "communicative reason" or "communicative rationality." Dmitri N. Shalin codifies the new paradigm of reason as follows:

1. An ideal speech situation provides every interested individual a chance to participate in discourse and argue one's viewpoint.

---

37. Habermas, *Knowledge and Human Interests*, 110.
38. Peirce, *Selected Writings*, 114.
39. Shalin, "Critical Theory and the Pragmatist Challenge," 246.
40. Peirce, *Selected Writings*, 72.
41. Habermas, *Theory of Communicative Action*, 1:390 While the old paradigm of philosophical consciousness is grounded in the familiar pair of *Verstand* and *Vernunft*, the new paradigm gives prominence to *Verstandigung*, which focuses on the interactive and procedural aspect of reason.

2. It is free from coercion, domination, and power play—all purely instrumental and strategic motifs.
3. It differentiates cognitive, normative, and expressive validity claims implicit in our assertions and redeems them through arguments alone.
4. It makes a freely reached consensus the sole foundation for democratic will formation and policy articulation.
5. It leaves a rationally motivated agreement open to revision in light of further deliberations.[42]

Indeed pragmatists' progressive and community-oriented philosophical stance encourages Habermas to develop his belief in a communicative rationality that engenders "a noncoercively unifying, consensus-building force of a discourse in which the participants overcome their at first subjectively biased views in favor of a rationally motivated agreement."[43]

It is true that Habermas's critical theory incorporates some of the key insights of American pragmatism into its own development, such as pragmatists' emphasis on the communal investigation of truth and the continuity of inquiry. This, however, does not necessarily mean that Habermas inordinately relies on pragmatism. Just as much as the pragmatists differentiate themselves from Habermas's critical theory, Habermas himself critically distinguishes his critical theory from Peircean pragmatism.[44] Despite his adoption of the pragmatist framework, particularly the process of inquiry, Habermas could develop his

---

42. Shalin, "Critical Theory and the Pragmatist Challenge," 251.
43. Habermas, *Philosophical Discourse of Modernity*, 315.
44. Habermas's critique of Peirce is somewhat extensively dealt with in chapter 6 of *Knowledge and Human Interests*. According to Habermas, Peirce's pragmatism is problematic for several reasons. First, Peirce's argument is circular because "if we assume that reality is not constituted independently of the rules to which the process of inquiry is subject, then we cannot refer to this reality to justify the validity of the rules of the process of inquiry, that is the modes of inference" (118). Second, Peirce's pragmatism is grounded in the behavioral system of instrumental action. Habermas writes, "By carrying out a cumulative process of inquiry according to rules of a logic that objectifies reality from the point of view of possible technical control, the community of investigators performs a synthesis. But if this synthesis falls under the operationalist [purposive-rationalist] concept of 'mind' and is dissolved objectivistically into a series of empirical events, then what remains is nothing but universal matters of fact existing in themselves and the combinations of signs through which these matters of fact are represented" (136–37).

critical theory primarily as a reconstructive endeavor expressing a transcendental, normative, and prescriptive stance.

From a different venue, Reinhold Niebuhr has a close tie to pragmatism, and his relation to pragmatism is as ambivalent as we have seen in Habermas. Niebuhr's serious study of pragmatism begins with his Bachelor of Divinity thesis, "The Validity and Certainty of Religious Knowledge," which he wrote under Douglas Clyde Macintosh's supervision in 1914.[45] In writing the thesis, Niebuhr encountered William James, reading his books *The Varieties of Religious Experience*, *The Will to Believe*, and *Pragmatism and the Meaning of Truth*.[46] The Niebuhrian scholar Richard Wightman Fox posits that the early encounter with James permanently rendered Niebuhr "a thoroughgoing Jamesian pragmatist." Fox epitomizes Jamesian pragmatism as follows: "Truth in the moral realm was personal, vital, a product of the will as much as mind, confirmed not in logic but in experience."[47] Niebuhr himself confirmed Fox's view in June Bingham's biography.[48]

According to Mark Douglas, however, Fox's interpretation is contested by Niebuhr interpreters such as John Patrick Diggins. For Diggins, Niebuhr is primarily a "Christian existentialist," not a pragmatist, because Niebuhr neither surrenders essentialism to nor believes in the promises provided by pragmatism.[49] Ethicists like Robin Lovin remark that "by 1957, Niebuhr himself acknowledged that his work could be called a 'Christian pragmatism.'"[50] According to Niebuhr, pragmatism is described as "the application of Christian freedom and a sense of responsibility to the complex issues of economics and politics, with the firm resolve that inherited dogmas and generalizations will not be

---

45. Brown, *Niebuhr and His Age*, 17.

46. Ibid., 18. According to Charles C. Brown, Niebuhr purchased and kept those volumes for the rest of his life.

47. Fox, *Reinhold Niebuhr*, 84.

48. June Bingham says of Niebuhr, "I stand in the William James tradition. He was both an empiricist and a religious man, and his faith was both the consequence and the presupposition of his pragmatism" (Bingham, *Courage to Change*, 224).

49. Douglas, "Reinhold Niebuhr's Two Pragmatisms," 222. Douglas introduces Diggins' argument that although Niebuhr's arguments are close to those of pragmatism, he should remain a Christian existentialist in that he grounds his theory in an essential account of Christian anthropology and theology.

50. Lovin, *Reinhold Niebuhr and Christian Realism*, 48. Niebuhr first identifies his work as Christian pragmatism in his 1968 *Faith and Politics*, 55.

accepted, no matter how revered or venerable, if they do not contribute to the establishment of justice in a given situation."[51] He goes on to say that social ethics is described as pragmatic "in the sense that it becomes increasingly aware of the contingent circumstances of history which determine how much or how little it is necessary to emphasize the various regulative principles of justice, equality and liberty, security of the community or freedom of the individual."[52]

Before we discuss Niebuhr's adoption of Jamesian pragmatism as a primary inspiration for his own social ethics, we need to take a look at Jamesian pragmatism itself. According to James, the pragmatic method makes an attitude of orientation as its subject matter, in that it has *"the attitude of looking away from first things, principles, 'categories,' supposed necessities; and of looking towards last things, fruits, consequences, facts."*[53] For James, the focus on last things, fruits, consequences, and facts renders truth one species of good rather than a category distinct from good. Truth now coordinates with good. He continues, *"The true is the name of whatever proves itself to be good in the way of belief, and good, too, for definite, assignable reasons."*[54] In his own account, *"unless the belief incidentally clashes with some other vital benefits,"* what is better for us to believe is true.[55] Perhaps the most important reason why Niebuhr found in James a favorable philosophical method lies in James's own assertion that pragmatism has no a priori prejudices against theology on the proviso that the abstraction of theological ideas has some practical benefits. James writes, *"If theological ideas prove to have a value for concrete life, they will be true, for pragmatism, in the sense of being good for so much. For how much more they are true, will depend entirely on their relations to the other truths that also have to be acknowledged."*[56] Openness to the religious claim can also be found in his statement: "Pragmatism is willing to take anything, to follow either logic or the senses, and to count the humblest and most personal experiences. She will count mystical experiences if they have practical consequences. She will take a God

---

51. Niebuhr, *Faith and Politics*, 55, cited in Lovin, *Reinhold Niebuhr and Christian Realism*, 48.

52. Ibid., 177, cited in Lovin, *Reinhold Niebuhr and Christian Realism*, 48 n. 39.

53. James, *Pragmatism and the Meaning of Truth*, 32 (emphasis original).

54. Ibid., 42 (emphasis original).

55. Ibid., 43 (emphasis original).

56. Ibid., 40–41 (emphasis original).

who lives in the very dirt of private fact—if that should seem a likely place to find them."[57] Following this Jamesian track, Niebuhr shows in his theological and ethical studies that a Christian view of life, order, and history can provide for us a better understanding and interpretation of the facts of experience proving its truthful values.

Niebuhr's Christian pragmatism reveals its most relevant sphere with regard to his conception of justice. As Mark Douglas claims, "Since Niebuhr's conception of justice is principally marked by his fundamental emphasis on the processive and open-ended quality of history, Niebuhr would happily call himself a 'Christian pragmatist'—at least while he writes about justice."[58] Niebuhr's pragmatist account of justice is well illustrated in his own account of justice as an approximation of the law of love. For Niebuhr, the law of love can only be approximated in human society and history because of the reality of sin as well as historical contingency. For this reason, Niebuhr is almost certain that the law of love as *agape* cannot be realized among human groups, although justice as an approximated love can be served as a realizable norm in economic and political society. Indeed, the approximation of love is closely related to the pragmatist's emphasis on the processivism toward a notion of truth.

For Niebuhr, unlike for the non-Christian pragmatist, what ultimately keeps Christian pragmatism on a processive track is *agape* as the foundation for the principles of justice, not pragmatism's philosophical method itself. Pragmatism, however, "provides the primary resource for clarifying and analyzing all the contingencies that make up the historical quest for social justice."[59] We can roughly say, then, that while pragmatism is beneficial to Niebuhr in that it enables him to recognize the degree to which ethical solutions for social, economic, and political problems ought to be approximated, it is limited, in that it does not account for the ultimate origin of the problem (original sin) or the final solution (love).

As we have seen in the above discussion, both Habermas and Niebuhr adopt the philosophical insights and methods of American

57. Ibid., 44.
58. Douglas, "Reinhold Niebuhr's Two Pragmatisms," 226. Douglas points out that Niebuhr would find kindred spirits in James and Dewey, in that both of them also "expressed similar concerns about justice, novelty, and historical contingency" (ibid.).
59. Ibid., 227.

pragmatism and use them in their ethical theories. Although their theoretic alliance with pragmatism is based on different methodological assumptions and intentions,[60] both thinkers seem to agree on an important ethical implication of pragmatism: "Pragmatism does not reveal the truth of systems, theories, or religions, but it does favor those that do a better job of *anticipating* how people and systems are likely to behave."[61] In my view, the ethical implication of pragmatism is greatly amplified in Habermas's discourse ethics in the form of universal solidarity, through its alliance with the universalizability principle and deliberative democracy. Pragmatism's emphasis on the "community of investigators" and the "inquiry process" nicely fits with Habermas's idea of the "ideal speech situation" and his procedural understanding of justice. By contrast, the ethical implication of pragmatism materializes in Niebuhr in the form of open-ended processivism toward the law of love by the moral subjects within the context of social, economic, and political relations and structures. Pragmatism's interest in the so-called last things, fruits, consequences, facts, and good is also cohesively connected to Niebuhr's concept of justice as an approximation of love and to his political realism. Regarding this theoretic alliance between Habermas and pragmatism as well as between Niebuhr and pragmatism, we notice that both thinkers adopt the philosophical insights of pragmatism primarily with regard to the metholological purpose. This becomes the reason why substantive claims of pragmatism such as embodied reasonableness, indeterminate reality, pragmatic certainty, reasonable dissent, and sane community are largely missing in both thinkers.[62]

Now our question is, what relevance does the commonality of pragmatism between Habermas and Niebuhr have in developing a moral norm for the positional self? First of all, our discussion on pragmatism has indeed helped us develop a conceptual tool with which we can cohesively integrate the minimal moral provision of "keep the law" (Habermas) and the "perfect justice as a discursive anticipation

---

60. While for Habermas, communicative-action-based transcendental pragmatics and the quest for universal solidarity in communicative society characterize his methodological assumptions and intentions, for Niebuhr, Christian realism and the quest for perfect love exemplify them.

61. Douglas, "Reinhold Niebuhr's Two Pragmatisms," 228.

62. For the case of Habermas, see Shalin, "Critical Theory and the Pragmatist Challenge," 253.

of universal regard of all affected subjects" (Niebuhr). In my view, the first lesson we learn from pragmatism is that it not only endorses law as an objective accumulation of the opinions of the community of investigators, but it also engenders a further critical inquiry toward the moral truth through "uncoerced discourse, rational argumentation, and consensus building."[63] It is important to point out that in the process of searching for truth, pragmatism does not limit the community of investigators to those who belong to a certain political society. This also fits with the logic of practical discourse that strives for universal solidarity on the basis of the idea of impartiality. Since the radical unilateralism between affecting agencies (the positional self) and affected subjects in economic and political society exists as a social fact against the backdrop of law, pragmatic effort to attain truth as well as the spirit of impartiality of the universalizability principle commands the positional self to go beyond the minimal stipulation to keep the law. This, of course, requires that both affecting agencies and affected subjects be members of the community of investigators. The logic of practical discourse justifies that both parties are legitimate members of the community of investigators, which seek a moral truth.

The force of pragmatism to go beyond the mere maxim to "keep the law" as a way of "advancing toward the truth" with regard to the radical unilateralism between the affecting agencies and the affected subjects sheds new light on Niebuhr's prescription for the positional self. In the above discussion, we have reviewed that Habermas's universalizability principle makes Niebuhr's perfect justice anticipatory as a moral norm for the positional self. Since perfect justice is "measuring the limits of interests and the relation between the interests of the self and other" by finding "the points of coincidence between the interests of the self and those of the other," perfect justice is what the Habermasian spirit of the universalizability principle projects as its goal with regard to doing justice to those affected by the actions of the positional self.[64] Niebuhr's perfect justice as an approximation of love substantiates Habermas's universalizability principle not as a positive moral norm but as an anticipatory moral prospect. This is an important point, because Niebuhr's idea of perfect justice can be understood as a

---

63. Ibid., 246.
64. David and Good, *Reinhold Niebuhr on Politics*, 157.

moral truth that "investigators are bound to come to in the long run" as "the object of their convergent opinion."[65] That Niebuhr's idea of perfect justice is anticipated means that the community of investigators in its practical discourse favors it as something that would "do a better job of anticipating how people and systems are likely to behave."[66]

Now, as a result of the above discussion, we finally come to realize how we can integrate Habermas's minimal moral provision ("keep the law") and Niebuhr's maximal moral prospect ("perfect justice as a discursive anticipation of universal regard of all affected subjects"). I will term this integrated moral norm for the positional self the "positional imperative." The positional imperative, I argue, is a moral law that all position holders are required to follow in managing and administrating organizations and corporations as a positional self. Just as the categorical imperative and the universalizability principle provide moral criteria for the individual moral self and for the intersubjective moral self respectively, so the positional imperative offers a moral guideline to the positional self. Uncovering the positional imperative also helps us see how the concept of positionality becomes a fundamental characteristic in portraying the positional self as a moral self. In sum, the positional imperative for the positional self can be constituted as follows: "Act in such a way that your positional action not only meet the standard of the law but also anticipatorily receive the approval of all affected."

Conclusion

In this book I have shown how the positional imperative becomes possible as a moral norm for the positional self through the co-reconstructive integration between Habermas's philosophical and Niebuhr's theological reconstructionism, centering on the concept of positionality. Through the method of co-reconstruction, which is designed to integrate two reconstructive agendas (Habermas's philosophical and Niebuhr's theological reconstructionism), I have demonstrated that the moral responsibilities of the positional self can be formulated as the positional imperative: Act in such a way that your positional actions not only meet the standard of the law but also anticipatorily receive the approval of all affected. For the positional self to establish itself as a

---

65. Peirce, *Selected Writings*, 114.
66. Douglas, "Reinhold Niebuhr's Two Pragmatisms," 228.

moral self, thus, it ought to seek the mutual benefits of all affected by its actions. Indeed the positional imperative requires the positional self to pay attention to the universal solidarity of human beings beyond their organizational boundaries protected by the laws of society.

In today's global world, in which business activities of multinational companies, and politics of international societies, increasingly characterize our lifeworld, we are also increasingly affected by many positional selves. As Helmut Peukert describes it in his *Science, Action, and Fundamental Theology*, "[Today's] society is also structured according to the concentration in individuals or groups of the possibilities for making decisions affecting many or all of the members of a society."[67] Although the present book does not extend its claim to universal solidarity, even to the "solidarity with the dead" as an "anamnestic solidarity" based on the faith in the resurrection of Jesus, it concurs with Peukert's claim that "this universal solidarity must be realized in concrete actions of individuals in relation to each other."[68] The concrete actions must include the actions of the positional self that definitely affect other individuals through positional mediation.

Ultimately, the responsibility that the positional self in organizations and corporations ought to take up is not merely a role responsibility: its moral responsibility lies not in its atomistic role performance as such but in its relation to itself as well as to others. Unlike the concept of the atomistic-role responsibility, which is externally and functionally stipulated, the responsibility of the positional self, formulated here as a positional imperative, is constituted by its own awareness of a new selfhood. If we, with this new concept of selfhood (that is, of the positional self) could overcome the conceptual impasse set by the moral dichotomy between "moral man" and "immoral society" and thus expand the horizon of morality and ethics into the systemic world, then this book would serve its most contributive purpose in both theological and philosophical ethics.

---

67. Peukert. *Science, Action, and Fundamental Theology*, 6.
68. Ibid., 227.

Bibliography

Albrow, Martin. *Bureaucracy.* Key Concepts in Political Science. New York: Praeger, 1970.

Antonio, Robert J. "The Normative Foundations of Emancipatory Theory: Evolutionary versus Pragmatic Perspectives." *American Journal of Sociology* 94 (1989) 721–48.

Apel, Karl-Otto. "The Common Presuppositions of Hermeneutics and Ethics: Types of Rationality beyond Science and Technology." *Research in Phenomenology* 9 (1979) 35–53.

———. "Discourse Ethics as a Response to the Novel Challenges of Today's Reality to Coresponsibility." *Journal of Religion* 73 (1993) 496–513.

———. "Normative Ethics and Strategical Rationality: The Philosophical Problem of a Political Ethics." *Graduate Faculty Philosophy Journal* 9 (1982) 81–107.

———. "The Problem of Philosophical Fundamental-Grounding in Light of a Transcendental Pragmatic of Language." *Man and World* 8 (1975) 239–75.

———. "Types of Rationality Today: the Continuum of Reason between Science and Ethics." In *Rationality Today*, by the International Symposium on Rationality Today, edited by Theodore F. Gereats, 307–40. Collection Philosophica 13. Ottawa: University of Ottawa Press, 1979.

Arens, Edmund. "Domination and Communication." In *The Influence of the Frankfurt School on Contemporary Theology: Critical Theory and the Future of Religion*, edited by James A. Reimer, 247–61. Toronto Studies in Theology 64. Lewiston, NY: Mellen, 1992.

Aristotle. *Nicomachean Ethics.* Translated by Martin Ostwald. The Library of Liberal Arts. New York: Macmillan, 1962.

Austin, J. L. *How to Do Things with Words.* Cambridge: Harvard University Press, 1975.

Baynes, Kenneth. *The Normative Grounds of Social Criticism: Kant, Rawls, and Habermas.* Albany: SUNY Press, 1992.

———. "Democracy and Rechtsstaat: Habermas's *Faktizität und Geltung.*" In *The Cambridge Companion to Habermas,* edited by Stephen K. White, 201–32. New York: Cambridge University Press, 1995.

Benhabib, Seyla. *Critique, Norm, and Utopia: A Study of the Foundations of Critical Theory.* New York: Columbia University Press, 1986.

Benhabib, Seyla, and Fred Dallmayr, editors. *The Communicative Ethics Controversy.* Studies in Contemporary German Social Thought. Cambridge, MA: MIT Press, 1990.

Bennett, Amanda. *The Death of the Organization Man.* New York: Morrow, 1990.

Berger, Johannes. "The Linguistification of the Sacred and the Delinguistification of the Economy." In *Communicative Action: Essays on Jürgen Habermas's "The Theory of Communicative Action,"* edited by Axel Honneth and Hans Joas, 165–80. Translated by Jeremy Gaines and Doris L. Jones. Cambridge, MA: MIT Press, 1991.

Bernstein, Richard J., editor. *Habermas and Modernity*, with an introduction by Richard J. Bernstein. Studies in Contemporary German Social Thought. Cambridge, MA: MIT Press, 1985.

———. *Praxis and Action: Contemporary Philosophies of Human Activity*. Philadelphia: University of Pennsylvania Press, 1971.

Bingham, June. *Courage to Change: An Introduction to the Life and Thought of Reinhold Niebuhr*. New York: Scribner, 1972.

Brown, Charles C. "Politics and Theology in the Postwar Years." In *Niebuhr and His Age: Reinhold Niebuhr's Prophetic Role and Legacy*, 124–64. New ed. Harrisburg, PA: Trinity, 2002.

Brown, Robert McAfee, editor. *The Essential Reinhold Niebuhr: Selected Essays and Addresses*. New Haven: Yale University Press, 1986.

Browning, Don S. "Altruism and Christian Love." *Zygon* 27 (1992) 421–36.

———. *Religious Thought and the Modern Psychologies: A Critical Conversation in the Theology of Culture*. Philadelphia: Fortress Press, 1987.

Browning, Don S., and Francis Schüssler Fiorenza, editors. *Habermas, Modernity, and Public Theology*. New York: Crossroad, 1992.

Chernilo, Daniel. "The Theorization of Social Co-ordinations in Differentiated Societies: The Theory of Generalized Symbolic Media in Parsons, Luhmann and Habermas." *British Journal of Sociology* 53 (2002) 431–49.

Chrystal, William G., editor. *Young Reinhold Niebuhr: His Early Writings, 1911–1931*. St. Louis: Eden, 1977

Cooper, Terry. "Citizenship and Professionalism in Public Administration." In *Democracy, Bureaucracy, and the Study of Administration*, edited by Camilla Stivers, 266–79. ASPA Classics. Cleveland: Westview, 2001.

Davis, Harry R., and Robert C. Good, editors. *Reinhold Niebuhr on Politics: His Political Philosophy and Its Application to Our Age as Expressed in His Writings*. New York: Scribner, 1960.

Dorrien, Gary. *Soul in Society: The Making and Renewal of Social Christianity*. Minneapolis: Fortress, 1995.

Douglas, Mark. "Reinhold Niebuhr's Two Pragmatisms." *American Journal of Theology & Philosophy* 22 (2001) 221–40.

Dowell, Richard S., Robert S. Goldfarb, and William B Griffith. "Economic Man as a Moral Individual." *Economic Inquiry* 36 (1998) 645–53.

Dunfee, Susan. "The Sin of Hiding: A Feminist Critique of Reinhold Niebuhr's Account of the Sin of Pride." *Soundings* 65 (1982) 316–27.

Early, Tracy. "Reinhold Niebuhr for the '70s." *Christian Century* 89, no. 24 (1972) 688–90.

Fichte, Johann G. *The Science of Ethics*. Translated by A. E. Kroeger. London: Kegan Paul, Trench, Trübner, 1897.

Fort, Timothy L. "The First Man and the Company Man: The Common Good, Transcendence, and Mediating Institutions." *American Business Law Journal* 36 (1999) 391–435.

Fox, Richard Wightman. *Reinhold Niebuhr: A Biography*. New York: Pantheon, 1985.
Gamwell, Franklin I. *The Divine Good: Modern Moral Theory and the Necessity of God*. San Francisco: HarperSanFrancisco, 1990.
———. "Reinhold Niebuhr's Theistic Ethic." *Journal of Religion* 54 (1974) 387–408.
Gardner, E. Clinton. "Character, Virtue, and Responsibility in Theological Ethics." *Encounter* 44 (1983) 315–39.
———. "Habermas and Apel on Communicative Ethics: Their Difference and the Difference It Makes." *Philosophy & Social Criticism* 23 (1997) 21–45.
Geuss, Raymond. *The Idea of a Critical Theory: Habermas and the Frankfurt School*. Modern European Philosophy. Cambridge: Cambridge University Press, 1981.
Giddens, Anthony. *Capitalism and Modern Social Theory: An Analysis of the Writings of Marx, Durkheim and Max Weber*. Cambridge: Cambridge University Press, 1971.
Gilkey, Langdon. *On Niebuhr: A Theological Study*. Chicago: University of Chicago Press, 2001.
———. "Reinhold Niebuhr's Theology of History." *Journal of Religion* 54 (1974) 360–85.
Glebe-Møller, Jens. "John Dewey and His Critics: A Lesson for Theologians?" *Studia Theologica* 54 (2000) 127–43.
Guyer, Paul. "Duty and Inclination." In *Kant and the Experience of Freedom: Essays on Aesthetics and Morality*, 335–94. Cambridge: Cambridge University Press, 1993.
Habermas, Jürgen. *Autonomy and Solidarity: Interviews with Jürgen Habermas*. Edited and introduced by Peter Dews. London: Verso, 1986.
———. *Between Facts and Norms: Contributions to a Discourse Theory of Law and Democracy*. Translated by William Rehg. Studies in Contemporary German Social Thought. Cambridge, MA: MIT Press, 1996.
———. *Faktizitat und Geltung: Beiträge zur Diskurstheorie des Rechts und des demokratischen Rechtsstaats*. Frankfurt: Suhrkamp, 1992.
———. *Knowledge and Human Interests*. Translated by Jeremy J. Shapiro. Boston: Beacon, 1972.
———. *Communication and the Evolution of Society*. Translated with an introduction by Thomas A. McCarthy. Boston: Beacon, 1979.
———. *The Inclusion of the Other: Studies in Political Theory*. Translated and edited by Ciaran Cronin and Pablo De Greiff. Studies in Contemporary German Social Thought. Cambridge, MA: MIT Press, 2000.
———. *Justification and Application: Remarks on Discourse Ethics*. Translated by Ciaran Cronin. Studies in Contemporary German Social Thought. Cambridge, MA: MIT Press, 1993.
———. "Law and Morality." In *The Tanner Lectures on Human Values*, vol. 8, edited by Sterling M. McMurrin, et al. 219–79. Salt Lake City: University of Utah Press 1988.
———. *Legitimation Crisis*. Translated by Thomas A. McCarthy. Boston: Beacon, 1975.
———. *Moral Consciousness and Communicative Action*. Translated by Christian Lenhardt and Shierry Weber Nicholsen, with an introduction by Thomas McCarthy. Studies in Contemporary German Social Thought. Cambridge, MA: MIT Press, 1990.

———. *The New Conservatism: Cultural Criticism and the Historians' Debate*. Edited and translated by Shierry Weber Nicholsen, with an introduction by Richard Wolin. Studies in Contemporary German Social Thought. Cambridge, MA: MIT Press, 1989.

———. "On Social Identity." *Telos* 19 (1974) 91–103.

———. *The Philosophical Discourse of Modernity: Twelve Lectures*. Translated by Frederick G. Lawrence. Studies in Contemporary German Social Thought. Cambridge, MA: MIT Press, 1987.

———. *Postmetaphysical Thinking: Philosophical Essays*. Translated by William Mark Hohengarten. Studies in Contemporary German Social Thought. Cambridge, MA: MIT Press, 1992.

———. "Reconciliation through the Public Use of Reason: Remarks on John Rawls's Political Liberalism." *Journal of Philosophy* 92 (1995) 109–31.

———. *Theorie des kommunikativen Handelns*. 2 vols. Frankfurt: Suhrkamp, 1981.

———. *Theory and Practice*. Translated by John Viertel. Boston: Beacon, 1973.

———. *The Theory of Communicative Action*. Translated by Thomas A. McCarthy. 2 vols. Boston: Beacon, 1984–1987.

———. *Toward A Rational Society: Student Protest, Science, and Politics*. Translated by Jeremy J. Shapiro. Boston: Beacon, 1970.

———. "A Reply." In *Communicative Action: Essays on Jürgen Habermas's "The Theory of Communicative Action,"* edited by Axel Honneth and Hans Joas, 214–64. Translated by Jeremy Gaines and Doris L. Jones. Cambridge, MA: MIT Press, 1991.

———. *The Structural Transformation of the Public Sphere: An Inquiry into a Category of Bourgeois Society*. Translated by Thomas Burger, with the assistance of Frederick Lawrence. Studies in Contemporary German Social Thought. Cambridge, MA: MIT Press, 1989.

———. "Transcendence from Within, Transcendence in this World." In *Habermas, Modernity, and Public Theology*, edited by Don S. Browning and Francis Schüssler Fiorenza, 226–48. New York: Crossroad, 1992.

Hauerwas, Stanley. *Wilderness Wanderings: Probing Twentieth-Century Theology and Philosophy*. Boulder, CO: Westview, 1997.

———. *With the Grain of the Universe: The Church's Witness and Natural Theology*. Grand Rapids: Brazos, 2001.

Held, David. *Introduction to Critical Theory: Horkheimer to Habermas*. Berkeley: University of California Press, 1980.

Hennig, Margaret, and Anne Jardim. *The Managerial Woman*. New York: Pocket, 1978.

Hegel, G. W. F. *Natural Law: The Scientific Ways of Treating Natural Law, Its Place in Moral Philosophy, and Its Relation to the Positive Sciences of Law*. Translated by T. M. Knox. Works in Continental Philosophy. Philadelphia: University of Pennsylvania Press, 1975.

———. *Phenomenology of Spirit*. Translated by A. V. Miller; with analysis of the text and foreword by J. N. Findlay. Oxford: Clarendon, 1977.

———. *Philosophy of Right*. Translated by T. M. Knox. Oxford: Clarendon, 1967.

Hess, Carol Lakey. "Gender, Sin, and Learning: A Response to Reinhold Niebuhr." *Religious Education* 88 (1993) 350–76.

Holleman, Warren L. "Reinhold Niebuhr on the United Nations and Human Rights." *Soundings* 70 (1987) 329–54.
Honneth, Axel, and Joas Hands, editors. *Communicative Action: Essays on Jürgen Habermas's "The Theory of Communicative Action."* Translated by Jeremy Gains and Doris L. Jones. Cambridge, MA: MIT Press, 1991.
Honneth, Axel et al., editors. *Philosophical Interventions in the Unfinished Project of Enlightenment.* Translated by William Rehg. Studies in Contemporary German Social Thought. Cambridge, MA: MIT Press, 1992.
Howell, Ronald F. "Political Philosophy on a Theological Foundation: An Expository Analysis of the Political Thought of Reinhold Niebuhr." *Ethics* 63 (1953) 79–99.
Humboldt, Wilhelm von. *On Language: The Diversity of Human Language-Structureand Its Influence on the Mental Development of Mankind.* Translated by Peter Heath. Texts in German Philosophy. Cambridge: Cambridge University Press, 1988.
Husserl, Edmund. *The Crisis of European Sciences and Transcendental Phenomenology.* Translated with an introduction by David Carr. Northwester University Studies in Phenomenology and Existential Philosophy. Evanston, IL: Northwestern University Press, 1970.
Janssens, Louis. "Norms and Priorities in a Love Ethics." *Louvain Studies* 6 (1977) 207–38.
James, William. "Pragmatism, A New Name for Some Old Ways of Thinking; and the Meaning of Truth," with an in introduction by A. J. Ayers. Cambridge: Harvard University Press, 1998.
Jay, Martin. *The Dialectical Imagination; A History of the Frankfurt School and the Institute of Social Research, 1923–1950.* Weimar and Now 10. Berkeley: University of California Press, 1996.
Joas, Hans. "The Unhappy Marriage of Hermeneutics and Functionalism." In *Communicative Action: Essays on Jürgen Habermas's "The Theory of Communicative Action,"* edited by Axel Honneth and Hans Joas, 97–118. Translated by Jeremy Gaines and Doris L. Jones. Cambridge, MA: MIT Press, 1991.
Judish, Julia E. "Balancing Special Obligations with the Ideal of Agape." *Journal of Religious Ethics* 26 (1988) 17–46.
Kant, Immanuel. *Fundamental Principles of the Metaphysic of Morals.* Translated by Thomas K. Abbot. Upper Saddle River, NJ: Prentice Hall, 1949.
———. *Critique of Practical Reason.* Translated by Lewis White Beck, The Library of Liberal Arts. 3rd ed. New York: Macmillan, 1993.
———. *Critique of Pure Reason.* Translated by Paul Guyer and Allen W. Wood. The Cambridge Edition of the Works of Immanuel Kant. Cambridge: Cambridge University Press,1998.
Kanter, Rosabeth Moss. *Men and Women of the Corporation.* New York: Basic Books, 1977.
Kegley, Charles W., and Robert W. Bretall, editors. *Reinhold Niebuhr: His Religious, Social, and Political Thought.* The Library of Living Theology 2. New York: Macmillan, 1956.
———, edtors. *Reinhold Niebuhr: His Religious, Social, and Political Thought.* 2nd ed. New York: Pilgrim, 1984.

Keul, Hans-Klaus. "Subjectivity and Intersubjectivity: Remarks on the Concept of Freedom in Kant and Habermas." *The Journal of Value Inquiry* 36 (2002) 253–66.

Kierkegaard, Søren. *"Fear and Trembling," and "The Sickness unto Death."* Translated by Walter Lowrie. Princeton: Princeton University Press, 1973.

Kierkegaard, Søren. *Works of Love*. Translated by Howard and Edna Hong. New York: Harper & Row, 1962.

Kohlberg, Lawrence. *The Philosophy of Moral Development: Moral Stages and the Idea of Justice*. Essays on Moral Development 1. San Francisco: Harper & Row, 1981.

Kroger, Joseph. "Prophetic-Critical and Practical-Strategic Tasks of Theology: Habermas and Liberation Theology." *Theological Studies* 46 (1985) 3–20.

Lakeland, Paul. *Theology and Critical Theory: The Discourse of the Church*. Nashville: Abingdon, 1990.

Leinberger, Paul, and Bruce Tucker. *The New Individualists: The Generation after "The Organization Man."* New York: HarperCollins, 1991.

Little, David. "The Recovery of Liberalism: *Moral Man and Immoral Society* Sixty Years Later." *Ethics & International Affairs* 7 (1993) 171–201.

Lovin, Robin W. *Reinhold Niebuhr and Christian Realism*. Cambridge: Cambridge University Press, 1995.

———. "Reinhold Niebuhr in Contemporary Scholarship." *Journal of Religious Ethics* 31 (2003) 489–505.

Maass, Arthur A., and Laurence I. Radway. "Gauging Administrative Responsibility." In *Democracy, Bureaucracy, and the Study of Administration*, edited by Camilla Stivers, 163–81. Cleveland: Westview, 2001.

Marsh, James L. "The Religious Significance of Habermas." *Faith and Philosophy* 10 (1993) 521–38.

Marx, Karl. *A Contribution to the Critique of Political Economy*. Moscow: Progress, 1970.

Mathewes, Charles T. "Reading Reinhold Niebuhr against Himself." *Annual of the Society of Christian Ethics* 19 (1999) 69–94.

Mathews, Matthew T. "The Persistence of Religious Meaning in the Critical Theory of Jürgen Habermas." *Soundings* 82 (1999) 383–99.

May, William F. *Beleaguered Rulers: The Public Obligation of the Professional*. Louisville: Westminster John Knox, 2001.

McCann, Dennis P. "Hermeneutics and Ethics: The Example of Reinhold Niebuhr." *Journal of Religious Ethics* 8 (1980) 27–53.

McCarthy, Thomas A. *The Critical Theory of Jürgen Habermas*. Cambridge, MA: MIT Press, 1978.

Mead, George Herbert. *Mind, Self & Society: From the Standpoint of a Social Behaviorist*. Edited by Charles W. Morris. Chicago: University of Chicago Press, 1934.

———. *Selected Writings*. Edited and with an introduction by Andrew J. Reck. The Library of Liberal Arts. Indianapolis: Bobbs-Merrill, 1964.

Meyer, William J. "Private Faith or Public Religion? An assessment of Habermas's Changing View of Religion." *Journal of Religion* (1995) 371–91.

Niebuhr, Reinhold. *Beyond Tragedy: Essays on the Christian Interpretation of History*. London: Nisbet, 1944.

———. *The Children of Light and the Children of Darkness: A Vindication of Democracy and a Critique of Its Traditional Defense*. New York: Scribner, 1960.
———. "Christian Faith and Natural Law." *Theology* 40 (1940) 88–94.
———. *Christian Realism and Political Problems*. New York: Scribner, 1953.
———. *Christianity and Power Politics*. New York: Scribner, 1940.
———. *Does Civilization Need Religion? A Study in the Social Resources and Limitations of Religion in Modern Life*. New York: Macmillan, 1928.
———. *Faith and History: A Comparison of Christian and Modern Views of History*. New York: Scribner, 1951.
———. *Faith and Politics: A Commentary on Religious, Social, and Political Thought in a Technological Age*. New York: Braziller, 1968.
———. "The Illusion of World Government." *Foreign Affairs* 27 (1949) 379–88.
———. *An Interpretation of Christian Ethics*. New York: Seabury, 1979.
———. *Leaves from the Notebook of a Tamed Cynic*. Hamden, CT: Shoe String, 1956.
———. "Letters to the Editor." *The Christian Century* (March 15, 1933) 364.
———. *Love and Justice: Selections from the Shorter Writings of Reinhold Niebuhr*. Edited by D. B. Robertson. Gloucester, MA: Smith, 1976.
———. "Love and Law in Protestantism and Catholicism." *Journal of Religious Thought* 9 (1952) 95–111.
———. *Man's Nature and His Communities: Essays on the Dynamics and Enigmas of Man's Personal and Social Existence*. Lanham, MD: University Press of America, 1988.
———. *Moral Man and Immoral Society: A Study in Ethics and Politics*. Scribner Library 28. New York: Scribner, 1960.
———. *The Nature and Destiny of Man*. 2 vols. Gifford Lectures. New York: Scribner, 1964.
———. *Pious and Secular America*. Scribner Reprint Editions. Fairfield, NJ: Kelley, 1977.
———. "Plans for World Reorganization." *Christianity and Crisis* 2 (1942) 3–6.
———. "Plutocracy and World Responsibilities." *Christianity and Society* 14 (1949) 6–8.
———. "A Protestant Looks at Catholics." In *Catholicism in America: A Series of Articles from the "Commonweal,"* 25–36. New York: Harcourt, Brace, 1954.
———. *Reflections on the End of an Era*. New York: Scribner, 1934.
———. *The Self and the Dramas of History*. New York: Scribner, 1955.
———. "Speak Truth to Power: Comment." *The Progressive* 19 (October 1955) 14.
———. "Ten Years That Shook My World." *Christian Century* (April 26, 1939) 542–46.
———. "World Community and World Government." *Christianity and Crisis* 6 (1946) 5–6.
Outka, Gene. *Agape: An Ethical Analysis*. Yale Publications in Religion 17. New Haven: Yale University Press, 1972.
———. "Universal Love and Impartiality." In *The Love Commandments: Essays in Christian Ethics and Moral Philosophy*, edited by Edmund N. Santurri and William Werpehowski, 1–103. Washington DC: Georgetown University Press, 1992.

Parsons, Talcott. *The Structure of Social Action: A Study in Social Theory with Special Reference to a Group of Recent European Writers*. 2nd ed. Glencoe, IL: Free Press, 1949.

———. *The Social System*. 1951. New York: Free Press, 1964.

Parsons, Talcott, et al. *Working Papers in the Theory of Action*. New York: Free Press, 1953.

Parsons, Talcott, and Edward A. Shils. *Toward a General Theory of Action*. Edited by Edward C. Tolman. Cambridge: Harvard University Press, 1951.

Paton, H. J. *The Categorical Imperative: A Study in Kant's Moral Philosophy*. London: Hutchinson's University Library, 1947.

Peirce, Charles S. *Selected Writings: Values in a Universe of Chance*. Edited by Philip P. Wiener. New York: Dover, 1958.

Peukert, Helmut. "Enlightenment and Theology as Unfinished Projects." In *Habermas, Modernity, and Public Theology*, edited by Don S. Browning and Francis Schüssler Fiorenza, 43–65. New York: Crossroad, 1992.

———. "Fundamental Theology and Communicative Praxis as the Ethics of Universal Solidarity." In *The Influence of the Frankfurt School on Contemporary Theology: Critical Theory and the Future of Religion*, edited by James A. Reimer, 221–46. Toronto Studies in Theology 64. New York: Mellen, 1992.

———. *Science, Action, and Fundamental Theology: Toward a Theology of Communicative Action*. Translated by James Bohman. Cambridge, MA: MIT Press, 1984.

Pierce, Ralph Milton, editor. *Preachers and Preaching in Detroit*. New York: Revell, 1926.

Plaskow, Judith. *Sex, Sin, and Grace: Women's Experience and the Theologies of Reinhold Niebuhr and Paul Tillich*. Washington DC: University Press of America, 1980.

Pope, Stephen J. "'Equal Regard' versus 'Special Relations'? Reaffirming the Inclusiveness of Agape." *Journal of Religion* 77 (1997) 353–79.

Porter, Jean. "De Ordine Caritatis: Charity, Friendship, and Justice in Thomas Aquinas' *Summa Theologiae*." *Thomist* 53 (1989) 197–239.

Pusey, Michael. *Jürgen Habermas*. Key Sociologists. Chichester, UK: Tavistock, 1987.

Pyne, Robert A. "The New Man and Immoral Society." *Bibliotheca Sacra* 154 (1997) 259–74.

Rawls, John. *The Law of Peoples; with "The Idea of Public Reason Revisited."* Cambridge: Harvard University Press, 1999.

———. *A Theory of Justice*. Cambridge: Belknap Press of Harvard University, 1971.

Rees, Geoffrey. "The Anxiety of Inheritance: Reinhold Niebuhr and the Literal Truth of Original Sin." *Journal of Religious Ethics* 31 (2003) 75–99.

Rehg, William. *Insight and Solidarity: The Discourse Ethics of Jürgen Habermas*. Berkeley: University of California Press, 1997.

Rice, Daniel F. "The Spirit of the Law in the Thought of Reinhold Niebuhr." *Journal of Law and Religion* 4 (1986) 253–91.

Ricoeur, Paul. *Husserl: An Analysis of His Phenomenology*. Translated by Edward G. Ballard and Lester E. Embree. Northwestern University Studies in Phenomenology and Existential Philosophy. Evanston: Northwestern University Press, 1967.

Roels, Shirley J., et al. *Organization Man and Organization Woman: Calling, Leadership, and Culture*. Abingdon Press Studies in Christian Ethics and Economic Life 4. Nashville: Abingdon, 1997.

Rosenthal, Joel H. "Private Convictions and Public Commitments: Moral Man and Immoral Society Revisited." *World Policy Journal* (1995) 89–96.

Saiving, Valerie. "The Human Situation: A Feminine View." *Journal of Religion* 40 (1960) 100–112.

Schlesinger, Arthur M., Jr. "Reinhold Niebuhr's Role in American Political Thought and Life." In *Reinhold Niebuhr: His Religious, Social, and Practical Thought*, edited by Charles W. Kegley and Robert W. Bretall, 125–50. New York: Macmillan, 1956.

Schweiker, William. *Responsibility and Christian Ethics*. New Studies in Christian Ethics. Cambridge: Cambridge University Press, 1999.

Shalin, Dmitri N. "Critical Theory and the Pragmatist Challenge." *American Journal of Sociology* 98 (1992) 237–79.

Simpson, Gary M. "Human Nature and Communicative Ethics." *Dialogue* 33 (Fall 1994) 280–87.

———. "Theologia Crucis and the Forensically Fraught World: Engaging Helmut Peukert and Jürgen Habermas." *Journal of the American Academy of Religion* 47 (1989) 509–42.

Sommers, Christina Hoff. "Filial Morality." *Journal of Philosophy* 83 (1983) 69–84.

Stackhouse, Max L., et al., editors. *On Moral Business: Classical and Contemporary Resources for Ethics in Economic Life*. Grand Rapids: Eerdmans, 1995.

Stivers, Camilla editor. *Democracy, Bureaucracy, and the Study of Administration*. ASPA Classics. Cleveland: Westview, 2001.

Thiemann, Ronald. "Political Liberalism: Religion and Public Reason." *Harvard Divinity Bulletin: Religion & Values in Public Life* 3 (1995) 1–11.

Thompson, John B. *Critical Hermeneutics: A Study in the Thought of Paul Ricoeur and Jürgen Habermas*. Cambridge: Cambridge University Press, 1981.

Thompson, John B., and David Held, editors. *Habermas: Critical Debates*. Cambridge, MA: MIT Press, 1982.

Tracy, David. *The Analogical Imagination: Christian Theology and the Culture of Pluralism*. New York: Crossroad, 1981.

———. "Theology, Critical Social Theory, and the Public Realm." In *Habermas, Modernity, and Public Theology*, edited by Don S. Browning and Francis Schüssler Fiorenza, 19–42. New York: Crossroad, 1992.

Tucker, Robert C., editor. *The Marx–Engels Reader*. 2nd ed. New York: Norton, 1978.

Weber, Max. *Basic Concepts in Sociology*. Translated by H. P. Secher. Secaucus, NJ: Citadel, 1980.

———. *From Max Weber: Essays in Sociology*. Translated, edited, and with an introduction by by H. H. Gerth and C. Wright Mills. New York: Oxford University Press, 1946.

Welch, D. Don, Jr. "A Niebuhrian Contribution to Normative Ethics." *Encounter* 44 (1983) 341–51.

White, Stephen K. *The Recent Work of Jürgen Habermas: Reason, Justice and Modernity*. Cambridge: Cambridge University Press, 1988.

Whyte, William H., Jr. *The Organization Man*. Garden City, NY: Doubleday Anchor, 1956.

Index

Agape,
    as equal regard, 9, 192, 194, 196, 219, 224, 225, 232, 233
    as self-sacrifice, 8, 181, 183, 184, 187, 188, 189
    as universal regard, 184–89
Albrow, Martin, 40, 42
Apel, Karl-Otto, 94, 97–101
Approximation (of love), 191, 197, 224, 225, 230–32; (pragmatic), 222; (of brotherhood), 194; (of moral idealization), 102; (as a dialectical realism), 183; (empirical), 37
Austin, J. L., 33, 35, 94–96

Baynes, Kenneth, 67, 118
Bendix, Reinhard, 43
Benhabib, Seyla, 22, 24, 33
Bernstein, Richard J., 27, 65

Colonization of the lifeworld, 78–89, 121
Colonizer (colonizer of the lifeworld), 5, 10, 85–89, 121
Communicative reason, 7, 8, 9, 45, 49, 67, 201, 213, 219–26
Co-reconstruction(ism), 1, 2, 6, 7, 9, 200, 201 (definition), 219–25, 233
Crisis
    Economic crisis, 51–54
    Legitimation crisis, 33, 51–56
    Motivation crisis, 51, 55
    Rationality crisis, 51, 53

Dewey, John, 130, 137, 230
Discourse ethics, 91–101, 201, 213, 214, 224, 231
Discourse principle ("D"), 89, 102, 105, 106, 108, 211, 212, 218
Dorrien, Gary, 142
Douglas, Mark, 228, 230–31, 233

Fichte, Johann G., 27–28
Ford, Henry, 125–26
Fox, Richard Wightman, 138, 228
Friedrich, Carl, 43

Gamwell, Franklin I., 100
Giddens, Anthony, 38, 41, 44
Gilkey, Langdon, 136, 138, 140–45
Group egoism (and the positional self), 7, 8, 19, 129, 135, 153, 154, 158, 164, 223

Habermas, Jürgen, 1, 4, 5–7, 21–36, 45–121, 135, 161, 177, 197, 200, 201, 206–33
Hauerwas, Stanley, 137–38
Hegel, G. W. F., 21–24, 27, 64, 161, 207
Held, David, 56
Hess, Carol Lakey, 150
Humboldt, Wilhelm von, 28–29, 94
Husserl, Edmund, 61–67

Janssens, Louis, 184
James, William, 228–30
Judish, Julia E., 185–86
Justice (principles of), 193–98, 229, 230

Index

Kant, Immanuel, 9, 15–26, 29, 36, 39, 48, 61, 129, 161, 177
Kierkegaard, Søren, 163, 185
Kirchheimer, Otto, 84
Kohlberg, Lawrence, 34, 76

Law
  as medium, 77, 78
  as legal institution, 77, 78
Lifeworld, 10, 46, 48, 59–68
Lovin, Robin, 146, 151, 194–98, 217, 228, 229

Macintosh, Douglas Clyde, 228
Maass, Arthur A., 43, 45
Marx, Karl, 41, 49, 50–53, 59, 78, 130, 131, 162, 194, 204
Mead, George Herbert, 29–31, 60, 68, 93, 226
McCarthy, Thomas, 51, 52, 57, 59
Money and Power
  as delinguistified media, 5, 78, 89, 136, 139
  as steering media, 5, 59, 74–76, 88–90, 115
  concentration of money and power, 1, 3, 6, 11, 138–44, 153, 158, 164, 197, 234
Moral norm
  Minimal, 10, 88, 119, 120, 177, 178, 200, 216, 221–25, 232, 233
  Maximal, 197, 200, 224, 225, 233
Moral faculty, 7, 8, 221, 223 (see communicative reason & positional freedom)

Natural law (Catholic), 130, 169–76, 194
Niebuhr, Reinhold, 5–11, 81, 121–210, 215–25, 228–33

Organizational self, 3, 6, 11, 127, 135, 189

Outka, Gene, 183–89

Parsons, Talcott, 68–75, 113, 189
Peirce, Charles S., 225–27, 233
Peukert, Helmut, 234
Piaget, Jean, 31, 32, 35
Pope, Stephen J., 184, 186, 187
Position (moral meaning of), 1, 2, 15
Position-mediated relation, 47, 187
Positional freedom, 14, 123, 157, 178, 190–92
Positional imperative, 2, 3, 11, 201, 225, 233 (definition), 234
Positional reflection, 213–16
Positional role, 3, 124, 127, 141, 143, 197, 210
Positionality, 2, 3, 4, 201 (definition), 219–23, 233
Power, see Money
Purposive rationality, 49, 57

Radway, Laurence I., 43, 45
Rawls, John, 97, 116, 117, 134, 217
Rehg, William, 102, 106, 107, 211
Reconstruction
  Philosophical reconstruction(ism), 6, 11, 177, 197, 200, 201, 219, 220
  Theological reconstruction(ism), 6, 11, 160; (definition), 161–68, 177, 178, 197, 198, 200, 201, 219, 224, 233
Reductionism
  Legal reductionism, 2, 220, 223
  Moral reductionism, 2, 220, 223
Responsibility
  Legal responsibility, 16
  Moral responsibility, ix, 1, 11, 14, 82, 127, 135, 222, 234,
  Positional responsibility, 3, 4, 82
Rice, Daniel F., 150, 173–75, 177, 179, 180, 190, 198

Ricoeur, Paul, 64

Self (tripartite moral self)
   Absolute self, 14–21
   Intersubjective self, 21–35
   Positional self, 1–15, 35–46, 200–206, 209–33
Sin
   as pride, 141, 148, 150–60
   as sensuality, 151–60
Smend, Rudolf, 42
System, 68–78

Uncoupling of the system and the lifeworld, 74, 77, 78, 83, 84, 87, 200
Universalizability principle ("U"), 97, 211–19, 223, 225, 231–33

Validity claim, 32, 33, 89, 90, 95, 99, 117, 227, 232, 233

Weber, Max, 9, 35–49, 57, 59, 69, 78, 82, 83, 91, 92, 95
Wittgenstein, Ludwig, 32, 94, 95
Whyte, William H., 38–40

www.ingramcontent.com/pod-product-compliance
Lightning Source LLC
Chambersburg PA
CBHW050850230426
43667CB00012B/2223